SQUADDIES

Portrait of a Subculture

SQUADDIES

Portrait of a Subculture

by

John Hockey

UNIVERSITY OF EXETER

First published 1986 by the University of Exeter

© 1986   John Hockey

ISBN 0 85989 248 4

Exeter University Publications
Publications Office
Reed Hall
Streatham Drive
Exeter
Devon EX4 4QR

Printed in Great Britain by A. Wheaton & Co. Ltd., Exeter

This one is for my folks in Wales, who were always there when I got a '48'.

Contents

Acknowledgements

This book started as a PhD thesis and the research would not have been possible without a grant from the Social Science Research Council, to whom I owe a debt of thanks. A similar thank you is due to the British Academy who provided a much needed publication subvention. Additionally, my thanks also go to the Ministry of Defence whose cooperation was vital to the completion of the research, and to all members of the Depot and the Battalion for their help. A special thank you to 'the lads' of 'A' Company whose story this is primarily. I am also indebted to the staff of the Sociology Department, Lancaster University, for providing me with a sociological imagination, and to John Hughes in particular, for introducing me to the 'awesome reflexivity' of social life. Additionally, I wish to express my gratitude to Barry Turner, Barbara and Stephen Mennell in Exeter and Andy Deseran in Baton Rouge for their help and support.

Lastly, a special debt of thanks to Anne, Sara, Silvi and Joe, who came along for the whole ride . . .

John Hockey
Lancaster

January 1986

Chapter One

The Army and the Private Soldier

This book is concerned with the lives of private soldiers in today's British Army. It is a study, more exactly, of infantrymen from initial recruitment onwards, as they encounter the constraints of military discipline and combat. I write as a sociologist, but my aim has been not so much to test sociological theories as to portray as accurately and faithfully as possible the routine, everyday world of private soldiers. I have tried in effect to tell *their* 'story'. Since that story is about *today's* private soldiers, the main source of evidence used in telling it comes from three months of participant observation with Army units during 1979-80. That involved my living with private soldiers, in barracks (in the north of England), on exercise in the field (in Alberta, Canada) and in a security forces' base during actual operations in Northern Ireland. With the exception of a fortnight spent at a basic training depot, the three months of fieldwork were carried out in a regular infantry battalion, and more specifically with one particular rifle company within that battalion. The battalion itself directly received manpower from the basic training depot.

One of my main aims was to examine two sides of privates' routine patterns of behaviour. On the one hand there is behaviour which is in conformity with the official organisational demands made upon them, or in other words involves co-operation with individuals of superior rank, both NCOs and officers, who are in command of them. Such behaviour is officially considered conducive to organisational objectives. On the other hand, there are unofficial patterns of behaviour which conflict with official organisational demands. Yet, as I hope to demonstrate, a balance is negotiated and struck between the two aspects of behaviour. I try to show what motivates privates to engage in *both* forms of conduct, and the consequences for the privates and for the military organisation when they do so. These are questions which ultimately have to be posed against the context of combat, when both privates and the organisation are liable to be severely tested. For, in the collective struggle to survive, social cohesion is a precondition for success, and the privates' conduct, whether it be deemed integrative or the opposite, is a decisive factor.

Behaviour which may be considered to conflict with official demands, commands and regulations is most easily understood if we first know what those demands and commands are. In any case, a good proportion of this book concerns conduct which is sympathetic to and in accordance with official regulations. So this is an appropriate juncture at which to acquaint the reader with the official structure, functions and goals of the Army.

THE ARMY: FORMAL STRUCTURE, FUNCTIONS AND GOALS

The Army has two primary functions: first, an external function to protect the state against an external enemy, and to aid in the pursuance of state interests in support of its foreign policy, by coercing other states. This may be manifested in a number of ways, such as in direct conflict, or by the threat of the use of such force, often by the display of military power. As Clausewitz (1968: 119) noted 'war is not merely a political act, but also a real political instrument, a continuation of political commerce, a carrying out of the same by other means'. The second function of the Army is an internal one and is to maintain the power of the state against possible internal threats.[1] The most obvious contemporary examples include the deployment of troops in Northern Ireland, and incidents ranging from the use of soldiers during public service worker strikes, such as those by ambulance drivers and firemen, to the storming of the Iranian Embassy by Special Air Service troops.

The formal structure of the Army closely resembles the model of bureaucracy as classically described by Max Weber (1977), and since its primary functions are the implementation and management of violence, its organisational structure is designed to effect this efficiently. Bureaucratic qualities such as reliability, impersonality, precision, routine and predictability, together with an emphasis upon the respect for traditions and obedience to authority, permeate the organisation. Although the Army's involvement in combat is, in the long term, episodic, outside these periods it is faced with maintaining a combat organisation through the long periods of inactivity. Therefore even during such times the bureaucratic qualities and the procedures which foster them still order the soldier's world. Training for war involves troops in a constant exercise of both the organisational authority structure, and the appropriate military procedures and skills. A. K. Davis's (1952: 383) comments on the United States Navy are just as applicable to today's British Army:

> It must keep in view a future moment which rarely comes, but which must be assumed as constantly impending. Hence it builds its routine on the abnormal, its expectations on the unexpected. This procedure affords a rational technique for war and an equally necessary rationale for peacetime.

Constant rehearsal of command, obedience and other relevant modes of behaviour ensures a readiness for war. The official rationale is that such constant training creates confidence and reduces uncertainty so that in moments of crisis troops will act predictably and routinely.

The Army thus displays numerous bureaucratic features, including a hierarchical authority structure, a formal, highly detailed, almost monolithic body of rules and regulations, and a specialised division of labour. The hierarchy of position or office is the hierarchy of rank; insignia and uniforms denote not only the individual's position in the bureaucracy but also his/her status along with associated rights and privileges. Position, rank, status, privilege, rights and duties, these features constitute the organisational authority structure and, by maintaining such a system in peacetime, control is more certain in combat.

One feature of the formal authority structure whose consequences permeate the story that follows is the division between officers and men, a division so profound that it almost resembles the legally entrenched divisions between the 'estates'—nobility and commoners—of medieval Europe. Visibly the divide is reflected in differences in uniforms and insignia, materially in differentials in remuneration and accommodation, and socially and legally in the greater privileges and status attached to officer positions. Within these two categories of officers and soldiers are the finer gradations between, for example, NCOs and privates, and similar, if less pronounced, inequalities are in evidence among the officer corps. Yet, despite these, the divide between officers and men is by far the most salient, especially with reference to recruitment, socialisation, and rights and privileges. The official arguments for such a division include: (a) the need for a strict discipline based on fundamental distinctions between leaders and led involving as they do two separate categories of duties and privileges; (b) functional differences such as those put forward by Huntingdon (1957: 18) who argues that officers are essentially concerned with the *management* of violence, while 'other ranks' are concerned with its application; and (c) that special privileges and rewards are required to motivate individuals to choose careers as military officers.[2] However, from the point of view of the private soldier, the important feature of the authority structure is not so much the divide between officers and men, significant as that is, but the division between himself and those who have power and authority over him, and *this* includes *all* those who hold rank.

Whatever its *formal* structure, however, no account of an organisation would be complete without mention of the *informal* structures that inevitably emerge within it, often in response to constraints posed by the formal structure itself. Sociologists have discovered such informal structures in organisations and occupations of many kinds, and armies are no exception. Although, strictly speaking, informal structures are not officially visible, researchers have found that informal structures are extremely powerful, for all members of military organisations.[3]

It must be stressed that informal patterns do not necessarily work against organisational purposes, since, at times, such actions may well assist official requirements while they simultaneously contravene rules and regulations. Thus, when assessing informal practices in the Army, such rule breaking must be looked at cautiously. There is a considerable body of literature on complex organisations which views informal group practices as being centrally orientated around resistance to control by higher authority. Undoubtedly, this viewpoint holds water in a large number of cases, yet the opposite may well be the case.[4] Therefore, when examining informal behaviour, there needs to be not only an awareness of both its negative and positive possibilities for the organisation and individuals, but that these consequences may well vary in the short and long term.[5]

SOME QUESTIONS ARISING

This book is concerned with the patterns of conflict and co-operation among private soldiers, and within this general research aim there are a number of more specific questions which need to be asked. First, what are the conditions and factors which motivate privates to behave in a fashion conducive to organisational goals, and, alternatively, what are those which influence them to engage in conduct which is not so conducive? Secondly, given that these forms of behaviour could be deemed antithetical, how is the tension or balance between them worked out in practice in the everyday lives of privates? Are there, for instance, informal limits placed upon behaviour which is conducive to organisational ends, and also upon conduct which is not so conducive to such ends? If there are such informal constraints why do they occur, and moreover when, in what kinds of contexts, and in relation to what kind of activities? If privates' behaviour violates such informal prescriptions, what are the consequences for them in terms of the sanctions likely to be imposed by their peers as well as those in authority? These are some of the main questions which motivated and informed the research. Other questions which also sprang to mind concerned the response of those in authority; for instance, are all informal practices which are not in accordance with regulations penalised? Or, are there, as Zurcher (1965) found in the United States Navy, types of informal action tolerated by authority on the grounds that whilst deviant in a technical sense, the consequences are in practice functional to the organization? If there are such patterns of behaviour which conflict with official ruling, to what extent do superiors operate a 'blind eye' policy? What forms of rule breaking will evoke such a response by superiors, and what actions will result in the military code of discipline being rigorously applied? Moreover if there are occasions when rule transgressions go unpunished, what are the motives and grounds which influence superiors in exercising this discretion? In addition, given that there is a potential conflict between formal organisational demands, and the informal, often deviant behaviour of privates, at what level is such conflict normalised, and what factors tend to mitigate an escalation of it to a point where organisational cohesion is seriously threatened? For as Salaman (1979: 151) has pointed out: 'The most common basis of intra-organisational conflict is that between superiors and their subordinates over the issues of domination and distribution of rewards'. Within the Army particularly, domination is well in evidence.

The organisation itself is an important arm of the state's power and, it can be plausibly argued, any disruption of the cohesion of the Army will ultimately threaten the power of the state. It therefore seems a worthwhile sociological enterprise to examine some of the basic factors which make the British Army a stable force in support of the state.[6]

The main exponents of military sociology have produced an over-whelmingly management-orientated body of research.[7] Given that, there seemed a pressing need to redress the balance somewhat, and for me to present *the privates' point of view*. They after all constitute the largest group of people who serve in the Army! Thus, the research perspective I have adopted is one which tries to show the reader army life from their standpoint. Therefore, whilst there are occasions where I shall describe and examine the viewpoint of officers and NCOs who command privates, this is done with the object of obtaining a deeper understanding of the privates' position. For how military law is enforced by superiors will in turn influence privates' reactions to military life. This is the sense in which this book is the privates' story: it is a story which takes into account the meaning of army life, as experienced and seen by them. The story within these pages is as close, and as faithful to their point of view as I can make it. If, for example, I invoke in the reader some understanding of the order and flow of the privates' living experience, I at least will consider the story to have been worth telling.[8]

At this point it needs to be stated that the storyteller cannot 'tell it as it is'. The best one can do as a researcher is to present an interpretation of reality to the reader, one which has itself gone through a highly personal and idiosyncratic interpretation in its conversion from the raw material of human experience to sociological knowledge. Furthermore, one reduces a reality that is massively complex into a relatively simple account, for there is no other way of getting it on to the page! Therefore, what I am presenting here is, in effect, a cardboard 'cut-out' of the private's reality. I have, so to speak, 'frozen the action' of the private's life for purposes of sociological explanation. What follows is my interpretation of how privates view army life, and all I can claim is, as I have already indicated, that this interpretation is as near to their own as I can make it.

Take for example the way my accounts are presented in this book. Much of the interaction was non-verbal—meanings being indicated by physical posture, gestures and facial demeanour. In this text there are incidents which illustrate a particular use of humour by NCOs in their relationships with privates. Written in cold print the conversation can be interpreted as being humorous *or* perceived as ridicule of subordinates by superiors. Much of its import is understandable only through accompanying non-verbal communications. So, what I have presented is a 'cleaner', more ordered, more sanitised version of events. In effect, when making the notes,

I 'prettied them up' in two stages: firstly, for my own purposes so as to make them more intelligible for analysis months later and, secondly, when inserting them in this text, for, without a whole store of background knowledge, their form would not be intelligible to the reader.[9] For much interaction between people does not take a straightforward linear form but doubles back upon itself in introspection, retrospection, trains of thought articulated and then cut-off in mid-sentence, or shot off at tangents to the main argument of the moment.

In an attempt to portray the reality of the privates' lives as faithfully as possible, I opted for a research method known in the sociological trade as 'participant observation'; a method which Florence Kluckhohn (1940: 331) has succinctly described as 'conscious and systematic sharing, insofar as circumstances permit, in the life activities, and on occasion, in the interests and affects of a group of persons'. My periods of participant observation were motivated by the desire to understand how privates saw and managed their military world, and by the belief that such understanding could not be obtained second-hand using purely secondary sources enlivened with doses of conjecture and introspection. Rather, I believe that only by 'getting involved', by experiencing as fully as possible the activities in which my subjects were themselves involved, could I gain a productive insight into their world. I undertook fieldwork because I conceived it to be a vehicle for entering reality, the reality of private soldiers,[10] my aim being, as I have stated, to explain their commonplace experiences, their commonsense world, and to reproduce their 'story' for the reader.

Participant observation represented the best methodological approach available to me, by which I could uncover the world of private soldiers. For it involves an analysis grounded in the day-to-day routine activities of privates' lives. And so it was these activities that I experienced with privates, as they marched, cleaned barrack rooms, dug shell-scrapes and so on. Readers who want to see the results and read the privates' story immediately may now turn straight to Chapter 2. But for the more technically-minded sociological reader, I will say a little more about the approach, the concepts, and the research techniques I have used.

THE RESEARCH PERSPECTIVE AND METHOD

As my main purpose is to portray Army life as it is experienced by privates, a chronological organisation of material seemed most appropriate, since it can clearly show the reasons for and consequences of their behaviour as they become increasingly experienced soldiers. I initially examine the various states through which privates are likely to pass, including basic training, peacetime soldiering and active engagement in conflict. Following this, I examine the focal concerns of their social life: the attitudes, beliefs and norms which structure their behaviour in all those stages. The final part of the work is concerned with an assessment of the contradictions or paradoxes I observed in the privates' conduct, the degree of subsequent conflict with organisational demands, and the impact of these two factors upon organisational functioning. Within the above framework, I also examine the conduct of privates which meets official organisational demands, and then follow with a chapter which discusses their deviation from these demands. Subsequently, I continue with these themes and show in the next two chapters how they are worked out in the context of an actual operational Army unit—an infantry battalion—in its peacetime role. These themes are also dealt with in the combat situation. This processual or sequential way of organising the material allows the reader to see the different official demands each stage of military experience imposes upon privates and how they respond to such demands, both officially and unofficially. For instance, the reasons which motivate privates to clean their weapons after a day's shooting on the rifle range are different from those which propel them to do so after a patrol in Northern Ireland.

In presenting and analysing the ethnographic material I make use of a number of analytical devices and concepts which I will now define. Given that I am presenting a chronological account of the private's experience, the reader will find frequent reference to their career. 'Career', as defined by Hall (1948: 327) refers to the patterned series of adjustments made by the individual to his/her 'network of institutions, formal organisations, and informal relationships'. In applying this concept to the private soldier I am doing so in a particular sense. The soldier moves through a series of different military environments depending on unit and location. He starts off as a raw recruit and should end up, ultimately, as a knowledgeable member of the organisation. The latter status is summed up by the cliché 'old soldier', a description which suggests that the individual possesses all the formal and informal knowledge needed to make him comfortable within the military system. The soldier's career progresses as he meets and comes to terms with a series of changing contexts—Basic Training making for different problems and demands from serving in South Armagh. The process of coping with these problems and demands has been termed 'situational adjustment' by Becker (1977: 282), and I use this concept to refer to privates' reactions to certain structurally imposed problems, and thus to illustrate the ways and means they devise of managing them. As Becker says:

A group finds itself sharing a common situation and common problems. Various members of the group experiment with possible solutions to those problems and report their experiences to their fellows. In the course of their collective discussion, the members of the group arrive at a definition of the situation, its problems and possibilities, and develop concensus as to the most appropriate and efficient ways of behaving. This consensus therefore constrains the activities of individual members of the group, who will probably act on it given the opportunity. (1977: 282)

By acting collectively and arriving at these situational adjustments together, privates have more potential to deviate from the standards demanded by those in command over them.

In defining the kinds of behaviour which privates display I make the classic sociological distinction between 'formal' and 'informal' conduct. The reader will find that I have made use of these two concepts particularly in the two chapters on Basic Training, the initial stages of the private's career. Such a distinction is particularly useful at this stage of the story as it contrasts informal conduct with the formal demands imposed upon recruits by organisational socialisation. Yet, as the private's career unfolds this distinction becomes sociologically less useful, for whilst still using a dichotomy to describe relationships between privates and their superiors which are *abnormal*, I increasingly use the private's own terms to portray the *normal* routine events which characterise such relationships. I do this for a number of reasons; first, there is a body of literature on complex organisations, some of it on the military, which provides the researcher with a number of useful concepts with which one can examine the process of initial socialisation, though these are less effective in attempting to examine the organisation's informal face. Secondly, as privates move through the various stages of their career, one finds a diminishing adherence to formal organisational processes by all concerned, including privates and their superiors, and that informal practices take over to a large extent—which is why I use members' definitions.

The next concept I wish to define is that of 'self-image'. This concept and the way I use it derives from the work of a number of writers. Cooley (1956: 184) for instance wrote about the 'looking-glass self', whilst in a similar fashion Znaniecki (1967: Chapter VII) uses the term 'reflected self'. However, it is the work of Mead (1972: 152–64) that is most commonly and directly associated with the concept I use. Mead maintained that the essence of the self was reflexive, and that a person was only a person because of his or her relations with others. Central to his argument of how the individual's personality and actions are shaped by society is the concept of the 'generalised other'. Individuals are seen to move through a process of role-taking, initially taking on the role of significant others, and, finally, as mature adults, the role of the 'generalised other'—the attitude of the whole community. Natanson (1956: 13) writing on Mead's conception of the self for the social actor comments: 'Only in so far as he takes the attitudes of the organised social activity or set of activities in which the group is engaged, does he develop a complete self'. Natanson notes that for Mead a real adult-self only arises when a 'generalised other' is internalised so that 'the community exercises control over the conduct of its individual members'. The self-conceptions that individuals hold of themselves are then not wholly independent of others, for they are in large part based on reflections of relationships with others. For Mead the development of the individual's conception of his or her self-image is a social process, a mature consciousness emerging out of interaction with others. Thus the self is not a static but rather a dynamic entity changing as the individual interacts with different situations and individuals. Individuals then possess a concomitant awareness of their selves in action. They possess both the capacity of knowing themselves as subjects, and, also as objects as known by others. I am therefore using self-image specifically in Mead's sense to show how privates develop a self-conception of themselves as soldiers as their career progresses through the stages identified earlier. This self-image gradually develops as the individual takes on the role and identity of being a military person.

The next concept I wish to elaborate upon is that of 'negotiated order'. What may be termed negotiated order theory has emerged as a result of studies in the sociology of occupations and in the field of medical sociology. As a theory it calls into question the more rigid and static rational-bureaucratic and structural-functional explanations of complex organisations. In contrast it stresses that there is a direct and reciprocal relationship between the formal and the informal aspects of organisations, each in turn influencing the other. It presents an interactional and processual picture of how work gets done in organisations. In its most succinct and theoretical statements, such as those by Strauss *et al.* (1963: 148), it presents a view of organisational order as being always revisable, and continually reconstituted: a dynamic process which involves constant negotiation between organisational members and, as Day and Day (1977: 131) note, this often involves lower level participants exercising power and influencing organisational processes. Therefore I use the concept of negotiated order to analyse and describe the routine relationships evident between privates and their superiors. Yet, as Hughes (1971: vii) has wryly noted: 'Society is interaction. Interaction involves sensitivity to others, but to some others more than other others.' And certainly in the privates' case, the 'some others' to whom they are particularly sensitive are all superiors: those who hold rank and thus have *power* over them. Therefore the area(s) of negotiation, the bargains that are made, broken and reformulated, have limits which are set by the power held by superiors. Such bargains are not bargains between equals, a factor which has caused Day and Day (1977: 127) to note that with negotiated order theory, 'the role of power (formal versus informal) is never pursued to its logical outcome'. Nevertheless within the boundary set by superiors to such negotiations, the concept of negotiated order is a valuable device for explaining certain crucial aspects of privates' lives.

The final concept I wish to remark upon is that of *deviance*. I am using it in a very broad sense, rather than narrowly, confining my definition to serious and obvious forms of criminal behaviour. This is primarily because I am interested in the *normal* events which constitute the private's world, and serious contraventions of military law, such as going AWOL (absent without leave) or striking a superior, are essentially *abnormal*. The normal events in terms of deviance are rather an endless series of misdemeanours, rule transgressions such as being late for parade, being unshaven on it, and so on. Moreover, when using deviance in the fashion I have outlined, I am not confined to actions which directly break law but which also encompass other forms of conduct. As Cohen (1973; 10) has observed there are a number of words which mean roughly the same as deviance—such as 'twist', 'drift', 'dodge', 'step aside', 'depart from', 'wander' and 'go astray' and I am using deviance in this wider sense. In addition when talking of deviance I refer not only to actions which violate formal organisational ruling, but also those actions which contravene the informal equivalents. Often when one uses the term deviance it immediately conjures up forms of behaviour which are labelled negatively, which are seen to constitute, in some sense, 'social problems'. By contrast, in telling the privates' story I show how, for them, such conduct is not a problem at all, but rather constitutes a *solution* to problems which have been imposed upon them by those who hold power over them.

All these concepts are grounded in a particular sociological tradition which stresses the importance of interpreting the behaviour of people in terms of their subjectively intended meanings. More specifically, the majority of the concepts I have used derive directly from the research traditions of symbolic interactionism and the work done in the area of occupational sociology by Chicago sociologists, who pioneered urban participant observation.[11]

Having outlined my research aims, method, and the organisational and analytical concepts I have used, it now remains for me to delve into the privates' reality. Before beginning the substantive part of this work based on my participant observation, there remains a central issue which readers need to be made aware of, and without which a real understanding of the private's response to the military environment would be incomplete—the nature of military law and its enforcement.

NOTES

1. Other functions of the Army sometimes identified but largely incidental for the purposes of this work are, respectively, economic and social. Economic in the sense that some writers (Cook (1963), Baron and Sweezy (1968)) view military expenditure as the only dependable system for controlling and stabilising capitalist economies, operating as it does outside the normal framework of supply and demand. The social functions include one not unconnected to the economic function in that during periods of economic recession the Army has traditionally served as a source of employment in areas hardest hit. But, above all, in times of war the Army and other military institutions become both a symbol of national unity and a means of promoting greater social cohesion within the nation state. For my purposes, however, the first two functions are of prime importance.

2. See Coates and Pellegrin (1965: 253); sociologists will recognise this as a familiar 'functionalist' argument.

3. An examination of the informal behaviour of the United States Navy Disbursing Officer is given by Turner (1947). See also Page (1946: 89). On informal structures within organisations generally, see Blau and Scott (1962).

4. See Goodrich (1975: 37) and Dalton (1959). Bensman and Gerver (1963) illustrate an example of informal patterns aiding official aims. See also Salaman (1979: 164) and Etzioni (1961: Ch. 8).

5. Paul Willis's (1979) study of the forms of resistance to institutional control, displayed by a group of male school leavers illustrates the potential for deviant actions in the short term to have organisationally positive results in the long term—in this case propelling pupils into specific parts of the labour market.

6. The British Army's stability, and by that I mean its lack of involvement in the internal politics of the state, has been due to a number of factors. The standard work on the subject, Finer's *The Man on Horseback*, points to two main reasons. Finer (1976: 20–26) argues that the professionalisation of the officer corps and the principle of civil supremacy have been powerful forces which have prevented the involvement of the military in British politics. Professionalisation resulted in the Army elite becoming more self-centred, and the attention of those in command has been concentrated on the development of increasingly sophisticated military skills. In other words, politics is left to the politicians. In conjunction with this trend, within Britain there has been as Finer (1976: 24:25) notes, a clear understanding by the military, 'that the civil power is paramount and must be obeyed'. The prime example of troops threatening to violate this axiom in contemporary times was the so called 'mutiny on the Curragh' in 1914, when the officers concerned threatened collectively to resign their commissions, rather than fight against Ulster civilians. As Finer (1976: 131–2) has argued, whilst rival sections of the military may have brought pressure to bear upon the British government (for instance the opposing factions within the Navy prior to the First World War), 'this is very different from other cases where the military have corporately opposed the civilian authorities, and advocated a policy which was less about professional matters than it was a general political programme'. One can of course argue on much more pragmatic grounds, that the British military (in essence the officer corps) has been supportive of the state, not so much due to any abstract notion of civil supremacy but because the state has never seriously pursued policies which were antithetical to the interests of the military elite.

7. See Sperber (1970: 62), also Becker (1977: 123–34). An exception is Marlowe's (1959) analysis of the American basic training process, in which he explores the initial socialisation of recruits from their point of view.

8. See the comments of Glaser and Strauss (1979: 230).

9. Klockars (1975: 221–222) has commented upon the problem of interpreting, and meaning when making field notes. A more detailed analysis is contained in Garfinkel's (1967: 38–44) work.

10. See Rock (1979: 184).

11. None more so than the concept of the 'self', for as Rock (1979: 102) notes, 'it constitutes the very hub of the interactionists' intellectual scheme. All other sociological processes and events revolve around that hub, taking from it their analytic meaning and organization . . . The doings and evolution of the self are elevated to a central place.'

Chapter Two

Military Law—Interpretation and Application

As I have suggested, the private's conduct is largely dependent upon how his superiors enforce military law. This is a relationship which is fundamental to an understanding of the substantive part of this work, and, therefore, in this chapter I examine in some detail the military law which serves to constrain privates' lives. First, I look at the nature of military discipline as well as its justifications and, second, I analyse the scope and powers embodied in the rules and regulations which are enforced to uphold discipline.

DISCIPLINE

In the previous chapter I remarked on how the formal organisation of the Army bears a close resemblance to the 'model or ideal type' of bureaucracy as proposed by Max Weber. According to him, the prototype of bureaucratic control requires that authority be exercised through a hierarchical command structure, within which subordinates are under obligation to comply with orders given by superiors. Weber (1977: 222) foresaw that 'military discipline and technical training can be normally and fully developed, at least to its modern high level, only in the bureaucratic army'. Control through a hierarchical chain of command is maintained by the operation of a code of discipline, which permits superiors, if only as a last resort, to enforce obedience by imposing coercive sanctions upon subordinates. Submission to authority is not limited to obeying verbal orders but also includes complying with rules and regulations, and with those procedures which govern general decisions and operations such rules being termed 'Standing Orders', or 'Standard Operating Procedures'.

As Spindler (1948: 86) remarked, 'the fundamental importance of this need for and exercise of discipline can scarcely be over-rated in the military'. The origin of this need lies in the demand for a ready predictability of behaviour, which is the paramount factor in the functioning of any large organisation. This is nowhere more evident than in the Army where the unpredictable may literally result in disaster and death. Uniformity of response to orders and thus concerted action are the desired ends of military discipline. Weber (1977: 253) summarised the matter as follows:

> The content of discipline is nothing but the consistently rationalized, methodologically trained and exact execution of the received order, in which all personal criticism is unconditionally suspended and the actor is unswervingly set for carrying out the command. In addition, this conduct under orders is uniform. Its quality as the communal action of a mass organization conditions the specific effects of such uniformity. . . . What is decisive for discipline is that the obedience of a plurality of men is rationally uniform.

Appropriate conduct in the Army is structured by a body of rules and regulations, which comprise military law. The object of such rules according to the *Manual of Military Law* (1972: 3) is:

> . . . to provide for the maintenance of good order and discipline among members of the Army . . . It is for this reason that acts or omissions which in civil life may amount to no more than breaches of contract (like failing to attend work) . . . become in the context of Army life punishable offences.

The Army Act (1955) comprehensively aims to cover every type of context and situation in which soldiers are likely to find themselves. Sections 24 to 69 of the Act cover the whole gamut of Army crime, ranging from such matters as 'misconduct in action' (section 24) and 'malingering' (section 42), to 'offences against morale' (section 63A). Depending upon the offence committed, Unit Commanding Officers may award soldiers any of the following: up to 28 days detention, or up to 60 days with the permission of higher authority; in addition he has the power to fine an offender up to 28 days pay, and also holds authority to award stoppages of pay up to the amount of 14 days, or more with the permission of higher authority. Commanding Officers may also impose upon soldiers restriction of privileges by confining them to camp and giving them extra work for up to 14 consecutive days. They also have the power to award extra duties— guards or picquets—not exceeding three in number for offences committed in connection with the aforementioned duties. A subordinate commander, such as a Major commanding a Company, has the power to fine soldiers up to seven days pay, to award stoppages of the same duration, and to impose restriction of privileges for up to a week, as well as to impose certain extra duties such as guards and picquets for offences relating to them. Offences of a serious nature such as 'assisting the enemy' (section 25) or 'mutiny' (section 31) require the convening of a court martial by an authority higher than a Unit Commanding Officer. The *Manual of Military Law* and its various sections covering the maintenance of discipline gives superiors enormous potential power and authority over subordinates in a way unparalleled in normal civilian life.

A CONCEPTION OF BUREAUCRATIC RULES

Much sociological analysis of bureaucratic oganisations has been influenced by Weber's (1977: 228–9) model of the rational application of formal rules in which the idea of efficiency governs the use of such rules in determining and assessing actions done by members of the organisation. Superiors command and subordinates obey and the outcomes are largely as predictable as clockwork. Moreover, the formal scheme embodied in the rules and procedures of the organisational plan are generally seen as an unambiguous description of actions within the organisation. In short, this is the way it happens. However, for my purposes a more appropriate way of looking at organisational members' actions can be found in the work of Egon Bittner. Bittner (1975: 71) has argued that such approaches fail to take into consideration how organisational members understand formal rationality, and how they relate to it in actual concrete situations. He goes on to argue that 'the literal interpretation of formal schemes is not only inappropriate but, strictly speaking, impossible'. It is impossible because rules and regulations do not operate in isolation from the actions of members. Rather, their application is determined by members' evaluation of ongoing situations. Thus, military law can be considered as a general set of guidelines which, like all rules, have to be interpreted and used in situations as they arise. In Manning's (1974: 239–56) terms:

> Rules within organizations, like grammatical rules and rules of logic, take on an indexical quality, that is they can be understood only contextually, as practical problems that arise out of the association of those people, facing those problems, in those periods of time.

In essence the contravention and application of rules arise out of specific social situations and, as such, organisational rulings do not emerge from particular contexts in any 'once and for all' sense. Rather, each situation has its own dynamic, depending on how context, rules and members interact and influence each other. Moreover, given the ever-changing content of members' organisational knowledge and practical interests, each interpretation of military law is what Mehan and Wood (1975: 75) call 'situationally absolute', based upon participants' understanding that later events may change the interpretation of how rules apply.

Once a person becomes a competent organisational member, he/she possesses a vast body of taken-for-granted knowledge and tacit assumptions which enable them to manage life in the organisation. These background expectations and commonsense typifications are rarely explicated, but are normally assumed and used as resources to accomplish interaction and manage events for all practical purposes. Bittner (1975: 73) describes the usage of such taken-for-granted knowledge in the following terms: 'While its content can be raised to the level of analysis, this typically does not occur. Rather the information enters into the commonplace and practical orientation to reality which members of society regard as "natural" when attending to their daily affairs'. The judgemental process inherent in rule interpretation draws heavily upon such tacit information, and to comprehend its nature fully one needs to understand the practical basis on which decisions are made.[1] These processes will be illustrated in the ethnographic sections of the work, but one or two remarks of a general kind are perhaps in order.

THE PRACTICAL BASIS OF RULE INTERPRETATION

I will now outline the practical contingencies that influence superiors in the Army in interpreting and applying military law. In the Army, as in all organisations, superiors are charged by higher authority with particular responsibilities and duties. Officers and NCOs are appointed to positions within their units commensurate with their rank and military experience. Regardless of rank every officer and NCO is subject to an annual assessment of his/her performance when their suitability for promotion is considered.[2] Since the Army is now an organisation made up of volunteers rather than conscripts, all superiors, even at the lowest level, are professional soldiers. The annual assessment of their competency is therefore very important for their careers, and so superiors are concerned with performing their designated tasks and responsibilities as efficiently as possible. 'Getting the job done' becomes their central concern.

Military discipline is legally the responsibility of all ranks, including privates. As the *Manual of Military Law* (1972: 351) declares:

> It is the duty of all ranks to uphold the good reputation of the service. Any conduct or neglect therefore which amounts to a failure in that duty by an individual may well prejudice military discipline although it has no direct bearing on the discipline of the unit to which the offender belongs.

Thus all officers and NCOs in the Army have, in effect, dual responsibilities. All are concerned with efficiently accomplishing their work tasks, and, at the same time, they have to maintain discipline amongst their peers and subordinates. Certain appointments in Army units, such as the RSM and the Adjutant, carry specific responsibilities for maintaining discipline. Others, such as the Cook Sergeant or MT (Motor Transport) Sergeant, are primarily concerned with catering or organising the unit's fleet of vehicles. Yet, all superiors are to some degree responsible for the conduct of their subordinates not only in their performance at work, but also in their general military demeanour. The scope of Army discipline is accordingly extremely wide and perhaps the most vivid illustration of this is the all encompassing scope of Section 69 of the Army Act (1955) as set out in the *Manual of Military Law* (1972: 350):

> Any person subject to military law who is guilty of any conduct or neglect to the prejudice of good order and military discipline shall, on conviction by court martial, be liable to imprisonment for a term not exceeding two years or any less punishment provided by this act.

The above serves as a 'blanket charge' used to punish offences which cannot be handled under any other section of the Army Act. 'Neglect', for instance, embraces 'neglect in handling firearms, failure to clean a weapon, to keep kit and uniform in good order or to have proper regard for personal turn out' (*Manual of Military Law*, 1972: 350). And, the Cook Sergeant is concerned both with his cooks' culinary skills and, according to *Queen's Regulations for the Army* (1975: 5. 366), the length of their hair.

While the maintenance and enforcement of such a wide ranging discipline is the responsibility of both officers and NCOs, in practice, there is very much a division of labour between the two strata. The day-to-day enforcement of discipline is carried out by NCOs. It is they who supervise soldiers closely, and who are directly involved in collective work-tasks. It is through them that orders from commissioned ranks are transmitted to the privates. Kahn (1944: 41) termed NCOs the 'immediate agents of discomfort', for in the main, it is they who decide whether or not formally to charge privates with contravention of military law and to initiate the official legal process. By contrast, officers are not often involved in maintaining and enforcing military law until formal proceedings begin. In the judicial process that ensues, an officer plays the part of both judge and jury, determining guilt and delivering sentence upon the accused.

Military law is usually interpreted by superiors in a fashion conducive to 'getting the job done'. This discretion is allowed by specific provisions within the rules and regulations themselves. The current Army Act, enacted in 1955, contains flexible provisions giving those in command some discretion in the interpretation of military law. Thus, the previously cited Section 69 of the Army Act (1955) states that offenders 'shall on conviction, by court martial, be liable to imprisonment for a term not exceeding two years or any less punishment provided by this act' (*Manual of Military Law*, 1972: 350). What form 'any less punishment' takes is then the prerogative of the officer judging the accused soldier. Another example of room for discretion being formally embodied in regulations can be found in the procedural guide for prosecuting a soldier under military law. Thus the *Manual of Military Law* (1972: 26) states:

> A C.O. (Commanding Officer) must, when signing a charge-sheet consider whether the charges preferred are oppressive, e.g. where a number of charges of insubordination are preferred against a soldier all arising out of one particular incident, the C.O. should consider whether some of these charges should be omitted.

The accomplishment of superiors' tasks, be they the setting up of a patrol base, ensuring that platoon vehicles are operating efficiently, that the barracks are kept in good order, or whatever, demands a flexible approach in their interpretation of military law in cases of rule breaking. Given the scope of military law, if a flexible approach were not adopted soldiers would almost constantly find themselves being charged under various sections of the Army Act. If such a state of affairs were to continue for any length of time, a unit's supervisory personnel would find their time taken up solely with judicial matters. As it is, the Army's code of discipline results in a considerable administrative burden. As Gibbs (1957: 258) noted during the 1950s:

> Delinquency varies in seriousness according to the nature of the offence and circumstances under which it was committed. Many minor military offences which are dealt with summarily cannot be categorized as crimes. On objective grounds, in fact, a high proportion of such delinquencies can hardly be regarded on a par with breaches of bye-laws. Though these increase the administrative burden they are unlikely to be greatly reducible owing to the range of possible offences . . .

Thus, on the very practical level of their own role performance, which is under constant assessment, superiors need to interpret military law flexibly in their own self-interest. A superior's degree of flexibility will have considerable effect upon the lives of his subordinates. If he is inflexible their existence will be harsh, and they will be subject to heavy punishment if found guilty of rule-breaking since an inflexible approach will mean that rules and regulations will be applied rigorously. An example would be how Section 69 of the Army Act is interpreted. The *Manual of Military Law* (1972: 350) states that neglect is an offence and that such neglect includes 'failure to keep kit and uniform in good order or to have proper regard to personal turn-out'. The problem is how does one assess 'good order'? In the eyes of a private, a pair of boots appears to be perfectly clean, a pair of trousers perfectly pressed, but to an inflexible superior these may appear as examples of neglect. Taken to an extreme length such inflexible rule interpretation may result in the lives of privates becoming intolerable. While mutiny represents the ultimate action of troops who are dissatisfied with the conditions under which they live, the more usual pattern is for soldiers to maintain a much lower standard of performance than that desired by superiors. Superiors are themselves well aware that the performance of those under them may well determine their own career prospects and, in combat, their survival. So, while they are extremely concerned to exact a high standard of performance from those under their command, they must strike a balance between an excessive adherence to the letter of the formal rules and a judicious exercise of judgement. Soldiers can be made to do their duty through fear of coercive sanctions alone. However, *how* they do their duty is the fundamental issue for their immediate superiors and the organisation as a whole.

Context, Offence and Offender

This generally widespread recognition of the inadequacy of a purely coercive approach by superiors helps to foster a more flexible stance towards discipline, although it is necessary to bear in mind that interpretations are liable to change according to both the actions and the context of these actions. Thus, for example, sleeping on sentry duty whilst on a Salisbury Plain exercise is likely to bring down a verbal reprimand, and perhaps a 'kick up the arse' from a Section Corporal. In contrast, the same offence whilst on patrol in South Armagh will invariably result in a much more severe and formal punishment being imposed upon the offender, to say nothing of the informal sanction of direct physical assault by all other members of the patrol. The transgressions of the private, his previous conduct as known to his superior(s), the context of the action, and the whereabouts of other superiors (if they are in the vicinity and hold higher rank, then the interpretation of law has to be negotiated with them) all influence how formal ruling is interpreted. Ions (1972: 236–7) who saw service as a regular soldier in the 1950s provides a good description of how NCOs can be flexible in dealing with deviance:

> The professional experience of these Warrant Officers and Sergeants had taught them that discipline must not be inflexible . . . They knew when to be iron hard with defaulters or trouble makers; how to distinguish individual viciousness from loss of temper; when to turn a blind eye if an old soldier of the regiment was helped back into camp blind drunk . . .

The Unit Milieu

Another important factor which influences how rules are interpreted is the particular milieu in which privates serve. Different kinds of Army units vary considerably in the degree of flexibility their members display in the maintenance and enforcement of discipline. Technical units, such as engineering workshops or communications squadrons, are primarily concerned with supporting and providing services for armoured, artillery, infantry, and combat engineer units. Compared for instance with the infantry, unquestioning obedience is not such a prime requirement. Generally such units, unlike the infantry, do not come into direct contact with enemy forces and the organisational requirement for instant collective action is not so marked. Furthermore, in the context of peace-time barracks such units have continuing administrative and support tasks. Unlike the 'teeth arms' (armour, engineer, artillery, infantry), their function is ongoing and, consequently, their time is more likely to be taken up with such tasks. Infantry units, by contrast, have no such outlet for their skills during peace-time, having only a round of training activities to occupy their time. As a consequence, there are periods of what may be termed 'dead time', during which no external training is possible owing, perhaps, to the weather, finance, or lack of facilities. During these periods superiors tend to lay more stress on the formal aspects of discipline. The barracks are the one place where the unit regimental policemen flourish and have considerable power in enforcing discipline.

Even within a particular 'arm' it is possible to discern further differences in the interpretation of military law. The following quotation is a satirical comment, from the magazine of the 3rd Battalion The Royal Green Jackets, upon the practices and attitudes towards discipline displayed by another infantry battalion, the 1st Battalion The Parachute Regiment, serving alongside them in Northern Ireland in 1972:

> At Echelon they have a rather unorthodox regiment—1 Para stationed with them. They look smart, have short hair, wear funny coloured berets with badges above the left eye. The men without anything on their arms call the soldiers with stripes 'Corporal' or 'Sergeant' and hold their hand above their right eye when men with little marks on their shoulders pass. We are trying to find out when these quaint customs started. (*Journal of the 3rd Battalion The Royal Green Jackets, 1972: 13*)

These details about appearance and forms of address are all examples of orthodox military behaviour. The Royal Green Jackets have a reputation within Army circles for being 'fly-boys' or unorthodox.In the above passage their collective rule interpretation is being contrasted with what they consider to be the more orthodox approach to discipline manifested by the 1st Battalion of the Parachute Regiment.

AN INFORMAL SYSTEM

The extent of a superior's discretion, that is, his freedom to interpret and apply rules, varies with the rank of the individual concerned. Officers who are in the position of having to pass judgement upon offenders when they are brought before them, are, as I have indicated, aided by provisions within the regulations which allow them to use some discretion. The normal context in which officers interpret law is characterised by drama and ceremony. The accused soldier is rapidly marched under escort into an officer's presence, in a stylised manner. The charge is delivered in formal legal terms. These procedures help to highlight the power of those in authority over the soldier. In contrast, an NCO's use of the same prerogative generally occurs with little ceremony, for it is they who confront first hand the common transgressions of military law committed by privates. It is invariably they who decide whether to start proceedings and charge soldiers, to punish the individual informally or to disregard the offence entirely. Informal punishment is generally preferred by privates on the grounds that the formal judicial sentence is liable to be much heavier than that imposed unofficially.

In fact, during my periods of field research informal punishments were constantly meted out by superiors, and the formal judicial machinery was set in motion only as a last resort. These informal punishments are not strictly speaking legal in that there is no official judicial process, nor documentation of the offence or the sentence delivered. In effect, delivering such informal punishments is 'off the record', though all superiors in the units I did research with, from the Commanding Officers downwards, understood and practised this system. In addition to the difference in the severity of punishment, no official record is kept and the soldiers' personal 'conduct sheets', will not reveal such instances of rule-breaking.[3] Since officers have access to these sheets when they are evaluating a soldier's conduct, either when judging him or assessing his potential for promotion, this absence of a record of deviance is not unimportant.

In the main, informal practices were resorted to, at least initially, by superiors when dealing with everyday transgressions such as being late on parade, drunk on duty and so on. Superiors who made constant use of the formal method of maintaining discipline created an administrative burden for their unit. In addition, given the prevailing 'man management' orientation of today's Army, such behaviour is liable to be looked upon disapprovingly by those of higher rank.[4] Significantly, during field research the comments by NCOs about peers who resorted continually to the formal judicial process, were of the 'he can't handle men' variety.

In conclusion then, rules and regulations in the Army are not inflexible. Rather they serve as guidelines for action which both officers and NCOs must interpret to maintain discipline which is necessary if military work is to be accomplished efficiently. The performance of subordinates in carrying out this work becomes the prime concern of their superiors, both on the battlefield and in barracks. To this end superiors interpret military law in a flexible fashion, evaluating both the offence, the context, and the biography of the individuals concerned. The rules themselves provide a certain amount of leeway for the personal discretion of the superiors, but they are also influenced in exercising this discretion by the particular disciplinary ethos of the unit in which they serve. The private soldier and his peers then do not adapt, react, and initiate informal practices in the face of a rigid set of organisational rulings. Rather, as I have explained, the fluid interpretation of institutional rulings means that the relationship between them and their superiors is dynamic and continually negotiated within certain bounds.

NOTES

1. The following studies illustrate the importance of the practical grounds for rule interpretation by members in various organisations: Zimmerman (1969), Sudnow (1965) and Manning (1977).

2. See *Queen's Regulations for the Army* (1975), part 12—'Confidential and Annual Reports'.

3. Each soldier has a 'Regimental Conduct Sheet' and a 'Company Conduct Sheet', kept amongst his/her personal documents by the unit administrative staff. The former document contains a record of any serious offence committed (such as going absent without leave—AWOL). The latter document records misdemeanours such as being improperly dressed on parade.

4. Certainly Warrant Officers and NCOs receive instruction in 'man management', much of it influenced by the social psychology of Maslow. See: *Education for Promotion: Students' Handbook* (1974) and *Education for Promotion Certificate: Students' Handbook* (1978). A formal statement concerning 'man management' is contained in *Queen's Regulations for the Army* (1975: 17).

Chapter Three

Basic Training—
Organisational Socialisation

Upon volunteering and being accepted for military service recruits enter the Army proper and undergo a period of Basic Training. During this period they are subject to processes which constitute organisational socialisation. In Berger and Luckman's terms (1976: 157–66) this is a form of 'secondary socialisation' which they see as 'the acquisition of role specific knowledge'. Recruits who join the Army enter it with what Goffman (1976: 23) has termed a 'presenting culture', in this case an interrelated set of expectations, beliefs, values, roles and norms, which is, in effect, a way of life based on the individual acting as and perceiving himself to be a civilian. The overall task of the instructional staff at the Basic Training Depot is to replace this presenting culture with one appropriate to the military way of life in which the recruit no longer thinks of himself as a civilian with all that this might imply. To this end Basic Training consists of a programmed series of activities, which Caplow (1964: 169) has defined as 'an organisationally directed process that prepares and qualifies individuals to occupy organisational positions'. Such a process will in time provide newcomers with new values, new accomplishments, new involvements, and new self-images. To attain this goal the Depot instructional staff teach the recruits what is demanded of them by their superiors. The recruit is trained to meet such role demands and motivated to practise the skills needed to fulfil them. After 18 weeks Basic Training ceases and, if successful, recruits are accorded full organisational membership. This step is celebrated, as the Depot's official handbook (1980: 8) informs recruits, with 'a colourful Passing-Out Parade, with military band in attendance. On this important day the *Trained Soldier* [my italics] passing out invites parents and relatives as his guests at the Parade'.

THE OBJECTIVES OF ORGANISATIONAL SOCIALISATION

The Army requires trained soldiers who are going to perform their roles effectively in conflict situations. To this end the Basic Training process has a dual orientation: to teach recruits soldierly skills (that is, how to engage in combat effectively) and to inculcate them with the canons of military discipline. As I have mentioned in Chapter 2, the Army's effectiveness is officially perceived as depending upon the collective obedience of its members. Soldiers may be fit and skilled in the practices of war but, from the standpoint of their superiors, if they are not disciplined they will be ineffective in combat. In practice it is difficult actually to isolate the teaching of military skills from disciplinary practices, except on those occasions when punishment is formally meted out for disobedience, since the adequate performance of many military skills—such as drill, section attacks, or ambushes—naturally involves discipline.

The round of activities which make up the recruits' training programme are all designed to inculcate discipline while at the same time ensuring that the recruits reach a certain level of skill in military activities. Nothing could better illustrate the importance of discipline in military training than the practice of drill. Drill, which involves the collective movement of a mass of men, was originally created as a means of controlling and deploying troops on the battlefield. It was particularly important during the eighteenth and nineteenth centuries when battles normally took the form of massed formations facing each other.[1] Twentieth-century warfare, however, has demanded a wider dispersal of troops on the ground, with a consequent devolution of command. Today drill has no place in an operational context, and its sole value for the organisation lies in its socialising potential, and it remains a central means by which recruits are conditioned to respond obediently to commands. Its importance can be gauged by the fact that during a recruit's training he will spend 82 forty-minute periods practising drill.[2]

Another instance of an activity with a dual purpose is that of 'locker-layouts'. New recruits are assigned a steel locker and issued with a large amount of equipment and clothing to keep in it. They are then instructed by their superiors on how to arrange these items in the locker. Items have to be folded, rolled, or arranged in a series of specific shapes, positions, and sizes. The extremely detailed nature of these instructions can be judged by the fact that all the buttons on uniform jackets, for instance, are supposed to be aligned in one direction, that is facing into the centre of the barrack room. Subsequent inspections by superiors are designed to test recruits' compliance with these instructions. The rationale for such practices given by superiors when questioned about them is that they are designed to train recruits to take care of and organise the equipment issued to them. A Corporal at the Depot commented

> If they [recruits] can't sort their kit out in a barrack room, then they're going to be up shit creek trying to find something from their packs in the middle of the night in a wood. No lights I may add! Suppose you're trying to find your can-opener then? If you're not organised you'll go hungry until dawn.

There is undoubtedly a logic to such explanations, but they tend to obscure the fact that one of the main aims of enforcing such detailed, and often petty, orders is to inculcate obedience to the military authority.

The term 'discipline' is used constantly in the Army by all superiors. The assumptions behind the term are, however, rarely made explicit. As Arkin and Dobrofsky (1978: 158) have noted of the American Army, 'it is difficult to isolate what is meant by military discipline'. Official interpretations centre on expectations concerning the recruits' appearance, cleanliness, and respect for rank and tradition; but, above all, unquestioning obedience is seen as the lynchpin of military discipline. There are also expectations about soldiers' personal standards such as their sobriety, honesty, as well as their loyalty to comrades and regiments, all of which are seen as affecting discipline.[3] Underlying the whole notion of discipline are the values of *esprit de corps*, and those of the military community. Both are indicators of the Army's official concern to maintain social cohesion, without which it would be unable to engage an enemy effectively.

THE BASIC TRAINING PROCESS

The basic training of an infantryman lasts eighteen weeks, at the end of which civilians have been transformed into soldiers 'ready to fight the enemy'.[4] I have found it most convenient to follow the typical recruit's passage through his 18 weeks of training and to separate it into two phases.[5] The initial phase which occurs during the first month largely involves the recruit being dispossessed of his civilian role. During the remainder of the training period (weeks 5–18) he gradually assimilates the new role expectations of being a soldier. I term this period the 'phase of adaptation and adjustment'.

The First Month—Civilian Role Dispossession

The Army needs to turn out recruits who are immediately ready to serve in conflict situations. In this respect the basic training process can only be described as socialisation under pressure. The first month involves civilian role dispossession in a hurry! Recruits arriving at the Depot are 'badged', formed into platoons (usually subdivided into four sections), and taken to meet their Training Team superiors who will supervise their time at the Depot.[6] The milieu of basic training closely fits Erving Goffman's (1976: 16) concept of a 'total institution'. In a famous essay (1976), Goffman used this term to embrace such superficially very different institutions as barracks, prisons, mental hospitals and monasteries. Among the most important features which all these institutions share in common are their lack of any 'offstage' area to which the inmate can withdraw for privacy and their tendency to diminish inmates' sense of individuality by moving them around in anonymous blocks and by stripping new recruits of their previous identity through such means as dressing them in uniform and, in some cases, giving them a new name or an identification number. In Goffman's (1976: 27–30) words newcomers to such institutions undergo 'role stripping procedures', which constitute the organisational means used to erode the recruits' civilian self-image.[7] Such procedures are much in evidence at the Basic Training Depot.

Upon meeting his Training Team, the recruit is informed that he is no longer a free agent, that all spheres of existence, in sharp contrast to his previous civilian work obligations, are now to be controlled by those who hold superior rank. As one observer of the U.S. Army commented: 'Aspects of daily life considered by civilians to be solely within the realm of private discretion are regarded as fit subject for regulation . . .'.[8] This introduces what Dornbusch (1955: 321) has termed, in the context of socialisation into the American coastguard service, a severe 'reality shock' from which most recruits suffer. It is induced by a series of measures enforced by the Training Team which facilitate civilian role dispossession and the undermining of the recruit's self-image. These measures erode:

(1) self-determination, the individual's freedom to make choices;
(2) autonomy of movement, where the recruit can go, when, and the time and pace of his movements;
(3) privacy: there is none in basic training, existence is collective;
(4) personal appearance, i.e. dress, length of hair, etc.[9]

I will examine these categories of role dispossession separately and show how they represent a massive challenge to the new recruit's civilian image of himself.

Change in physical appearance

On the second day of basic training the recruit's civilian clothing is taken away from him and placed in his platoon store. (He will next see it in a month's time.) He then dons uniform and equipment—the clothing is not yet tailored to his personal measurements, nor has he the knowledge necessary to make his appearance as presentable as those of his superiors or even those peers who have been at the Depot some time. As one recruit succinctly put it, 'you feel like a sack of spuds tied up with string'. Dressed in dungarees and a soft-peaked camouflage cap normally only worn on field exercises, recruits then submit to a close haircut. The result is a physical appearance which is collectively identical, and anonymous. Within the space of a few hours the former individualised civilian appearance has been obliterated.[10]

An end to privacy

The recruit now finds his existence is massively collective, there being no privacy in Basic Training.[11] He resides in a barrack room with 14–16 others of his section, possessing nothing but a large steel locker and one tier of a two-tier bunk. Toilet and shower facilities are shared with a whole platoon and meals are also taken collectively. As a consequence, all members become aware of each other's naked physical selves. In addition both the recruit's physical self and his belongings are open to daily inspections by superiors.[12] A senior NCO issued the following warning to new recruits: 'Don't hide any dirty washing in your lockers, I'll find it on inspection, I know all the tricks . . . I know everything that goes on in this Depot, everything!' Surveillance specifically by the recruit's Training Team and generally by all other superiors is the order of the day. The recruit's privacy is violated to such an extent that he may well begin to think that those in authority know more about him than he does himself. An example of this occurred during an initial medical inspection. The recruits were lined up holding documents containing their medical biography. As one recruit began to open and peruse the reports, he was immediately reprimanded by a Warrant Officer, 'Don't read that lad—it's *about* you not *to* you'. Privacy then is a thing of the past; it is civilian. Going to the toilet represents the one action where it is possible to be alone. As one recruit, no doubt wistfully, explained, 'it's the only place you can have a wank in peace!'

Restrictions on personal movement

Wherever recruits go within the Depot they do so in a squad and individual movement is initiated only on the authority of a superior. The training programme is at its most intense during the first four weeks. In the words of one Platoon Sergeant, 'Reveille is at 0530 hours and work starts then. You stop at lights out' (usually 10 pm). The pace of life is hectic, the Training Team constantly chivvying their charges through a programme of activities, each period overlapping with another. There is in effect no free time for recruits. Their evenings are devoted to cleaning kit and accommodation, and a member of their Training Team is in attendance 24 hours a day and all this continues for the full 18 weeks. Life is like being on a perpetual escalator, and there is a constant frantic, collective scrabble to change from one form of dress to another to the accompaniment of their NCOs' threats of 'outside and changed for PT in 3 minutes, last man will get a special dirty job tonight!' The following comment by a Platoon Sergeant to recruits illustrates this pattern of existence:

> Whilst you are at the Depot you'll never get the order to 'Dismiss', although it will be given to you when you leave here and go to your Regiments. 'Dismissed' means you are finished work, here you will be given only the command 'Fall Out'. That means you go to your next period of work. In the Depot you are never dismissed!

Constraint upon personal movements, however, is not confined to movement from place to place. Individually and collectively the recruit's

whole posture, demeanour and motion become the subject of control and
critical surveillance by superiors. Everything has to be carried out in a
'smart and soldier-like manner'. As soon as the recruit learns the rudiments
of drill, starting the first week, personal movements takes on a different
meaning for him. Error in physical deportment, both on the drill square
and off it, brings ridicule and threat of sanctions from superiors. The
recruit finds that even facial movements are now subject to control. A vivid
example of this was the case of recruits who were caught smiling at
instructors during drill practice. The Corporal instructing at the time
reprimanded the recruit concerned in the following fashion: 'Don't smile at
me lad—you can smile all day at the Provo Sergeant if you want'[13] Other
examples observed of superiors controlling the personal demeanour and
movement of their subordinates included:

> *On Drill:* CORPORAL (to Recruit): Stop picking your nose your head will cave
> in.
> SERGEANT (to Recruit): Who gave you permission to scratch your
> arse? I'll tell you when you can, until then stand still!

> *Prior to Parade:* CORPORAL (to Recruit): That wall's been up for 30 years it
> doesn't need your help, stand up straight, stop fucking
> leaning!

Absence of self-determination

The recruit encounters a totally structured environment within which his
capacity to make choices, to determine how his life should run, is
drastically reduced compared with his former civilian existence. As
indicated, recruits rise early and retire to bed early. Washing and shaving
times are similarly controlled. Even the speed of eating a meal is not up to
the individual recruit. The NCO in attendance decides when to leave the
dining room and all members of his platoon also have to leave, regardless
of whether or not they have finished eating. The recruit's dress is specified
for each period of instruction, and so is how he stores his uniforms and
equipment and how he makes his bed. Each day inspections of personal
dress and equipment are carried out by the NCOs of his Training Team.
Personal responsibility for the maintenance of the self is, then, severely
challenged. How one washes, shaves, and cleans one's boots are subject to
control. Absence of self-determination can at times be carried to extreme
lengths. I observed a recruit being reprimanded by a Corporal for having a
'love-bite' on his neck, who commented: 'No more of that! Tell your boy-
friend to stop biting you, it's not soldierly'. On another occasion a
Corporal dragged a recruit out of a toilet whilst he was in the act of
urinating. He then bundled the recruit into squad formation and told him
in front of his assembled peers: 'Take a piss at the right time, and not when
I say you're to get on parade, got it? I don't care if you piss yourself.'
   The processes which I have described all challenge the recruit's civilian

self-image, and are imposed upon recruits who are totally isolated from the wider civilian society and the supports it offers to such a self-conception. For the first month recruits are not allowed to leave the barracks, nor are they allowed to visit the NAAFI canteen within it. Constant surveillance by their Training Team also prevents contact with other recruits who are at more advanced stages of training. The new recruits' existence is bounded by the locations where they train and their barrack accommodation. Unable to visit the canteen, they have no access to newspapers, the use of radios was severely controlled by NCOs.[14] All of this constitutes a planned isolation, as the following comment by an officer in charge of a Training Team indicates:

> The first four weeks, it's not so much that we've a lot to teach them, which is true enough. Rather it's more to isolate them, so we can really instil into them the new way of living. They can't run off the first weekend, go back home and lose it all.

The isolation and the package of structured constraints imposed upon recruits systematically assault their 'presenting culture', and facilitate role dispossession. The impact of this dispossession now needs to be examined.

THE IMPACT OF ROLE DISPOSSESSION

Fatigue

Role dispossession involves what some observers on U.S. Army training procedures, such as Brotz and Wilson (1946: 374) termed 'a knifing off of past experience'. Previous expectations, practices, perceptions of the self, all have been undermined since the recruit entered the gates of the Depot. The long hours of work, the swift pace of activities, the constant surveillance and control by their Training Team, induce fatigue in the recruits. Their arms hurt from swinging them when marching, as well as from medical injections. Their feet are tender from new boots and the stamping of drill practice. Their skin is chafed and sore, a consequence of donning an Army uniform that is 'too fucking rough' in the words of one. They complain constantly of being 'knackered' and hungry, despite three meals a day, and their leg muscles ache constantly from the unaccustomed physical training.

Anxiety

Overlying these physical problems is a high degree of anxiety generated by the Training Team's threat of collective and individual sanctions if commands are not obeyed. An individual who has failed to obey an order may bring down a collective punishment upon his platoon or section, an extra evening inspection of equipment for instance. There seemed to be no established criteria by which superiors chose to punish either collectively or individually. Such practices varied widely, with particular superiors, particular offences, and particular contexts. This in fact reinforced levels of anxiety, as recruits were thus uncertain about the incidence of punishment.

During the first four weeks, possessing scant knowledge about the actual legal powers superiors have to enforce sanctions, recruits display much apprehension whenever their superiors are present. They exist in a constant state of anxiety. Isolation from their former civilian environment heightens the recruits' awareness of their present situation.[15] The world of the recruit has been narrowed down to the relationship between himself, his peers, and the Training Team. Actions of no consequence in civilian life take on a crucial importance in this new milieu. Recruits display extreme anxiety over the cleanliness of their clothing and equipment, and whether or not it will pass inspection.[16] A clear example of the anxiety felt about their Training Team involved the recruits playing a joke upon each other which depended, for its point, on the high level of anxiety. During basic training, when a superior enters a barrack room, recruits are expected immediately to jump to attention. The first recruit who perceives the superior is expected to shout out the order 'attention', or 'stand up'. In their own platoon, recruits were constantly shouting out these phrases when no actual superior was present. As a consequence the whole barrack room would jump to attention for no reason, behaviour which caused much mirth for the 'joker', and increased anxiety for those who were his victims.[17]

Disorientation

Fatigue and anxiety combine to facilitate role dispossession with another factor, disorientation.[18] Recruits have entered a new social world whose structure, norms, values, and practices are all largely unfamiliar. The recruit in 18 weeks has to assimilate a large volume of information rapidly, while simultaneously using this information to cope with life in an organisation which imposes sanctions upon those who contravene its rules. Berger and Luckman (1976: 173) have stressed how 'language objectifies the world transforming the panta rhei of experience into a cohesive order . . ... In the widest sense, all who employ this same language are reality-maintaining others.' The problem for recruits during their initial stages of training is that they do not have an adequate grasp of the Army's language. They cannot name the artefacts, structures, establishments, nor even the individuals around them, and therefore their comprehension is limited. This state of affairs is at its height very early on in the training process. The following conversation was recorded during the first week of a platoon's service:

RECRUIT: Is there a Corporal here Sergeant?
SERGEANT: Which one?

RECRUIT: The one who took us to the place where we got our trousers.
SERGEANT: What do you want him for?
RECRUIT: The Corporal who gave us the trousers says he's finished with us now.
SERGEANT: O.K. hold on and we'll find Corporal ————— for you to go back down with.
RECRUIT: What are we going to do then Sergeant?
SERGEANT: You're going to the place where you get given injections son (smiling).[19]

Fatigue, anxiety, disorientation, as Zurcher points out (1967: 89) in his equivalent study of the United States Navy, 'softens up' recruits and makes them receptive to the role expectations of the organisation. Suffering from a 'reality shock' induced by this process, recruits are simultaneously informed by all other members of the Depot of their particularly lowly status within the establishment's hierarchy.

Recruits for the first month are allowed to wear only one particular form of head-dress, a soft-peaked camouflage cap that is normally only worn by troops when on field exercises. Wearing this cap symbolises that they are in their first month of service and are the most inexperienced recruits in the Depot.[20] As such they are instantly recognisable by more advanced recruits and by all instructional staff, as 'Trogs': a term deriving from troglodyte—a prehistoric cave dweller—and applied, according to a Depot NCO because 'new recruits are all thick and ugly'.[21]

Their general military ineptness also marks them out as novices. The most visible sign of this ineptitude occurs during their practice of drill. When proficient in drill, soldiers execute movements at a word of command—silently, swiftly and in concerted time. Absolute beginners to the art are taught drill movements by sequence: that is, each movement is divided up into parts, and each part is given a number. Recruits then practice each part separately and, when proficient, combine the parts to effect a full movement. They are made to shout out these numbers together at the required pace as they execute movements. Their reaction is one of extreme self-consciousness. Phrases such as 'you don't half feel a prick' abound. Instructors exhort, encourage, and ridicule as confusion initially reigns when recruits discover that they no longer know how to walk, turn, stop and start correctly. Only 'Trogs' practice drill in this fashion and their collective ineptitude is on display to all who pass the drill square. Reduced to a clumsy and childlike state they are, in the eyes of themselves and their more competent peers, mere 'Trogs'.

New Role Models

Disorientated, fatigued, anxious, and conscious of their lowly status, recruits are swiftly made aware of the expectations of their new role. On the first available Wednesday morning they are taken to the edge of the

Depot's main drill square, where they are positioned and allowed to watch the 'Depot Dance'. This is the argot used to describe the once weekly formal parade in which all recruits (380 at the time of my observation) and their instructors take part. As the massed platoons march smartly past what is ultimately demanded of the new recruits by their Training Team becomes clearer. The cliché 'in a smart and soldierly fashion' becomes defined and the role expectations less opaque.[22]

Isolated as they are from the mass of recruits, 'Trogs' turn to a much more accessible and impressive source for role models, namely, the members of their own Training Team.[23] It cannot be overemphasised that basic training is crucial for successful organisational socialisation. As Van Maanen (1976: 79) has noted, when 'a person first enters an organization that portion of his life space corresponding to many of the specific role demands of the organization is blank.' During this period of time (the first month) the recruit has few guidelines, other than those emanating from his immediate situation, to order and evaluate his actions. In consequence this is the period when organisational processes are at their most persuasive.

In this context, Training Team members are influential figures for recruits on a number of levels. I have explained how recruits are propelled into a state of bewilderment while their comprehension of official demands is limited. At this stage, they also experience anxiety over their ability to perform the role of soldier, and it is the instructors of their Training Team who provide the necessary guidelines for adequate military performance. Recruits are swiftly introduced to what Goffman (1976: 51–4) called the 'privilege system'. The boundaries of good behaviour are defined by encouragement, praise and incentive. Thus on the drill square a Sergeant remarks: 'Good, now that's good. Much better than when we started. Keep it up and I'll fall you out for a smoke-break.' Disobedience or bad performance brings immediate sanctions, the ultimate one being a period of detention in the Depot Guard Room. The horrors of this particular punishment are demonstrated and dramatised for the new recruits by the spectre of cropped-headed, dungaree clad prisoners running past them, accompanied by the Depot Regimental Police, who utter a tirade of verbal abuse, whilst one's platoon Sergeant warns, 'that's what you get if you get into trouble, time in the Provo Sergeant's Hotel!'[24] Rather than this ultimate sanction, however, most disobedience is met by extra inspections of the recruit's person, equipment and accommodation.[25] Dirty jobs and verbal reprimands are also common practice. In addition, NCOs may officially 'charge' recruits, and sanctions such as fines, restrictions of privileges and extra duties may well be imposed.

The Training Team is also the sole source of information about existence at the Depot. The NCOs provide the newcomers with all the facts pertinent to coping with their new life: the name of the Commanding Officer, the system of ranks, the building next to the Guardroom, its function and purpose, when 'No 2 Dress' is worn and when it is not, how to 'Bull' boots, how to make a bed in the Army fashion and so on. The Training Team are, then, the source of incentives and sanctions as well as the interpreters of reality for recruits. They are also the principal role models available to newcomers: superiors who present an image of soldierliness par excellence.[26] Their boots are always shining, uniforms tailored and pressed. They instruct recruits in all the military skills they need to learn displaying at the same time a high degree of expertise and fitness. Nowhere is this combination of appearance and proficiency more apparent than in the figure of the Training Team Sergeant, and no other context dramatises these qualities more than the occasion of drill. Each drill movement is expertly demonstrated by the Sergeant, broken down into parts and numbers. Recruits are then made to carry out the drill movements, minutely criticised and encouraged by the Sergeant. During drill the Sergeant wears a particular form of dress which again dramatises his role. A peaked parade cap instead of the normal beret, trousers instead of dungarees and a scarlet drill sash, topped off by a polished cane.[27] Shining boots completes a performance which is all that recruits are not—efficient, experienced and smart.

In effect Training Team NCOs become 'significant others' for the recruits in their charge. The average age of the recruits I observed was 18 years and 4 months. These individuals were in transition between adolescence and adulthood, a particularly impressionable period in their lives.[28] Basic training sharply cuts off communication with their neighbourhood and their family, as well as the social control they have hitherto derived from such sources. Training Team NCOs are usually anything from 5 to 14 years older than recruits, and in addition have usually seen active service, mostly in Northern Ireland. Age, authority, expertise, knowledge and appearance, are the factors then which make members of the Training Team significant others and role-models for recruits.[29]

WEEKS FIVE TO EIGHTEEN—ADAPTATION AND ADJUSTMENT

The Challenge

At the initial formal address given by a Depot NCO, recruits were told: 'This is your apprenticeship, once you pass off that square in 18 weeks time, you are a soldier. Until then you are recruits.' This apprenticeship is presented to recruits as a direct challenge to their character and competence. In their accommodation various notices of the following kind are displayed: JOIN THE PROFESSIONALS—NOW YOU ARE HERE, ARE YOU GOOD ENOUGH TO BE ONE? NCOs constantly inform recruits that if they work hard and put in a lot of 'effort', they would graduate as 'Trained Soldiers'. In the terms of one Training Team commander, 'you're here for us to see if you've got what it takes—there's plenty of people outside who'd like to be in your position'. The recruits are informed that if they get through the first four weeks they will have passed a considerable hurdle on the way to graduation. They are told that the first month is the hardest period of Basic Training.[30] At the end of the first month they are then presented with a test termed 'Passing Off the Square'. They are collectively drilled in front of the Commanding Officer and then inspected for smartness. They have to answer questions individually about the Army. If they are judged successful they are credited as having 'passed off the square'. They are then awarded the cap-badge of their particular regiment and allowed to wear berets. The last item signifies a major status improvement, for they no longer have to wear the soft-peaked combat cap about the Depot. Their Trog status has now been relinquished and they are now no longer on the bottom of the Depot's hierarchy.

As a result life becomes easier to cope with. The hours of work diminish as the Training Team is no longer faced with a platoon who have to be dispossessed of a civilian role but a platoon which has at least a minimum of military achievement, and who are beginning to understand the military system.[31] Consequently there are fewer inspections, less surveillance after work hours and therefore less harassment. The level of individual and collective anxiety and disorientation diminishes as many of the training activities become commonplace, routine, and accomplished daily. A simultaneous assimilation of Army jargon and argot enables the recruits gradually to classify and order their newly encountered experiences.[32]

Having passed the first major test, the recruits throughout the remainder of their training are presented with a series of challenges right up to the day they graduate with a full ceremonial parade which visibly impressed them. One articulated it to me: 'D'you know John, that to become trained soldiers, we've got to pass over 97 tests? That's more than I did all the time I was at school.' Recruits are tested upon a range of weapons for their firing and handling ability, nuclear, biological and chemical warfare procedures, first-aid, map-reading, military tactics, radio-operating skills and various other subjects, by the Depot's instructional staff. Between weeks 16 and 17 the recruits live in the countryside amid wild moorland at a 'Battle Camp', where their 'fieldcraft' is practised and tested. At this venue there are also live firing exercises (using live ammunition in tactical situations, rather than on the much more controlled location of a rifle range), where war is simulated as nearly as it can be without their actually engaging in it. The physical testing of their abilities, and the activities they undergo, is very much in line with the 'action-image' scenario current in Army advertising. Recruits expect such activities to be rough and tough. Yet this does not dispel anxiety over fear of failing. The 'Battle Camp', for instance, was part of training mythology and its reputed severity reaching a dreaded extreme in the recruits' expectations by the end of the first month of their service, when it was actually two months distant at the time.

Fear of failure, of being discharged from the Army for incompetence, was prevalent. Just as onerous was the fear of being 'backsquadded', that is, being made to repeat the training programme or parts of it.[33] This apprehension motivates recruits to expend considerable effort and energy upon the activities in which they are engaged. They actively desire to do well, to achieve graduation from the Depot. Being 'backsquadded' is onerous to recruits for a number of reasons. Firstly, there is a loss of status at being backsquadded (peers often describing those who were so as 'Mongs'—Mongols—congenital mental defectives). Secondly, the individual is removed from his immediate peer group with whom an effective relationship has been built up. He is then faced with 'finding new mates'. Thirdly, he has to repeat part of the training process, which is itself arduous. At the beginning of the second week I was frequently asked: 'Are we getting better at drill now John? Not so much cow-kicking?' (cow-kicking is an incorrent drill movement, involving bringing the foot down at an angle, when it should be straight). In the platoon accommodation the results of tests and the individuals' competence are publicly displayed. This increases both individual and collective awareness of progress being made towards a new and valued status. At their first lecture given by their Company Commander, recruits were told: 'You, when you pass out of here, will be the number one guys. As Infantrymen you are vital to the success of the whole Army. All the other parts of the Army support you, for your job is to close with and destroy the enemy.' [34]

A Rite de Passage and Masculinity

This journey through a series of tests towards a new status closely resembles Van Gennep's (1960) concept of a *rite de passage*. Both Mouzelis (1971: 117) in Greece and Arkin and Dobrofsky (1978: 154) in America have noted the currency given to the popular cliché that entry into the Army turns 'boys into men', and that it 'makes a man of you'. It is difficult to gauge whether or not this form of belief is prevalent within contemporary British society. As it is the mass media and the publicity issued by the Ministry of Defence all stress a relationship between being a soldier and being a man. This action-image is the epitome of aggressive masculinity, none more so than in the case of the infantryman—the combat soldier. While current Ministry of Defence publicity stresses the learning of a skill or occupation, as part and parcel of its definition of manhood (and the soldierly role), the main focus still remains upon traditional conceptions of masculinity (toughness, aggressiveness etc). The skill factor has merely widened the Army's appeal, coopting the work ethic and productivity as part of masculine behaviour. The other combat arms of the Army (armour, and artillery) kill the enemy at long range, but it is the Infantry alone who destroy the enemy face to face: the ultimate test of courage, aggression, endurance, of manhood. Infantry socialisation is much more intense, and lays greater stress upon weapon skills, physical endurance and aggression, than the process undergone by recruits bound for other spheres of the Army. Yet all Army recruits are socialised through the same general process. The difference is in the duration and intensity, rather than in the form and content of the socialising experience. Becoming 'Trained Soldiers' and passing out of the Depot fits Van Gennep's formulation for it entails not only a change of status from civilian to soldier, but also from being a boy to being a man. As I shall show, role effectiveness is integrally linked with masculine potency in Basic Training.

Masculinity and Military Effectiveness

Military socialisation involves the development of a number of qualities and of a particular self-image in the recruits by their Training Team. These qualities, such as toughness, aggressiveness, endurance, loyalty, are seen by superiors as being the attributes required for recruits to function effectively in their new soldierly role.[35] The following are some of the comments elicited from officers and NCOs:

> OFFICER: You expect them [recruits] to behave like soldiers, to get involved in fights and to get drunk and so on. In a way you are disappointed if some of them don't, but of course you can't acknowledge it, or inform them.[36]
>
> CORPORAL: Soldiers should be young and fit, rough and nasty, not powderpuffs!
>
> OFFICER: Southern Regiments have polite soldiers. That's why they are not so effective as us. We don't aim to turn out polite soldiers here!
> [laughing].

The 'right' qualities are developed by propelling recruits through a programme of activities designed to cultivate and test them. These include physical training, road runs, assault courses, forced speed marches, carrying heavy loads of equipment, classes in aikido and bayonet fighting. Field-craft training, involving simulated infantry patrolling in rural conditions, is also a part of the recruits' programme. The overall character of these activities is that they are physically hard upon the recruits.[37] Endurance is built up by gradually increasing distances and loads, and thus the degree of physical effort. Toughness can be described as a particular state of mind, which, in a soldierly context, means achieving a high level of tolerance to various forms of deprivation such as fatigue, lack of sleep, being very hot, cold, wet, and—on occasion—fearful. This quality is fostered by repeatedly exposing recruits to such conditions in training.[38] Some examples observed include: first week: an NCO marching recruits through a puddle of water deliberately, and telling them 'a little water won't kill you, you'll get a lot wetter than this later on'. The same week: squads of recruits awaiting medical examination, clad in vests and shorts, standing to attention outside the Depot Medical Centre, in freezing weather for prolonged periods.[39] Later in the training, on arms-drill (drill with rifles and bayonets) recruits were instructed to 'throw that rifle up and break it. If it does we'll give you a new one!' Subsequent displays of pain at the sore hands they were developing from smacking the stock of the rifle with their palms, was met with the response: 'You're supposed to be soldiers—are you going to stroke it like a baby's bottom?'

Aggression, another of the qualities highly valued by instructors, is built up as recruits are exhorted and encouraged to display it in all of the activities which I have just described. Nowhere was this more apparent than during the periods devoted to the art of bayonet fighting, in which collective screams in response to the question 'what's the bayonet for?' were of the kind 'to kill the enemy!' Recruits were taught to perceive aggression as a valuable commodity, needed by them as individuals, for, in battle, it is only the aggressive soldiers who will survive. If recruits display endurance, toughness, aggression, and the requisite degree of skill, adequate military performance is liable to follow. The recruits are then soldiers and by definition thoroughly masculine.

Inadequate Performance and Femininity

Failure to perform a task adequately often resulted in members of the Training Team deriding individuals or the platoon. A means often used was to equate poor performance with being feminine and, thus, the antithesis of soldierly behaviour.[40] Some instances I recorded follow:

Bayonet Fighting Class
CORPORAL (to Recruits): I want to hear you scream, you sound pathetic, like a bunch of Mary's, no balls at all. Now let's hear some aggression!

Bayonet Fight Class
CORPORAL (to Recruit): J——— stop behaving like a fanny, and get a grip of that rifle, thrust it, thrust it in!

Outside platoon accommodation. Recruits are indulging in horseplay
CORPORAL (to Recruits): Get fell in and stop fucking about! Act like men and not like a bunch of wet tarts!

Drill square, the platoon are in the middle of a drill movement
SERGEANT (to the platoon): Come on, come on, faster, harder! Bang those feet in when you halt. Some of you are like old women coming around that corner.

The soldierly role is often presented to the recruits as being the epitome of masculinity, and in contrast inadequacy is associated with being feminine. Moreover, during various activities the soldierly role was explicitly portrayed to them as one which requires heterosexual potency:

Arms Drill
SERGEANT (to recruit who was having great trouble in releasing his bayonet from its scabbard): Stiff is it? As stiff as your cock should be when you go on leave. Get a hold of it!

Rifle Range
CORPORAL (to recruit firing an automatic rifle): Now let's see you squeeze it gently. Never jerk the trigger, always squeeze it softly, like your girl's tit.[41]

Sexual potency is reaffirmed constantly by the practice of swearing. Numerous recruits during the first week of training commented upon this since it pervaded their new environment. Their response was certainly not one of shock but a puzzlement at its pervasiveness. When they questioned their instructors about such practices, retorts of the following ilk were forthcoming:

> SERGEANT: Swearing's part of the Army lads, it's been going on for hundreds of years, you'll find it's just something everyone does. They don't mean anything by it, so don't take offence.

Swearing is indeed a generalised practice with obscene terms being often used in ways more or less devoid of their sexual meaning. Thus, 'fuck' can be used positively, negatively, or neutrally; as an adjective, noun, verb, or expletive.[42] Recruits as they assimilate the Army's jargon and argot also pick up and use obscene terms; real soldiers after all are expected to swear! The wholesale use of such language, taboo in much of civilian life, reinforces and symbolises their new status as soldiers, constituting a release from certain restraints evident in wider civilian culture.[43] Moreover, given the age group of the majority of recruits, such expressions would appear to express a still developing masculine self-image, which has been reinforced by their acquisition of the infantryman's role.[44] The image of soldierly masculinity and its connotations of sexual athleticism, admittedly of a brutal kind, is reinforced by instructors who, I again stress, are both role-models and significant others to young recruits. The following comment from an SNCO's address to new recruits exemplifies this point:

> It's been a good life. I've been all over the world for free, shagged them all, black white and . . . [mass laughter by recruits].

Loyalty to the Team

Successful military effort is dependent upon concerted action by a mass of individuals. To this end the basic training programme is aimed at creating a team-work perspective amongst recruits. Colonel Sprung (1960: 39) succinctly describes the relationship between the recruit and his peers in the following fashion:

> From the first soldiers' breath he draws the recruit learns that his own labours flow together with those of other recruits towards an end result which is credited not only to himself but to a collective thing known as his squad. The recruit must be trained as an 'individual' of course, but even so he learns that in drill as in the barrack room excellence is meaningless unless the entire squad attains it.

This loyalty of the individual to the group is variously described by those in command as 'team spirit', esprit de corps or good morale.[45] Interdependence and identification with his immediate peers is, then, a salient feature of the recruit's existence. The skills in which he is trained emphasise collective endeavour as a means of ensuring survival in the combat situation. Failure to perform efficiently in concert with others threatens the group as a whole. Cooperative effort is encouraged by instructors from the first days of training and it is presented to recruits as a necessity. Moreover, without such cooperation coping with military life becomes more difficult in barracks, as well as to lower survival chances in combat:

> CORPORAL (to Recruits): If you've finished putting your webbing together, help someone who hasn't finished. You're not civvies any longer, everyone has to help each other in the Army. The best way is to work in pairs.

> CORPORAL (instructing on sentry duty): If you don't do your job properly and follow the correct procedure, you may be responsible for your whole section being wiped out. Your mates! All it needs is for you to slip up for an instance, and the enemy will tag on as Tail End Charley [last man in a patrol], and get inside the perimeter. Everyone depends on you when you are on sentry, remember that!

Loyalty to the team involves the individual's commitment in both peace and war. Its antithesis is behaviour which draws from superiors the threat of both immediate official sanctions, and tacit approval for unofficial measures aimed at imposing retribution for breaches of such loyalty:

> SNCO (addressing recruits): If you steal off your mates that's the worst offence of all in the Army. If we catch you it's gaol for sure. And when you get out, well you can see blokes walking around with their fingers in plaster. Where they've caught them in doors, if you get my meaning?

Identification with immediate peers is fostered by the totally collective existence, living and working within the section and platoon. On a wider level recruits identify with the particular regiment they are destined for after passing out of Basic Training. They have little if any personal knowledge of such units, yet they represent the future—'real soldiering' after the apprenticeship has finished. Consequently they can be heard praising the worth of their own regiment and denigrating those for whom other recruits are bound. Identification at the section and platoon level is reinforced constantly by sporting and military skill competitions, which create mutual rivalry.[46]

Recruits then are presented with a thoroughly masculine challenge when they enter basic training. Adequate performance as demanded by instructors calls for the manifestation and development of the qualities which I have described. As recruits are socialised in this manner, their perceptions of themselves begins to change. Achievement towards shedding the demeaned 'Trog' status fosters confidence, and as the various tests are successfully passed, a new self-image begins to emerge.

A new self-image

This self-image is one which combines traditional masculine values with a competence in the techniques of survival and liquidation.[47] Recruits perceive themselves very much in the same fashion as the Corporal who said that 'soldiers should be young and fit, rough and nasty, not powderpuffs!' As Park (1931: 37) says 'the conception which men form of themselves seems to depend upon their vocation', and the trade of soldiering is centrally concerned with toughness, ruthlessness, aggression and proficiency in various homicidal techniques. Gradually as recruits assimilate and develop these qualities, a new self-image develops, as their following comments indicate:

> RESEARCHER (to Recruit): What's that like?
> RECRUIT: It's a good gun, makes you feel powerful when you've got it in the shoulder. You can make it do what you want to. You can blow things to bits!
>
> RECRUIT (to Researcher): Hey John we all passed the test run this morning, dead chuffed! I couldn't have done that when I started, came eighteenth.
>
> RECRUIT (to Researcher): Well it's the seventh week now and I reckon I've cracked it. The Battle Camp that's going to be the real test, it's as rough as fuck up there. Still I've got this far, it's just a question of keeping on going now, keeping thinking I can do it all.

This enhanced soldierly self-image is now compared favourably with those new recruits who inhabit their former lowly status. As one recruit observed:

> Trogs don't know anything and they all look like shit. . . . Well their combats are sort of like pregnant dresses and they're always putting their puttees on wrongly. We're not allowed to get our gear really tailored-up like the NCOs, but at least we pull our combats round, tighter like, shrink our berets and shape them. . . . Everyone's got to be a Trog but you're glad when you're not.

Simultaneously their particular military speciality, that of combat infantrymen, is contrasted strongly with other roles which are judged to be inferior. As I was informed by a certain recruit: 'Well we are the infantry and we get it the roughest. It's not like being a blanket-stacker . . . Being in the QM stores, that sort of thing. . . . Well, take the cooks—you can't really call them soldiers.' This then is the self-image the trained soldier takes with him to his regiment, along with a whole gamut of soldierly skills, upon completion of Basic Training. It indicates the power of military socialisation to change recruits' perceptions of themselves, with the individual now accepting an altered view of himself, as a participant in Army life as distinct from being a civilian outsider.

The organisational process I have presented in this chapter constitutes military socialisation. What I have described are recruits complying with official demands designed to produce behaviour which was integrative for the organisation. If this were the whole picture, then Dennis Wrong's (1977: 31–54) conception of the 'oversocialised man' would indeed ring true. Yet as I noted in Chapter 1, the Army, like civilian organisations, has a flourishing unofficial face counterbalancing behaviour which adheres to official regulations, and which is potentially disintegrative from the official organisational standpoint. Basic Training is, then, also a period of unofficial socialisation for recruits into what are often deemed deviant practices.

NOTES

1. See Blatchford's account of nineteenth-century recruits' drill in Palmer (1977: 96–9).

2. The time spent by recruits on drill outweighs the time devoted to teaching them 'fieldcraft' (57 periods), the skill of using the environment for cover and protection, which is a central part of the soldier's trade. See: Adult Recruit Training Syllabus (1980).

3. For official views on discipline generally, see Franklyn (1953), Pannett (1964), and Watkins (1960: 396–8).

4. This was the phrase used by the Depot SNCO during his initial address to recruits. It was no exaggeration, for I encountered recruits whom I had met at the Depot, subsequently on patrol in Crossmaglen. They had been posted to this operational location, almost immediately after the completion of their 18 weeks' basic training. Berlin (1961: 53) recalls troops fighting in Normandy, after only six weeks' military service.

5. The sociological importance of these two stages in military basic training has been noted by American researchers. See Zurcher (1967) and Marlowe (1959).

6. The term 'badged' means that recruits are designated as potential members of particular regiments, which they are to serve with after basic training. The Depot furnishes recruits for 7 infantry regiments. A Training Team generally consists of one officer, usually a lieutenant, a sergeant, and usually four corporals.

7. Goffman's definition is most applicable to the context of the Basic Training Depot. Other contexts described in this work also share the features which Goffman describes but, to a lesser degree. Goffman's position on the results of role-stripping procedures is that inevitably they are destructive consequences for the inmates self. 'Mortification' is a word which crops up again and again in his work, *Asylums*. Other researchers on total institutions, such as Lifton (1962) and Bettelheim (1960), describe a similar process of regimentation and the tyrannisation of everyday life. However, as Mouzelis (1971) has accurately pointed out, Goffman's theory is only relevant to one type of total institution, namely those which are characterised by involuntary recruitment, and whose members are in some fashion stigmatised by those outside in the wider society.

One obvious feature which Goffman omits to deal with is the meaning of such processes to the actors who undergo them. Thus, the shaving of someone's head is an act which is likely to mean something different to a monk than to a convicted prisoner. The Army is an institution which recruits volunteers, and, at the moment, the Army's public image is a positive one (McCann, 1976: 243). Thus there is generally little social stigma in 'going for a soldier', unlike in previous times, when the popular image of the soldier was based on reactions to 'Peterloo' (Higham, 1962: 38), and the knowledge that the Army's lower ranks were recruited from the unemployed and also the unemployable (see Maitland (1951: 32), Mays (1969: 75), Griffin (1937: 215–7), and Roland (1955: 107)). Moreover, soldiers are no longer viewed by the military authorities as objects needing to be kept in line by the lash, but as a valuable commodity eagerly sought after. As volunteers, their training programme is geared to the presupposition that they desire to participate in military life. I am not denying that mortification occurs in Basic Training, and particularly so during the role-stripping phase. The point I wish to make is that Goffman's thesis appears to perceive the effects of such a process as being irreversible, i.e. that they are always going to have destructive implications for the individual's self-image. What needs to be taken into consideration, however, are factors which are not negative, but positive for the individual's identity. Recruits are not stripped of their civilian role and left with nothing, rather they are immediately presented with the soldierly role. A role for which they have volunteered, into which they have self-selected themselves. The impact of role-stripping procedures, and the mortification which accompanies it, must be balanced against what recruits gain from acquiring the soldierly role. How they view the soldierly role and the positive meaning it has for recruits, are factors which counterbalance the destructive potential of role-stripping.

The reality is in effect more complex than Goffman's model allows for. As I have previously mentioned elsewhere, the Army is an organisation which combines various forms of compliance. In particular, the normative factor must be looked at carefully when examining basic training. It may be stating the obvious, but individuals who suffer an ongoing lack of self-respect, i.e. possess an impaired self-image, are hardly likely to perform effectively in combat. It would appear more accurate to accord recruits more resilience and resistance to mortification than Goffman allows his inmates. One realises this very quickly when observing recruits being verbally abused by superiors one moment and then, as soon as their backs were turned, Nazi-type salutes of derision were automatically in evidence. Vidich and Stein (1960: 506) conclude their examination of American recruit training during the Second World War, with the claim that 'the soldier's self exists in shifting and disparate layers of consciousness . . . the civilian past, the defeated self of the training period, the magnified or falsified self of combat . . . all combine in various ways to produce a workable self-mechanism.' Notwithstanding that Vidich and Stein looked mainly at conscripts to the military, their dynamic approach would appear to be more useful in trying to understand the impact of basic training upon recruits, than a standpoint which sees only destructive implications for those undergoing initial military socialisation.

8.   Anon. (1946: 366).

9.   See Goffman (1976: 24–6) for the classic exposition of such procedures in a mental hospital.

10.   Some members of training teams tended to pursue this policy of altering the recruits physical appearance to a greater extent than others. Some NCOs ordered recruits not to wear their watches, whilst others made no such command. When questioned on the rationale for such an order, answers were of the form that recruits had no need to know the time as everything was arranged for them.

11.   It is interesting to note that, during the SNCO's lecture to recruits they were instructed to 'respect each other's privacy'. Military and civilian conceptions of the term are markedly dissimilar.

12.   The rigours of Army inspections which appear to have changed little since National Service days, are described in detail by conscripts in: Johnson (1973: 94) and Baxter (1959: 13).

13.   The Provo (Provost) Sergeant is the NCO who is in charge of the Depot Guardroom, in which offenders serve limited terms of detention.

14.   One recruit who brought a portable television with him to Basic Training, had it taken from him by the Training Team, and placed in his platoon store.

15.   See Marlowe (1959: 86–7) for a similar observation about American recruits.

16.   Datel and Lifrak (1969: 876), examining the stress levels evident among American Army recruits, concluded that their findings suggested that the stress of basic training may well be as high as levels experienced under actual combat conditions. See also Stouffer (1965: Vol I: 209), and Chambers and Landreth (1955: 53).

17.   Janis (1945: 166–8) examining the adjustment of American recruits to Army life during the Second World War, observed similar forms of mimicry. He attributed to them a tension reducing function. That is, by actually practising amongst themselves the act which causes anxiety, mastery of such fear is gained.

18.   See similar comments by Stouffer (1965: Vol I: 210).

19. Graves (1958: 12) presents similar evidence of initial bewilderment caused by not knowing an occupational language amongst apprentice pipeline construction workers.

20. Vaught (1980: 166) cites the wearing of an orange tin hat as the item which denotes a 'new man' in the American mining industry, lowly status automatically accompanying the wearer.

21. The use of the term is completely unofficial. I was told that the Commanding Officer of the Depot had forbade the use of the term, nevertheless it was used constantly by all members of the Depot.

22. Zurcher (1967: 91) describes a similar instance in American Navy training. It is interesting to note that amongst Training Team(s') members, there was a collective perception of new recruits being childlike. Many of them were unable to carry out the simple domestic functions required of them to prepare their equipment, i.e. sewing buttons on uniforms. Instances like this gave rise to various jokes amongst instructors about them occupying roles akin to father and mother. Cogswell (1968: 427) uses the term 'disabled' to describe this perception of newcomers held by instructional staff.

23. I am referring to the NCO members of the Training Team. Recruits in effect, see very little of the officers who nominally command the teams. Certainly in the context of activities which are meaningful to the recruit, e.g. those in which he has to be proficient in to pass-out of basic training, the NCOs are by far the main socialising agents, and thus the central role-models.

24. The scenario of prisoners being 'doubled' (run) about by Regimental Policemen, is a familiar sight in every Army unit. It is an ongoing and particularly potent warning to soldiers of the fate that potentially awaits them if they seriously break military law. As Scott (1972: 29) has observed: 'To contain and control deviance, and thereby master it, is to supply fresh and dramatic proof of the enormous powers behind the social order. The visible control of deviance is one of the most effective mechanisms by which a social order can tangibly display its potency. The act of harnessing things which are dangerous helps to revitalize the system by demonstrating to those who live within it just how awesome its powers really are.'

25. Perhaps the most disliked of these 'extra' inspections are the so-called 'changing parades'. If the platoon or section has not performed well, NCOs will impose another parade after normal working hours. They then order recruits to parade in a certain specified dress, e.g. in physical training kit in five minutes time. When the recruits do so, they are then ordered to parade again in five minutes in full combat equipment or perhaps parade dress. Such practises can be carried on as long as the NCO desires. It causes, amongst other things, a total disarray of the recruits' equipment, clothing and locker—all of which then have to be prepared for inspection next morning.

26. Jones (1968: 354–6) in a study of Canadian infantry recruits makes some similar comments.

27. Faris (1976: 21) has observed a similar process in the American Army, where Drill Instructors wear a special 'Smokey-the-Bear Hat'.

28. Interestingly, Berger and Luckman (1976: 177) stress the point that emotional dependency (which replicates the childhood experience) on significant others, is required to radically transform an individual's subjective reality.

29. There is also the charismatic element to be considered. Military experience, as it was understood by recruits, resulted in the Platoon Sergeant particularly being endowed with much charisma. Comments by recruits in the vein of, 'he's been to Ireland half-a-dozen times', were commonplace. Weber (1977: 245–52) commented long ago upon this form of authority.

30. Recruits themselves held a perception of the first month similar to the view propagated by their Training Team(s). The following comment comes from a recruit in his second week of service: 'I reckon this is the worst part of it all, this month. They are out to try and break you. It's just that everything's so different . . . Well they've got different ways of doing things, like lacing up your boots in a certain way. Not any old way mind. All of it, it's all a test.'

31. The actual training time settles down to nine 40-minute periods, from 0830 to 1710 hours. However with a parade at 0800, various night training periods, and the time spent cleaning equipment and clothing for the next day, recruits still work a very long day.

32. Sykes (1958: 85) has made a similar comment, concerning the convicts' assimilation of prison argot.

33. In effect the fear of not making the grade held by recruits, was found to be grossly exaggerated. The Ministry of Defence concern to maintain manpower levels, results in a policy operating at the Depot, which superiors at both officer and NCO level, termed the 'numbers game'. That is the acceptance and graduation of recruits who, in the training staffs' eyes, are not as competent as they would like. One officer expressed the matter in the following fashion: 'We pass out of here material which ideally we, would send back to civilian life. We backsquad recruits, give them extra training, to bring them up to standard. It's a minimum that we hope to instil into a lot of them. If we can do that, then hopefully their Regiments with more training will turn them into adequate soldiers. It's the numbers game.' Conducting research in the U.S. Army, Faris (1976: 22) observed a similar process in operation.

34. This apprehension is of course not confined to causes internal to the organisation. Failure has possible external repercussions such as a loss of status with civilian friends or family. Recruits' apprehension is concerned, in this case, with what Becker (1977: 285) has called 'the need to save face'. Such external consequences are what Becker has called 'side bets'.

35. The qualities officially demanded have changed little in forty years, judging by an examination of official publications. See: HMSO (1941: 6).

36. Behaviour such as the officer describes cannot be formally acknowledged as desirable or productive for the organisation as it contravenes military law as well as the image of disciplined troops which Army publicity projects. Officially, such behaviour is regarded as deviant. The following extract is taken from a Company Detail (printed daily orders): 'All recruits are reminded that their behaviour out of Barracks and in particular in town must be of the highest standard. Rowdiness will not be tolerated.' In effect those in authority are in a dilemma: they wish to produce soldiers who are capable of wreaking carnage on the battlefield, yet expect them to behave like angels when on the local high street. The most explicit statement I have come across, which actually raises the question of this contradiction, is that made by Major Tugwell (1969: 78). See concluding chapter for a fuller discussion of this issue.

37. Pleck (1976: 18–27) has noted that the major forms of achievement which validate masculinity are physical.

38. Being fearful can never really be simulated, it occurs only in a real operational context, wherein there is the possibility of being killed by the enemy.

39. Obviously some of these practices are explicitly designed to toughen such as assault courses, and the like. Others, like standing outside in cold weather, occur not so much because superiors have thought out that such actions will toughen recruits, but simply that it is part and parcel of life at a Training Depot. Recruits have always lined up outside the medical centre and there is a quality of naturalness about the affair. By civilian standards it is a harsh action, by military it is normal; an indicator of how far concepts of masculinity (and of toughness) have permeated the consciousness of all instructional staff.

40. This pattern of negative association between inadequate military performance and femininity, has also been observed by Eisenhart (1975: 13–23) in American Marine Corps training. However, judging by his account such practices were taken to much more extreme lengths than I observed at the Depot. See also Bagnall (1947: 133).

41. Very similar use of sexually loaded language by instructors can be found in the memoirs of those who served in the Army during the nineteen-fifties. See: Johnson (1973: 35) and Ions (1972: 50).

42.   Soldiers' conversation is then far from monotonous or limited in its use of language. Parker (1974: 146) in his study of working class adolescents, reports a similar subtle and flexible pattern of speech.

43.   F. Elkin (1946: 414) commenting upon obscenity in the American Army has noted that 'the most significant feature of such expressions is that . . . they give . . . a unique universe of discourse which helps distinguish him (the member of the military) and thus they become a binding-in-group force.'

44.   This feature has been noted in the American Army by H. Elkin (1946: 408–13). See also Janis (1945: 172–4), Mays (1975: 34), and Johnson (1973: 34). The pervasive use of swearing has been noted amongst other very masculine occupational groups. See for instance Dennis (1974: 214–5), also Mead (1955: 230) on the relationship between youth and military service.

45.   See for example the handbook issued to all soldiers in 1980, called 'Basic Battle Skills'. Ministry of Defence (n.d.: 49). Janowitz (1964: 191) has also commented extensively upon the military's prime need to generate high levels of solidarity amongst its members.

46.   Good descriptions of rivalry being used to generate *esprit de corps* and solidarity, can be found in Johnson (1973: 32) for the period of post-war conscription, Byrom (1957: 145) for the second world war, and Griffin (1937: 88) for the inter-war period.

47.   The recruits' desire to achieve, to pass tests and perfect military skills, was nowhere more evident than on the shooting ranges. In between taking their turn at shooting, they invariably and quite spontaneously, without orders from superiors, practiced IA's (immediate actions); procedures which they had been taught to remedy faults in their weapon's functioning. Spontaneous competitions developed, one recruit checking another to see if the IA's were correct. Similar behaviour has been reported by Zurcher (1967: 94), Warren (1946: 205) and Solomon (1954: 90), in the U.S. and Canadian armed forces. I maintain that such behaviour is another clear indicator of the development of a soldierly self-image.

Chapter Four

Basic Training:
Its Unofficial Face

AN UNOFFICIAL CAREER

Just as Basic Training constitutes the first period in the recruit's official Army career, it also represents the initial step in his learning the unofficial ways of a soldier's life. This unofficial socialisation takes place simultaneously with recruits undergoing their official training programme. As Everett Hughes (1959: 457) has noted: 'A career consists, in one sense, of moving—in time and hence with age—within the institutional system in which the occupation exists. Ordinarily, career is interpreted as progress upwards in the system, but a man can make progress in a number of ways.' This chapter focuses upon why and how recruits learn these 'other ways' of coping with Army life so quickly. Successfully learning these unofficial practices constitutes a different kind of career achievement to that looked at in the previous chapter.

As I have shown, officially the soldier's training career involves a rapid change from civilian to soldier and it is through an examination of the problems and contingencies the recruits encounter in these early stages that the formation of unofficial practices can be understood. Basic Training presents recruits with some of the most severe problems they will encounter in their Army service, short of involvement in combat. On the one hand they are shaped to institutional demands by instructors using the means described in the previous chapter. On the other hand, the harshness of these institutional demands encourage recruits to seek ways of easing or evading organisational constraints by using ploys which either make their role performance less arduous, or by deliberate circumvention and evasion to mitigate the impact of such constraints.

Situational Constraints and the Unofficial Response

As I have described, under the impact of various role-stripping procedures, recruits suffer disorientation, fatigue and anxiety. No amount of presocialization in their civilian life has prepared them for the shock they suffer, particularly in the way their previously taken for granted civilian

44

freedoms are swiftly abolished. In addition the instructors who propel them through their training programme treat them in a fashion which is far from civil. Legally superiors are required to behave towards their subordinates in the following manner, and here I quote from *Queen's Regulations for the Army* (1975: 5–5):

> Officers, Warrant Officers and NCOs are to adopt toward subordinates such methods of command and treatment as will ensure respect for authority and foster feelings of self-respect and personal honour essential to military efficiency. They are not to use intemperate language or adopt an offensive manner.

This statement is the official brief on the treatment of troops but, in practice, conformity with it is, to say the least, flexible. Instructors are charged with resocialising recruits under the pressure of an 18-week deadline. In acquainting recruits with the harsh nature of military discipline instructors' behaviour and language is far from temperate. As every 'old sweat' knows ridicule is frequently employed by NCOs to gain compliance from recruits, particularly in the first weeks of training. Without this compliance recruits cannot be instructed in the various military activities which make up their training programme and presuppose concerted and collective action.

In comparison with earlier times—judging by my own recruit experience in the 1960s,—ridicule and humiliation are used less. Yet, as Abrams (1965: 253) has noted, how disciplinary control is viewed by subordinates must be judged not by the 'past practices of the armed forces' but by 'the present expectations of the men they hope to recruit'. The recruits' expectations are given a severe jolt and the imposition of military discipline comes as what can only be described as a 'reality shock'. The central image which they are liable to hold of Army life is one of 'action', of being involved in real or simulated combat activity. Therefore, when confronted with both severe constraints and activities which seem a far cry from action some disjuncture in their perceptions is inevitable, as the following comments by various recruits demonstrates:

> I expected it to be hard, after all it's the Infantry. I expected that we'd get straight into training, out into the country on exercises, instead of being stuck here inside the barracks.
> I though it'd all be putting a gun into your hand and training, not all this bed-making lark!

While the degradation and ridicule recruits suffer is generally of a verbal nature, I did on occasion observe physical abuse, such as the instance of an NCO stopping a recruit urinating or another example when a Corporal forced recruits to eat cigarettes, after he had caught them smoking without permission. While such examples are selected ad hoc, there was evidence of a degree of planning and calculation in the operation of such practices by superiors. For instance, during the first week when I arrived in the recruits' accommodation in the morning, it was commonplace to find their bedding on the floor of the room or scattered in disarray as their NCOs had found faultwith their bedmaking, despite strenuous attempts to meet the required standard.[1] The planned and deliberate use of ridicule and humiliation to compel obedience and foster an awareness of the power of superiors to control subordinates is further illustrated by the following extract from a conversation with an officer in charge of a Training Team:

> Platoon Commander's Inspection, that's when they get their first dose of me. I make a point of not seeing them very much early on. Then I have an inspection and go through their accommodation like a whirlwind. That's when kit goes flying all over the place. It's from that point on that they really know who I am.

Such occasions have a strong negative impact upon the recruits for they cannot be escaped. In Goffman's (1976: 41) terms, the recruit 'cannot defend himself in the usual way by establishing distance between the mortifying situation and himself'. Face-saving devices such as sullenness, expressions of discontent or irony, constitute behaviour which itself may be penalised on the grounds that it is insubordination.[2] Subjected to these forms of degradation and ridicule, fatigued and disorientated, considerable resentment is felt by recruits:

> The discipline like, it's a bit fucking much. O.K. so you can't go out of camp for a month, but not even to the NAAFI for a cup of tea, that's stupid. That's treating you like nothing!
> Permission to wipe my arse sir? That's the only thing I haven't been told to ask permission for so far!

Mutual resentment and anger at their instructors over the way they are being treated, together with an awareness that they are suffering a common fate together, creates a dichotomy: a division of interest between 'us' and 'them' is established within the military unit. An 'us' or 'we' feeling amongst recruits develops, directed against all those who are causing the fatigue, humiliation and ridicule; in effect all those who hold rank. What Bryant (1974a: 250) has observed of the American military, applies also to the British Army:

> Initial training in the military succeeds in separating the neophyte from his former identity and ties. Military discipline is demanding and often oppressive, and military life not infrequently stressful. Enduring and coping with military discipline and life is made easier by the presence of a strong supportive informal culture.

Solidarity

Whereas the Training Team constantly exhort their Platoon to display collective effort to facilitate official goals, recruits quickly come to realise that collective action and support for each other in the face of their instructors' demands can make life easier to cope with. This awareness and the cooperative action that emanates from it is as Marlowe (1959: 93–4) notes a 'defensive investment'. Recruits exhibited instances of unofficial cooperation very early on in their time at the Depot. Displays of mutual aid were well in evidence, such as lending each other mugs in the dining hall, loaning each other money, sharing items such as polish, soap, shampoo, chocolate and cigarettes even though it is well to remember they had never met each other before. The following dialogue between myself and a recruit happened during the second day of his service. I had asked him about sharing amongst his peers:

> RECRUIT: You've got to help each other in this place, you need friends to help you get through it all. I won't have any fags sometime, and someone will help me out.
> RESEARCHER: How d'you know that, you've never been here before, you don't know any of these blokes.
> RECRUIT: You just sort of know, everyone sort of knows that sort of stuff.

The overriding situational contingency of the first month is that recruits are not allowed anywhere apart from work and training locations. Therefore, such items as 'fags' (most prized) were in extremely short supply.[3] Mutual aid—the *sharing* of various items and money—is then a group adaptation to constraints imposed upon them. The constraints of their common situation, its enforced communality and propinquity, broke down the everday social barriers of civilian life and encouraged behaviour between recruits of the order normally only found between individuals who have known each other for some time.[4] Initially, not knowing anything about his peers, the recruit uses a number of gambits to gain information and establish mutual *rapport* quickly, including 'where d'you come from?', and 'which team d'you support?'. The barrack rooms consequently soon echo with cries of 'Bolton Cunt', 'Man United are wankers', and the like.[5] Relations within their living accommodation are as one would expect of a group of male adolescents and or near adolescents, noisy, bawdy, with much banter and horseplay, such as 'you're so ugly even the dog wouldn't play with you when you were a kid!' Intensive interaction of this type reinforces the recruits' sense of togetherness, and the realisation that self-interest is best achieved by *cooperating* with other peers. Previous civilian experience of being in subordinated positions at school or work are a resource upon which recruits draw, when faced with constraints imposed by their instructors. For example, when questioning recruits about the incident of a Corporal making some of their peers eat cigarettes, the group agreed with the following statement made by one of their number.

> RESEARCHER: Your smokings' stopped now, lads?
> RECRUIT: Not fucking likely—we've just got to keep a better lookout!

Again we have a common, cooperative solution to a problem imposed upon them, and this on the second day of the recruits service.[6]

Confronted with a new world filled with unfamiliar activities, all peers have difficulty in managing the tasks put before them by their superiors. Some recruits find the physical tasks easier than others and offer encouragement and assistance during road runs or traversing the assault course. Others are more dexterous and in the time available can competently finish a locker lay out or make a 'bed-block', whilst others still stare bemused and fumble ineptly. To some the art of 'bulling' boots comes easily while others spend frustrating hours as they attempt to acquire the demanded degree of shine. In an environment that is wholly communal, an individual's strengths and weaknesses soon become known. Advice and help is keenly sought after and given, for few recruits are adequate in all the official tasks they are required to perform, and coping in isolation is, at best, problematic.[7]

Shortcuts

Civilian experience is a resource upon which recruits draw in their attempts to evolve strategies to deal with the problems they encounter. Yet while some ploys and gambits are likely to be similar to those previously used in civilian life, others are the product of innovation, created as new problems are encountered. Life for recruits is hectic, and the fulfilment of the demands of the Training Team places recruits in a state of constant stress. To ease the pressure, to cope without so much anxiety and sheer physical effort, recruits develop 'shortcuts'.

One fairly common one concerns the 'bed-block'. Making a morning bed-block takes the inexperienced newcomer about 15 minutes, time in which he could be scrambling for a clear basin in the line to wash and shave, or completing his 'room job', a cleaning task he has to accomplish every morning prior to work, or making last minute adjustments to his dress prior to inspection. To save this time he develops the practice of making his bed-block the last thing at night before lights-out. Or, if the Duty Corporal is in the habit of checking the beds, the recruit may perform the task in the dark. He then sleeps wrapped in a single blanket on his mattress, his bed-block residing neatly on the floor. Faced with the programme of physical activity, the recruit accumulates dirty laundry at an alarming rate. Given limited facilities and limited time available for washing this clothing, constant inspections demand a solution.[8] Thus on occasion the recruit meticulously folds and irons dirty items of clothing, placing them clean-face outwards in his locker, and hopes his instructors will not inspect these items too closely. He also discovers that although he has two pairs of boots which he has been told to 'get broken in', that is, wear each pair alternately, no one will check if he keeps one pair as 'best' and proceeds to 'bull' them assiduously, thereby saving considerable time and effort, when called to wear them during a particular inspection.[9] During film shows at the Depot recruits recognise that with darkness surveillance by superiors is diminished, and so often use such periods to catch up on their sleep. On the assault course they dodge around obstacles rather than go over or under them just as soon as their instructors gaze lingers elsewhere and much the same pattern of behaviour takes place within the gymnasium. Even when practising drill, recruits soon understand that there are limits to what superiors can see and they learn to make the activity easier for themselves by completing drill movements in an unorthodox fashion when superiors are on their 'blind side'. This practice was particularly evident during arms drill, and especially so during the movements when recruits were learning to fix bayonets. As the bayonet is held in a scabbard behind the recruit's back, and therefore out of sight of the instructor's gaze, unorthodox and easier movements were the order to the day.

Picking up Tips

The beginning of the second month of training sees a large change in the recruits' circumstances. Upon 'passing off the square', they are no longer confined to their work and living locations. The NAAFI becomes open to them, and they are allowed out of the Depot during their off-duty hours. Their civilan clothes are also returned to them. Shedding 'Trog' status opens up new sources of unofficial information to the recruits which, during their first month of service, were denied to them. Whereas the unofficial practices developed by recruits during the first four weeks were heavily dependent upon prior civilian experience and assessment of situations as they arose, a new stack of unofficial information now becomes accessible. Quite simply, recruits emerging from total confinement now come into contact with other recruits in more advanced stages of the 18 week training process who pass on knowledge which both adds to and reinforces the unofficial potency and legitimacy of unofficial 'ways' in common usage.[10] Such information is passed on benevolently as proof of the giver's superior status, and is eagerly sought after by the less experienced recruits, seeking as they are better ways of making their life easier to cope with.[11] One recruit describes the business of gaining such unofficial knowledge:

> You learn things from blokes who've done more time than you have. I'm from Liverpool and I've got a couple of scouse mates in A————platoon, and they're always telling me things, stuff that will get you past a test . . . Well on the ranges when you have to hit a target so many times to pass, you get given so many rounds. Well it depends on the NCO, sometimes they'll give you what your supposed to have. Others they just tell you to go to the ammo box and fill up your mags (magazines), with so many rounds each. Well my mates told me that if that happens, just put a couple extra rounds in each mag. Then you've got more chances of passing the test. There's no way they can really tell, not with so many of us shooting at the same time.[12]

Recruits learn that hours may be saved on 'bulling' boots, by the

application of 'clear', a liquid floor polish, which produces a crystal-like
shine instantly. The tip is passed on that after an extensive day's firing on
the range, the carbon deposits on one's weapon can be quickly removed by
the use of a little 'Genolite', an industrial cleaning fluid, thereby saving
much time and energy compared with the wire brush of the regulation
method.[13] Advice is rendered about the problems recruits will encounter
when carrying out their first guard duty, for which they become eligible
after the first month of service, about locations around the Depot that
afford covert shelter and warmth such as various stores, boilerhouses etc.
The recruit is also informed that if such shelters are used, he needs to be
careful about answering the radio which he has to carry and which
connects him with superiors in the Guard Room. 'If you are in a building
go outside and answer the radio', he is told, since the sound differs when
transmissions occur inside buildings, thereby informing superiors that the
individual is off his patrol beat: a transgression which will inevitably bring
trouble down upon him.[14] As a result of this contact with their more
advanced peers, the new recruits' understanding of the division of interests
in their new environment widens. 'Us' is no longer confined to their own
platoon but now encompasses all peers in the Depot, as the following
extract from my field-notes illustrates:

> Talking to a recruit outside a weapon training classroom. He suddenly halted
> the conversation and whistled to another who was leaning against the wall of
> a store awaiting its opening. The whistle was followed by a muted call
> 'Officer', and an indication by a jerk of the head. The other recruit ceased
> leaning against the wall immediately, and assumed a more 'soldierly' posture,
> as an officer appeared around the corner of the building. Asking the recruit
> who gave the warning later, it turns out that he did not know the other
> recruit, but gave the warning anyway, as in his terms the other was 'one of
> the lads', and liable to be in trouble if caught in the act of being unsoldierly.

All the unofficial practices I have so far elaborated upon can be seen as
solutions to particular problems recruits encounter. All these solutions are
officially deviant in that they either contravene written military law, or
disobey verbal directives given by superiors. I now wish to examine in more
detail this relationship between problem, activity and these unofficial
practices.

Action, Domesticity and Boredom: A Disjuncture

Recruits enter the Infantry very much with an 'action-image' perception of
their new military selves. And while some of the activities they encounter
match the expectations they hold, there is a variety of other activities used
by superiors primarily to inculcate discipline, some of which I have already
described. There is, for example, a sudden immersion in activities of a
domestic nature, all, as Bugler (1966: 5) has noted, involving a near-
pathological concern for cleanliness, neatness and uniformity. These are

activities which, set against an 'action-image', are seen as female in character. These are imposed upon recruits who have been promised an action packed, adventurous life, filled with masculine challenge. The official justifications which are fed to recruits—the need of being organised, and that this period of service is an apprenticeship not 'real soldiering'—are rarely powerful enough to mitigate the negative view recruits develop about such activities. I will now examine some of these activities more closely from the point of view of the recruits.

First, I wish to focus upon the example of dress and the degree of smartness demanded by superiors. While the shaming ineptness of dress they show in the first month motivates nearly all recruits to smarten themselves up, this aspiration is rarely in strict conformity to the standards of neatness, cleanliness and uniformity demanded by their Training Team superiors. Recruits do want to appear less inept in their dress, but they also want to achieve a better standard with style. They shrink their berets, adjust their combat smocks, place their trouser bottoms in their puttees so that they hang over their boots in a certain fashion, bend the peaks of their parade-caps, and so on. Style in the context of the Depot denotes above all that the individual has passed the 'Trog' stage. Its creation and its maintenance are unofficial—its features are not demanded by the Training Team. Style is a means by which recruits can express some small autonomy, some individuation, by a particular slant to the beret, a certain method of positioning their cap-badge, and so on. The terms 'Bull' or 'bull-shit', used by recruits (by all soldiers for that matter) to describe their superiors' overriding concern for appearances, point to the recruit's attitude to disciplinary control in direct contrast to the importance that 'style' has for recruits.

The recruit's response to these dress demands is resentment and annoyance, particularly when he perceives them to have no other purpose than pure discipline. To appear glittering and shining in front of parents and relatives on one's Passing-Out Parade has some logic, and perhaps some personal benefit for the recruit in a sense of corporate pride. However, when the same kind of demands are made without such personal benefits, they invoke the following form of response from recruits:

> You know John, we've got to have the toe-caps of our boots bulled every day. There's no sense in it. Some days we're on the ranges, on the assault-course, or doing field-craft. You're bound to get your boots really fucked-up when you do all that, so you've got to get them bulled for the next morning's inspection, it's a real pain in the arse, no sense in it! [15]

Time and energy are being spent to no real purpose from the recruit's viewpoint, in an environment where both factors are in short supply, particularly for satisfying his own needs.

In a similar category to the detested 'bull' recruits place 'fatigues'—washing dishes, moving stores, cleaning equipment and accommodation, or similar tasks designated by superiors. Within the Depot with its

concentrated training programme, time is precious to the instructional
staff, and during the day time recruits are rarely officially given periods of
fatigue duty. Rather, fatigues are imposed as punishments for misdemeanours. This can occur as the result of being officially charged before an
officer. In addition, there is the wholesale usage of unofficial punishments
by superiors, which are sanctions imposed without the effort and
paperwork of the official process. The recruit may be told to 'parade behind
the Guard' which will involve being inspected for his dress, and will thus
require an extra spate of cleaning and shining. Alternatively, unofficial
evening fatigues may be given to him on the occasions when the various
support and administrative echelons of the Depot require manpower, to
fulfil various tasks. NCOs may also order the recruits to complete fatigue
tasks within their own living accommodation, such as cleaning toilets, or
giving the floor an extra polish. Again such activities clash with the action-
image of 'real soldiering', as well as taking up precious time and energy.
Nor can the recruit see how a dose of fatigues will help him become a
marksman. Also, given that such activities are enforced upon recruits as a
punishment, it is then hardly surprising that they view them pejoratively.

Recruits place in the same category the one 'duty' they are called upon to
perform regularly whilst being at the Depot, namely that of acting as a
member of the Unit Guard which is maintained to exercise security patrols
around the barracks.[16] During this duty recruits are ordered to man static
positions or to operate roving patrols within the confines of the Depot. The
organisation of the Guard is that on weekdays it starts at 1800 hours and
terminates at 0700 hours the next morning, while on weekends it operates
for a full 24 hours. Recruits who are members of the Guard do two hours
on patrol termed a 'stag', and then four hours resting in the Guardroom,
where they are not to undress but are allowed to sleep on a mattress. 'Stags'
involve either standing stationary in a sentry-box or roaming the Depot
checking the security of stores, etc. in all weathers and throughout what the
Army calls the 'silent hours'. Recruits view being on Guard with distaste,
for it harbours a number of all too obvious disadvantages. First, the activity
involves them in an extra spate of polishing and pressing, since the Guard is
inspected by the Orderly Officer at 1800 hours. Secondly, it erodes even
further the small amount of real free time they have, particularly if the duty
is of the weekend variety. Thirdly, the shift system involves broken sleep
and when there is any sleep it is liable to be uncomfortable (sleeping fully
clothed usually is). Moreover, recruits have to be back to complete a full
day's work with their platoon just a couple of hours after the Guard has
terminated. That few hours is the only time they are allowed off, and, as
one recruit informed me, 'you're fucked for the rest of the day, all you want
to do is to go to your bed'. Fourth, the actual periods when the recruit is on
stag, are liable to be cold, often wet and, above all, deadly *boring*. Fifth, the
Depot itself covers a large area and is protected by a single, less than
daunting, wire fence which means that any serious intruder could easily
gain access to the Depot. Recruits rapidly realise this fact, and as a

consequence are fairly cynical about the official aims and achievements of doing Guard-duty. They perceive it very much as an act of tokenism despite official warnings of IRA activity. With this combination of factors which spell boredom, discomfort and a loss of their free time, it is no wonder that recruits regard Guard negatively. Walking a lonely beat in Northern England equipped with a pick-axe handle is also a far cry from the action-image!

These activities then are viewed negatively by recruits and, as a result, recruits evolve for themselves or learn from others a whole gamut of unofficial practices which are aimed at meeting the problems posed by such activities. These ploys are generally known by recruits—by all soldiers—as 'skives', and involve either evading the activity, or simply not doing it in the officially prescribed fashion, both of which run a high risk of official disapproval. Smoking when one should be sweeping a floor, or sitting in a boiler-room when one should be out there on stag roaming the Depot, are both examples of such skives and which, in the context of the Depot, require considerable work, thought and anticipation on the part of recruits due to the high degree of surveillance by superiors in the establishment.

Scrounging

Another form of unofficial activity flourishes at the Depot, and again is a solution, albeit unofficial, to a common problem. Upon entering the Depot recruits are issued with a full 'scale' of military equipment. While there are provisions for replacement of this equipment when it becomes unserviceable, the loss of such items leads to recruits having to replace them out of their own pockets. As soon as recruits are issued with their equipment they are told to mark it with their own name and service number, and warned that thieving is endemic to Army life.[17] Thus 'going diffy' (going deficient—when recruits have to pay for missing equipment) constitutes an economic problem for recruits, particularly so when one considers that the replacement of a set of battle-webbing cost in the region of £80.

Recruits 'lose' equipment in basic training primarily through the activities of others, activities which constitute a practice known as 'scrounging'. If a recruit suddenly becomes deficient of equipment or clothing, then he proceeds to scrounge replacements, the normal assumption being that a competent 'squaddie' will repeat the process upon others.[18] Scrounging, then, within the confines of Basic Training is often a solution to a possible economic problem. Yet there is another factor which can motivate recruits to scrounge. The demand by their Training Team for a constant high degree of smartness, and the subsequent frequent inspections, means that clothing and equipment used during one day's training has to be clean and sparkling by the next: a problem for recruits since most days they spend at least some period getting themselves covered in mud and dirt.

The advantages of scrounging extra kit become quickly clear to the recruit. Spare items can be prepared and kept up to the high standards of smartness demanded by superiors. They can be used and produced for inspection, with none of the recurring late night effort required if one just possesses the standard issue of clothing and equipment. The following statement by a recruit illustrates such advantages:

> RECRUIT: I've got six pairs of them [lightweight denim trousers]. I just keep one for Monday parade, and take the rest home for my mother to wash on the weekend. You always have a clean pair for the next day, you don't have to spend all night cleaning kit.
> RESEARCHER: How did you get all them extra pairs?
> RECRUIT: I borrowed them off the Depot! (winking).

The attitude of recruits towards scrounging is mirrored by the following comment made by one of them:

> If you see a waterbottle or see a belt laying around loose, well it's spare naturally, and you give it a home don't you? I mean one thing you learn quickly around here, is to never leave your kit about. If you do and get stuff knocked-off, no one gives you any sympathy. I'm not saying that blokes will say to you that you deserve to lose your kit, but they'll think you're a bit thick asking for it!

DISCIPLINE AND ITS ENFORCEMENT

The successful accomplishment of the unofficial and deviant practices I have described is facilitated by the amount of knowledge recruits have of their superiors. As Hilmar (1965: 298) has noted of the American forces so the same applies to the recruits at the Depot, 'they will have had considerable experience in testing the limits of deviation in various structured situations'. How far recruits can go, how much they can 'get away with things', involves a very similar process of assessment, whether the superior in charge of one is a teacher, foreman or Platoon Sergeant.[19] From an early date—even before recruits really possess the knowledge to assess competently a particular NCO's power and character—they quickly become aware that all commands need not be taken literally.[20] A common example is the case of NCOs threatening recruits who lag behind with dire punishments as they hustle their charges through the tightly scheduled training programme. Often this takes the form of NCOs threatening those who are slow with extra dirty jobs, and the like. Initially, when this kind of threat is uttered, recruits are filled with anxiety, and rush about madly, fumbling and falling over each other in their haste to comply with the order. After a while, however, it becomes apparent to them that in the main such threats are not carried out. Such an awareness both diminishes the level of anxiety for recruits, and allows them to take an extra drag on a cigarette, put a stamp on a letter, or listen to the football results on the radio—the kind of activities which, in the context of Basic Training, are *achievements*. In the situation I have just described, recruits understand that NCOs are only liable to carry out their threats against habitual late-comers.

Gradually as recruits and instructors spend time together, the former gain a more intimate knowledge of the latters' characters, idiosyncracies, and above all, the degree of flexibility which they display when enforcing discipline. This knowledge is used by recruits as a resource when they decide whether or not to engage in unofficial practices. To understand fully the growth of this knowledge, one needs to understand the development of the relationship between superiors and subordinates. Since, in no small measure, this task involves a consideration of the NCOs position and motives, the focus of my analysis will concentrate upon them for a moment.

Recruits' Relationships with NCOs

As I have mentioned, for a variety of reasons the 'book' is interpreted flexibly by superiors. Faced with the task of turning civilians into soldiers in 18 weeks, instructors evolve their own unofficial practices to aid them in completing their own role performance. In the early stages of Basic Training the severe deprivation and constraints suffered by recruits cause them to view instructors in a decidedly negative fashion. Jones (1968: 301) has described a similar process in Canadian Army training: 'By virtue of the focus of their camp roles on the problems of discipline, the incumbents of the socializer role acquired a strong punitive significance to the recruits.' However, NCOs need to elicit from recruits levels of performance which they are not likely to display if those who socialise them are perceived solely in this way. Coercion alone will not bring about the kind of commitment to training activities that superiors wish to create. The basis on which to build a strong normative commitment to the recruit's new role is already in evidence; they have, after all, volunteered to be soldiers. Yet cultivation of this orientation, this predisposition, cannot be effectively reinforced until the recruits' solely negative view of the instructors has been diminished.[21] There are a number of ways instructors accomplish this, and I will now go on to show how their role performance shifts as their relationships with recruits develop.

The initial strategy employed by NCOs, once recruits begin to understand and comply with their commands, is to *display* that they can be lenient and flexible in how they interpret military law. Whilst recruits are verbally abused, given extra inspections, or fatigues, during the first few weeks of their service, they are not likely to be officially charged.[22] Flexibility and some permissiveness in dealing with subordinates is explicitly made known to recruits at this stage, as the following remarks by a Sergeant illustrate:

> You can't put them in front of the Company Commander, not at that early stage of the game. They don't know what the score is then, so you fuck them

around in other ways, without charging them. You tell them, 'O.K. you're
new and I'm prepared to be easy on you, until you know how things work'.
Once they pass off the square things are different, they should know by then,
that if they step out of line it's going to be a charge.

Often this 'period of grace' involves NCOs disregarding minor acts of
deviance by recruits, an indulgence which, given that their own duty is to
maintain discipline, is itself technically in breach of regulations, for in the
Army ignorance is legally no excuse for failure to comply with a
command.[23]

Contexts, Formality and Informality

As the training programme progresses recruits become aware that their
superiors' treatment of them changes with particular contexts. Especially in
barracks, interaction between recruits and their superiors is characterised
by a high degree of formality. Recruits address all those who hold rank by
their official title. In all public places—that is in contexts where other
superiors are likely to be present—recruits also stand to attention when
addressing or being addressed by a superior. In contrast within the
barracks, during lectures and periods of instruction other than drill,
superiors exhibited a degree of permissiveness in their dealings with
recruits. In my own observation, classrooms and outdoor training areas
were locations where a greater degree of informality was in evidence.[24]
Recruits asked questions and initiated a degree of interaction themselves.
This informality by superiors not only lessens their punitive significance for
recruits, but simultaneously reduces the degree of impersonality and the
degree of social distance between them and their superiors. At the same
time and, as a consequence, the degree of deprivation suffered by recruits is
lowered and constraints upon their posture, demeanour and language, are
no longer so strictly imposed. As well as reducing their punitive significance
through such relatively informal contact, superiors promote solidarity
between recruits and themselves by sharing the same tough field conditions
or by freezing together on the same windswept rifle ranges. Instructors in
these contexts are then not only NCOs but also fellow soldiers coping with
the same problems.

Recruits are keenly aware of the changes in treatment that occur within
different locations, as one put it whilst on the final Battle Camp on the
northern moors: 'It's better out here, not as strict as in barracks, you can
have a laugh with the NCOs out here. Everyone's more relaxed in a way.'

The Importance of Humour

Humour permeates the relationship between recruits and their Training
Team, and is a useful indicator of how this relationship is progressing.

Ridicule is used extensively by instructors during the role-stripping phase, to demean and to correct the recruits' behaviour. Gradually, as recruits begin to function more adequately in their new roles, as informality begins to be displayed between superiors and subordinates, so also humour becomes less censorious. Ridicule gives way to a 'joking relationship' characterised by much banter and repartee.[25] At this stage, if a recruit commits some misdemeanour, humour is used to correct and warn rather than ridicule. The following comment comes from a Platoon Sergeant addressing a recruit who is talking whilst standing in Platoon formation 'All right J——— shut it up, or they'll hear you gobbing off in Newcastle. Any more of it, and I'll shovel shit into it, it's big enough.' This form of humour is not confined to the correction of misdemeanours, for occasionally recruits initiate it themselves. The following example happened during a Section's last training period on a Friday before finishing work for the weekend:

> CORPORAL (to Recruits): O.K. children get fell in and let's go and play soldiers!
>
> RECRUIT (answering): Will you buy us all ice cream Dad? (all participants laugh).

A Working Relationship

As recruits discover that NCOs can be flexible in how they interpret formal rulings, a working relationship is developed between them. This relationship is based upon a largely implicit and rarely explicitly formulated bargain. On the NCOs' side they expect recruits to perform adequately in their new roles so as to graduate from Basic Training in 18 weeks. While NCOs expect a percentage of recruits to be backsquadded, they view the majority as being capable of passing-out on time. Something else which reinforces the NCOs' demand for an adequate performance from their charges is the series of inter-platoon and inter-section competitions in which they are all involved. Such military skill competitions obviously cast light upon the competence of the instructors who train recruits. A bad performance by recruits in such competitions does their Training Team's own careers no good at all. The recruits' expectations in such a bargain is that their instructors interpret formal ruling in a flexible fashion and, as a result, the deprivation which they suffer is relatively reduced.[26] This means that the recruits find themselves with a little more time, less direct surveillance, less harassment, etc. Any increase in the degree of autonomy recruits enjoy is very valuable to them. As one recruit explained to me:

> It takes about 15 minutes to make a bed-block in the morning, and that's 15 minutes less sleep. We didn't have to make one this morning, our Section Corporal told us just to make our beds down. You really look forward to something like that.

The bargain is struck and reinforced by instances such as these. Others, while not so graphic, nevertheless contribute to the building of a working relationship. Instances such as a Sergeant sharing his homemade soup and biscuits with recruits on the rifle-range, or a Corporal allowing recruits to keep the ring and locking-pin, from the first grenade they throw: 'They like that, it means a lot to them, they take it home on weekends to show their civvie mates'. Those superiors who do interpret rules flexibly are then contrasted strongly by recruits with those who either do not do so or are less prone to do so, as in the case below, concerning an officer.[27] The context is a military skills competition and one recruit is expressing his ire over the behaviour of a certain Captain:

> That Captain's a real shit—everything's by the book for him. He asked a guy how many items were in a cleaning kit (weapon cleaning kit), and the guy told him the right number. Then the bastard told him he wasn't right, and said he'd missed one—he should have counted the box!

Breaking the Bargain and Renegotiating it

The agreement, the bargain, is as I have stated rarely made fully explicit in any formal sense—unless the expectations of either party are breached. For instance, if an NCO perceives recruits to be slacking at drill and cancels their smoke break, the contract is being called into question. At such a point the crucial issue in the business of renegotiating a working relationship is whether or not recruits perceive any justification in the NCO limiting the degree of flexibility he normally shows. A bargain between two parties implies a degree of obligation on both their parts. Once a working relationship has been established, the obligation to fulfil one's part is felt and understood by recruits. The following incident illustrates a case where recruits have failed to meet such an obligation from their NCO's viewpoint, and accept fatalistically his return to a more rigorous approach to rule interpretation. I have just asked the recruit what his Section Corporal was like:

> He's a decent bloke generally, but he's a bit pissed-off with us today, giving us a hard time. . . Well, we were all late getting up this morning after he'd given us a call. We had to rush like mad to get on parade in time. Half the blokes didn't make it to breakfast, and the room-jobs didn't get done either, so the place was in a bit of a state. He's been giving us fuck-all today, bollocking us for everything, no smoke-breaks, doubling us everywhere. Tonight we've got a room inspection, 'beasting' us he is. He'll settle down in a bit. Fair enough like, we fucked it up, could have got him in trouble if the Platoon Commander had come around and inspected the room. It's just that we were really knackered, been out on exercise on the common last night.

If, however, recruits perceive no justification for NCOs' reverting to a more rigid approach to discipline, their motivation to fulfil their part of the bargain, their sense of obligation, will in its turn be reduced. Recruits then do their duty, perform the task set them, first because they wish to graduate from the Depot, to get on with 'real soldiering', and secondly through fear of coercive sanctions being employed against them by superiors. Their level of performance, however, is liable to be far less than the standard which those in command desire.

Whether or not recruits perceive any justification in the NCOs' actions is important then in influencing the renegotiation which occurs as the working relationship is once more re-established. Such negotiation and renegotiation, made up of flexible rule interpretation on the NCOs' part, and differing levels of military performance on the recruits' part, is a central feature of the relationship between them. The bargain is made until the next time some disjuncture, some violation of expectations occurs.[28] Thus it is never made in a 'once and for all sense'. As Strauss (1975: 304) has noted of the hospital, so the same applies to the context of the Depot and its members:

> For the shared agreements, the binding contracts—which constitute the grounds for an expectable, non-surprising, taken-for-granted, even ruled orderliness—are not binding and shared for all time.

The term Strauss and his colleagues use to describe such a set of social relations is that of *negotiated order*, and it is just as relevant and useful a concept for this study also.

Understanding NCOs

Against this background, recruits accrue information about superiors. A biographical profile of each superior is established, for, from the recruit's viewpoint, knowing the degree and limits of tolerance of each member of his Training Team (and if possible, others outside it) is crucial to the successful evasion of the often onerous officially prescribed duties. Recruits learn that their NCOs' tolerance extends further in relation to some activities and to some contexts than to others.[29] The form of deviance and the context intermesh, and the recruit's knowledge acts as a complex resource to guide his actions. Categories of behaviour which NCOs are known to display little flexibility towards include all aspects of weapon-handling and occasions when their own status is directly in jeopardy. The former category includes maintenance, safety and security of arms and ammunition. In the latter category, an incident such as a joke which has been taken too far by a recruit, or a particularly ineffective performance, whether it be intentional or unintentional, are instances which are liable to provoke a more rigid rule interpretation by superiors.

Thus if a recruit makes a joke at the instructor's expense in the classroom, the informality of the context, together with the likelihood that there will not be any other higher-ranking superior present, allow the instructor to exhibit a degree of permissiveness towards the recruit.[30] The same behaviour by a recruit where a high degree of formality is expected, for instance on the drill square, is liable to bring down severe sanctions upon his head. Behaviour of the latter kind in a 'public' place where other superiors may be passing, not only contravenes the situational proprieties of the drill square, but also places the superior's own status in jeopardy, positively broadcasting the fact that he is being permissive with those whom he is supposed to discipline. Similarly, if a recruit is slack on the drill-square and drops his weapon during rifle-drill, he will more than likely receive a torrent of abuse from his instructor, though, unless a repeated offender, he is not likely to have any other sanction imposed on him. In contrast the same inept performance with a weapon on a rifle range where live ammunition is being used may well see the offender officially charged. So whilst the formality of the occasion outside the barracks is considerably reduced in one sense, in another, especially regarding safety procedures, it is heightened, and the NCOs' attitudes towards rule enforcement alter accordingly.

Possessing both the knowledge and techniques to effect deviant practices to evade the all-pervasive surveillance of Basic Training, recruits are then constantly evaluating the possibilities for making their lives easier— assessing the gains, the dangers, and the consequences of becoming involved in 'other ways of doing things'.

So far I have shown how recruits are socialised both officially and unofficially during Basic Training. As a result, when leaving the Depot they are in possession of a dual set of norms, values, knowledge and skills, one of which is integrative for the official goals of the organisation, and is centred on techniques of survival and liquidation. The other is potentially disintegrative for organisational goals, and is primarily concerned with facilitating an easier existence within the training environment. These unofficial practices are solutions to the problems recruits encounter in Basic Training and, as such, are examples of 'situational adjustment'. In the next chapter I follow the recruits to their designated Regiment—the next stage in both their official and unofficial careers.

NOTES

1. Recruits had to make their beds in a specific manner, known as making a 'bed-block'. An intricate process of folding, measuring and stacking blankets and sheets together which requires considerable effort on the part of newcomers to the practice.

2. Goffman (1976: 41) has used the term 'looping' to describe this process.

3. This is not to say that members of the Training Team did not in time, about the forth day of training when I observed it, escort selected representatives of the Platoon, who were armed with funds and a long list, to the camp NAAFI. However, the frequency of these official shopping expeditions, were far too few to satisfy the recruits' needs, particularly for cigarettes and chocolate.

4. A study by Loether (1960) of American Air Force men suggests the importance of propinquity as a prerequisite for solidarity amongst small-groups.

5. Marlowe (1959: 77) notes similar gambits amongst American Army recruits. The comments of Johnson (1974: 115) reveal the same sort of identity formation techiques amongst workers in a food processing plant. It is likely that such gambits are common devices for 'opening' interactions.

6. See for instance Jackson (1972: 75) and Sykes (1973: 207–8) for similar instances recorded in the work place, and also Willis (1979: 18) who has noted such behaviour in school.

7. See Ions (1972: 59) for a National Service example of mutual aid.

8. There was a newly opened launderette at the Depot, which was totally inadequate for the number of recruits it had to cope with. Given the restrictions placed on the recruits, particularly in the first month, time and opportunity to visit the launderette depended upon their superiors allowing such visits. These visits were far from as frequent as the recruits would have liked. The alternative was for recruits to wash a large amount of clothing by hand. The average age of the recruits I observed was 18 years and 4 months and I suspect that most of them lived at home prior to entering the Army. Washing and ironing would then be an onerous and unfamiliar task given their background. After the first month, a large number of recruits hoarded dirty washing until the weekend, whereupon they would take it home to be washed and ironed. See, Sullivan et al.(1971: 97–8) for American Air Force examples of 'shortcuts'.

9. See Marlowe (1959: 88) for a similar instance in the U.S. Army.

10. During the first month the socialisation process may be termed 'disjunctive'. That is, recruits enter a situation where they are of a kind, and where they have no access to peers gone before them. Upon completion of four weeks service, the socialisation process may be described as 'serial'. Recruits here have access to others who have already been through the training they are about to encounter, and thus they can gain information about future events from their more experienced peers. Cogswell (1968: 431) uses these terms in her article on the structural properties of socialisation processes.

11. A conscript describes National Service recruits seeking ways of making life easier, in Johnson (1973: 30). See Cain (1973: 72) and Holdaway (1983: 52) for examples of 'easing behaviour' amongst policemen.

12. If recruits have more holes on a target than rounds they have been given, and are subsequently questioned by instructors, there is a stock retort, 'Some silly bastard's been firing on my target!' (a mistake which does occur).

13. The use of 'clear' and 'Genolite' is officially frowned upon, to say the least. 'Genolite' has an acid base, and while effectively cleaning carbon off a weapon also tends to decrease its operational life.

14. Two recruits were fined £140 between them, for being off their designated patrol path during guard duty, while I was observing at the Depot. This practice of resting or sleeping whilst on duty has been reported elsewhere. Burnham (1969: 68) reports it as a routine practice amongst New York police, where it is known as 'cooping'.

15. As I have noted before, it is no good myself (based on my own service experience) and other observers stating that 'bull' or discipline has been reduced in today's Army. Recruits have no personal knowledge of such times or the practices which were current then. The meaning of and resentment at such features of their existence come from their own immediate experience and difficulties.

16. All tasks soldiers are commanded to perform are officially termed 'duty'. Technically servicemen and women are 'on duty' 24 hours a day. However, in practice, in a peacetime barracks context, the normal working day is usually between 0800 and 1630 hours. There are, however, a number of 'duty personnel' who remain on duty, providing security, administrative and transport facilities. Thus within the average unit, there are duty clerks, duty drivers, and a unit guard, all maintained overnight. Such duties are run on a roster basis, rosters for weekend and daily duties operating separately. See Bagnall (1947: 42–3) on guard duty.

17. See Ions (1972: 35) and Mays (1969: 4) for examples of such warnings, during the 1950s and inter-war years respectively.

18. There are numerous illustrations of this scrounging practice, contained in the literature written by ex-soldiers. See for instance Coppard (1969: 8) from the era of the First World War, and from nearly a half a century later, the recollections of Ashton-Braithwaite (1969: 16).

19. For a National Service recruit's realisation of how far to go with NCOs, see Chambers and Landreth (1955: 56).

20. This is important in the process of recruits' learning about Army life. They begin to understand that a literal interpretation of a command is not always necessary. Official social norms, as Stouffer (1949: 717) has noted, need an inbuilt flexibility to make group behaviour possible. See also Mechanic (1962: 362).

21. The other important influence on how superiors treat recruits is that recruits can quite easily terminate their service during the initial period of training. If under 18 years, all that is required is for the individual to give a few days' notice. If over 18 years he has to serve for a trial period of a month, and then pay a nominal fee. Application for this form of discharge from the Army must however be made within the first month of service.

22. Ridicule has long been recognised and used by training NCOs as an effective means of making recruits amenable to discipline. See Ions (1972: 61) on his training in 1952, Graham (1919: 58) on the First World War period, and Lyndon (1978: 21) commenting upon his Territorial Army training (under Regular Army instructors), just a few years ago.

23. Van Maanen (1976: 78) has pointed out that various organisations display such a period of time where the newcomers actions are 'relatively free from censure'. Jones (1968: 361) has noted a similar process at a Canadian Army recruit centre.

24. The greatest degree of informality occurs when recruits live in the field with their instructors, and simulate tactical conditions. This, however, is something that happens at the very end of their training, and then only for a few days.

25. Examples of such banter from other times can be found in Ions (1972: 49), Mays (1969: 60) and Wilson (1951: 108). The original anthropological use of the term 'joking relationship' was by Radcliffe-Brown (1940). See also Bradney (1957) who has carried out research on the topic in industry, and Faris (1976: 20–21).

26. Sykes (1958) has described how prison guards and inmates maintain a similar kind of bargain.

27. Stouffer (1965: I, 405) recorded similar findings concerning superiors who were viewed positively by subordinates, and the degree of flexibility and informality they exhibited amongst American troops.

28. Gouldner's (1965: 27–39) study of an unofficial strike in the American mining industry, is a good example of conflict arising from the violation of expectations, held by workers. The position of troops in the Army is of course different there being no legal right to strike, such an occurrence being classified as mutiny.

29. Blau (1966: 73) and Blau and Scott (1970: 143) have noted this, when commenting in general upon styles of supervision in industry.

30. Solomon (1954: 92) records such an instance in a Canadian Army lecture to recruits.

Chapter Five

'Real Soldiering' in the Battalion

The Regiment the private joins is in effect a single Battalion of infantry, with an establishment of 650 including all ranks. Unlike the Depot it is not a fluctuating and transient community. There are, for instance, no mass exits of whole platoons as is normal at the Depot. Granted, soldiers do leave the Battalion as they terminate their service in the Army, or when they are posted off to some other temporary work, but (and this certainly applies to privates) most members spend the majority of their service time within this one Battalion. An infantry Battalion is internally divided up into a number of rifle companies, in addition to which there is an administrative and support echelon including medical, transport, engineering and police elements, as well as various specialist platoons which have signals, mortar, and anti-tank functions. The core of the Battalion, both in terms of numbers and importance for its operational role, are the Rifle companies, which receive support from these various other subdivisions. Each Rifle company is divided into a number of platoons and each platoon, in turn, divided up into sections. The number of companies and, in turn, the number of subdivisions, and the number of soldiers in each, varies with the overall strength of the Battalion. That fluctuates according to the numbers discharged from the Army, and the strength of recruitment at any particular time. The Battalion is commanded by a Lieutenant Colonel, and each Company by a Major. Platoons are usually led by 'junior officers' ranging from Second Lieutenants to Captains. As for non-commissioned officers (NCOs), each Company has a CSM and each platoon a Sergeant. Sections are usually commanded by a Corporal, with a Lance Corporal as his second in command. So the newly arrived private soldier will for instance find himself serving as a rifleman in 3 Section, 2 Platoon, X Company.

Simply put, an Infantry Battalion's mission is to engage and destroy the enemy. In conventional mechanised warfare this would usually involve operating with the support of armour and artillery. In practice, the Battalion is far more likely to be involved in an operational tour of Northern Ireland. This deployment is closer to counter-insurgency campaigning than conventional war, in which surveillance, intelligence gathering, small-scale patrols and ambushes are the order of the day.[1]

When not actually engaged in a conflict the unit's time is taken up in preparing for it. As a company training directive concerned with an extended field exercise in Canada stated: 'The forthcoming training period is a unique opportunity for the Platoon Commander to train, exercise and test his platoon and himself in many phases of war'.

On occasions, such as a major field exercise, training will be conducted by the Battalion as a whole. More frequently, however, training activities are decentralised to the Company level, and often even further down to the Platoon and Section.[2] Training may involve the private in anything from a 10 mile run with the rest of his Company around the vicinity of the barracks, to a month's field exercise by the whole unit overseas. During my periods of research with it, the Battalion practised intensive counter-insurgency tactics in preparation for Northern Ireland, while a little earlier it had undergone an inspection by higher authority, and had undergone Nuclear, biological and chemical warfare training.

The aims of the training that the Battalion carried out are a continuation of those in the Depot: efficiency in soldierly skills, the promotion of endurance, toughness, aggression, and a strong identification with the group. All these then remain the central concerns of those who command the privates. At the same time, underlying these concerns is the continuing demand for obedience, and conformity with military discipline. The Battalion's training and the accompanying efforts to foster particular qualities are based upon several assumptions. One of these is that the newly arrived private possesses to a certain degree soldierly skills. This is taken for granted, and newcomers are gradually introduced to a wider range of weaponry and activities such as infra-red night sight equipment, river-crossing techniques, urban patrolling, and exercising with live supporting fire from mortars and artillery. An increased degree of endurance and toughness are demanded and fostered by exposing newcomers to the vagaries of infantry work, often involving prolonged periods living in the field. Whereas the recruit's ultimate test at the Depot was a 'Battle Camp' of little more than a week, as a fully fledged private he now finds himself as a matter of course spending long periods enduring a primitive existence in the countryside, when it is not unusual for him to be marching fully loaded with up to 80lb or more on his back.

Often cold, wet and muddy—more rarely baking hot as it was in Alberta during the field research—usually without a shower for prolonged periods, all members of the Battalion suffer considerable deprivation. Such periods consist of military work and little else, and the work is itself invariably accomplished on a chronic lack of sleep.[3] Exercise planning staff deliberately simulate combat conditions. Again to quote the Company Training Directive: 'The aim of our training here is to practise the company in all its skills in as *realistic* [my italics] as possible a setting'. Thus the toughness fostered in Basic Training is built upon and reinforced by the continuing training of the Battalion, and along with it aggression, physical endurance, and loyalty to the group.[4] The last involves creating in the privates a high level of identification with their Section, Platoon, Company, and, ultimately, the community of the Battalion. This identification is made more potent by, once again, the private soldiers living in something resembling a 'total institution'. For, as at the Depot, he sleeps, eats and works with the same members in his section and platoon.[5] Furthermore, a considerable period of his leisure time is also spent in the company of these same individuals. Such an identification with the structural levels most immediate to him is again cultivated by various officially arranged competitions involving sporting or military skill.

Discipline and the New Environment

The second presupposition held by those who have rank above privates is that the official socialisation process has been successful. Newly trained soldiers are considered to be disciplined troops who will generally comply with the canons of military law. As a consequence, upon entering the Battalion, the newcomer—usually called a 'sprog' by those privates who are already members of the unit—encounters a number of pleasant changes.[6] Overall there is a considerable reduction in the concern by superiors for 'bullshit'. Bulled boots, for instance, are unknown on morning parade, the norm expected being functional cleanliness rather than a shining display. Inspections of personal equipment and accommodation are also now rare occurrences. Drill is confined to a few perfunctory movements each morning. So much so that a Corporal could joke with a Platoon, 'that surprised you, didn't it? Asking you to come to attention, half of you can't remember how to do it!' The private finds that his hours of work are less in the barracks than the Depot, the normal day being from 0800 to 1630 hours. Moreover, unless on duty or on a 'working weekend', everyone is free of work from 1300 on Friday until 1200 on Monday.[7] There are no restrictions on the time privates have to be back in camp prior to a working day, nor do they have to book in and out of barracks at the Guardroom, as they did at the Depot. No longer are there 'reveille' or 'lights-out', nor do privates have to make 'bed-blocks' each morning. Although the single junior NCOs may live in the same accommodation, they are not resident there for the sole purpose of maintaining surveillance over their subordinates, as was the case at Basic Training.

An Extension and Deepening of Working Relationships

This relative relaxation of discipline is motivated by superiors acknowledging that the organisation's socialisation process has been successful, and also by the fact that those in command have an even greater need to establish working relationships with their subordinates. The tasks which face all members of the Battalion are both more arduous and more complex than those facing them at the Depot, and so greater and closer cooperation is needed for the efficient completion of these tasks. A Training Team at the Depot may not establish a particularly satisfactory relationship with a Platoon of recruits. That may not be desirable, but it is not likely to be disastrous for the Team members' individual careers. All their eggs are not all in one basket, for they will train other recruit platoons, and so have other chances to show their expertise as instructors. In contrast, superiors in the Battalion are in charge of a particular Company, Platoon, Section, or whatever. There is, for them, no real second chance to display their military competence. Movement to another platoon may come with promotion, or as a result of a manpower re-allocation, and the reason will be known instantly by all ranks. Likewise failure and incompetence becomes instant news in such an insular community. Inadequacy may well result in the NCO or officer being reprimanded, 'busted', or transferred to some other less demanding job within the Battalion. For their own personal career then, there is even greater need for superiors within the Battalion to arrive at satisfactory working relationships with their subordinates. In addition, because the tasks involving the members of the Battalion are more arduous and more complex, the role of superiors is somewhat different from that in evidence at the Depot. There the superiors occupied an instructional role, they taught and then watched and guided the recruits' performance. As a result, they were in a sense detached from the recruits' performance as a direct function of the need to achieve a high degree of surveillance and control over them. To a certain extent this happens within the Battalion, especially in activities such as a weapon-training lectures or shooting practice on the ranges. However, during simulation of combat activity, superiors' and subordinates' relationships are not simply of this instructional kind. Tactics require a high degree of coordination and team work, and there is high degree of decentralisation, the infantry being primarily concerned with cover, shelter, dispersal—in short, survival! There is no time or opportunity for superiors to supervise intimately the performance of their subordinates. Orders are given and privates are expected to perform adequately and 'do their job'. Not doing so could result in casualties, while during a simulation disapproval and sanctions from even higher authority are likely for *all* concerned. There are also innumerable instances where privates have to make tactical decisions swiftly, without recourse to their superiors: to cross a path or not, to move left or right, to fire upon an enemy or to hold fire and wait for a better target. Janowitz (1959: 37–8) aptly sums up the needs of the modern military organisation in this direction:

> The combat soldier, regardless of military arm, when committed to battle, is hardly the model of Max Weber's ideal bureaucrat following rules and regulations. . . Rather his role is one of constant improvization, regardless of his service or weapon. Improvization is the keynote of the individual fighter or combat group . . . The military organization dedicated to victory is forced to alter its techniques of training and indoctrination. Rather than developing

an automatic reaction to combat dangers, it requires training programmes to
teach men not only to count on instruction from superiors, but also to
exercise their own judgement . . .[8]

The private's decisions and use of a qualified initiative are not trivial, for
even during a simulation the wrong decision may result in himself and his
section being captured or even assulted by members of another unit.
Bruises, black-eyes, and sore ribs are then the likely result. During actual
combat the results could be fatal. Immediate superiors are too involved in
deploying those under their command, and assessing the intentions of the
enemy, to be able to maintain close supervisory and institutional control
over their subordinates. So, within the Battalion there is an even stronger
set of reasons for superiors to arrive at a satisfactory working relationship
with privates, for without it efficient military team work is impossible. It is
therefore in the superiors' direct interest to obtain the maximum degree of
performance from privates. Blau and Scott (1970: 237) have noted of
industry, and the same pertains to those who hold rank within the Battalion
that 'The successful supervisor must do more than maintain discipline and
compliance with official orders—he must encourage his subordinates to
exert effort, to assume responsibility, and to exercise initiative'. To put it
bluntly but not too inaccurately, the difference between the Depot and the
Battalion is that the superior's role is one of command and leadership
rather than being primarily instructional.

The removal of a number of constraints and the reduction in various
activities employed at the Depot primarily to inculcate obedience is
accompanied by a more relaxed disciplinary ethos in Battalion life. At the
Depot all supervisors, including those outside the recruit's particular
Training Team, acted as agents of disciplinary enforcement. In the
Battalion privates soon become aware that this state of affairs is not
normal. In the main, suppervisors concentrate their energy on the
subordinates for whom they have *direct* responsibility. Transgressions of
military law by those for whom they only have an indirect responsibility
merely by virtue being an NCO or Officer tend to be overlooked,
disregarded or 'not seen', especially if the transgressions are not serious.[9]
Offences of this sort are the norm in the Battalion. Going AWOL, extensive
damage to civilian or military property, assaults on those who hold rank,
are serious and abnormal; and when they occur they involve superiors
acting in accordance with their duty as embodied in military law. But
superiors often turn a blind eye to the host of misdemeanours which it is
possible to commit under the all-embracing code of military law, ranging
from not shaving on parade in the morning to gambling in barrack rooms.
There are exceptions to this, of course: there are some individuals who do
not or cannot overlook such minor infringements of discipline, particularly
those who have specific responsibility for the general enforcement of
discipline within the Battalion, such as the RSM, the Adjutant, and the
Regimental Police. In spite of these exceptions, one can see that the milieu
of the private is different from that he inhabited whilst at the Depot. Not

only are there fewer constraints upon him, but the working relationship established with his superiors has deepened and widened, and, moreover, other superiors who have no direct responsibility for his conduct adopt a far less rigorous and more indulgent attitude towards his behaviour.

INFORMALITY: THE NORM

Despite the degree of informality I have described between instructors and recruits at the Depot, the vast majority of interaction between them was of a formal nature. In contrast, within the Battalion informality was, in some senses at least, a *normal* state of affairs.[10] Perhaps the easiest way of illustrating this is to focus upon terms of address between privates and those who commanded them. At the Depot modes of address were overwhelmingly formal. Only at the recruits' Battle Camp (the most informal context in which recruits found themselves) did Corporals allow themselves to be addressed as 'Corp'. Back in the lecture room, or on the firing range even if superiors of higher rank were not present, the mode of address reverted to 'Corporal'. On the drill square or in overtly public places, not only did recruits use the formal title, but stood to attention when doing so. Within the Battalion, however, the normal practice for junior NCOs was for them to be on first name terms with privates of their own Company, and those outside of it if known. This form of mutual address occurred in all contexts where higher authority was not present with the exception of the drill square. Senior NCOs and officers also displayed a marked degree of informality with privates, often referring to them by their nicknames, although this was not reciprocated, privates responding with the rank of their superior or 'Sir'.[11] The Company Clerk of the Company with which I did participant observation, for instance, was known and referred to by all ranks as 'Flash'. It is not surprising that junior NCOs in particular displayed the greatest degree of informality, for they are the group which has the most immediate need to negotiate a working relationship, being the last links in the chain of command and the people who are ultimately responsible for privates completing their military work.

The further away from barracks, the more informal do relationships between all ranks become. In the field there are no longer separate eating and accommodation facilities for officers and senior NCOs. Privates and all their superiors eat the same 'C' rations and sleep on the same hard ground. Moreover, for tactical reasons, saluting and standing to attention is no longer practised, and all members wear the same featureless camouflage clothing on which badges of rank are minute.[12] The private finds that the more his Section is detached from any form of centralised authority, be it the Battalion, Company or Platoon, the more informal do relations with his immediate superiors become. So the sociological distinction between formal and informal behaviour is of more limited use within the Battalion than the Depot. In making any analysis of 'how things get done' it rapidly became apparent to me that informal behaviour was the general *modus operandi* for all members—in fact the basis of all working relationships established between privates and their superiors. Yet it is still useful to distinguish formal behviour from the other variety, for when things 'do not get done'—when they go wrong, when working relationships become fraught and are called into question by either party—formality emerges and those in authority resort to the officially prescribed organisational practices for dealing with subordinates. The most marked examples of this during my periods of observation with the Battalion concerned, as at the Depot, privates violating safety procedures on weapons, or placing their superiors' own status in jeopardy. Here is an example from my field notes:

> The squad is formed up and about to move off. The Sergeant in command is joking with a private about the latter's beret, maintaining that its style is that of a raw recruit. The private's nickname is used by the Sergeant, and there is lots of laughter from the squad. As the Sergeant turns away the private who has 'lost' the joke, points his weapon at the Sergeant's back in a mock fashion, grinning. The Sergeant perceives it out of the corner of his eye, spins around and in a very loud, fierce and serious tone, tells the private—using his surname—that if he ever points a weapon at a person again, 'you won't have a head to put your hat on, and what's more I'll gaol you!' The Sergeant then orders all members of the squad to assume the correct position of attention. The squad is very quiet.[13]

Other Parts of the Bargain

A flexible approach to discipline, and the informal behaviour which is part of it, often involves superiors themselves, as I have noted at the Depot, in rule-breaking. Formally speaking, privates have the power to report such instances to higher authority; to use privates' argot, this is to 'drop someone in the shit'.[14] Consequently superiors expect private soldiers not only to give an adequate military performance as their part of the bargain, but also to play their part in the display and management of the required formal front, when higher ranked individuals are nearby. Protection of the official status óf the superior is perceived to be part of the bargain. An example which illustrates this concerns privates addressing junior NCOs by their first names, and failing to display the formal form of address when in the presence of a superior of higher rank:

> Sitting in a shellscrape (small trench) with a Lance Corporal and a private, somewhere in the wilds of Alberta, the conversation centres on returning to the UK. About five yards away an officer—the Platoon Commander—is sitting eating a can of cold stew. Argument breaks out about the exact duration of the flight home, and the private announces in loud tones to the Lance Corporal, 'sometimes you're fucking stupid Billy, thick as shit'. Simultaneously the officer turns around and looks sharply at the three of us: conversation stops abruptly. The officer finished his stew and walks off. The Lance Corporal turns to the private and curses him. He then turns to me and

says, 'that's the trouble with some of this lot John, you're a decent bloke to them, and then they go and fuck it up. I'll probably be getting a rifting [verbal reprimand] later on for being too familiar'.[15]

Fully aware that by behaving informally and interpreting military law flexibly, they are often putting themselves in the path of possible trouble, NCOs are therefore on occasion at pains to remind privates of their half of the bargain, as the following instance illustrates:

> Sitting in a wood with 4 privates as they prepare to move down to its edge and board a helicopter. As they begin to file out past their Section Corporal towards the Landing Zone, they are laughing and joking, and not in partol formation. The Corporal calls to them, 'when you get about half way down go tactical [assume patrol formation], the O.C.s there, so use your heads O.K?' They reply 'O.K., O.K., Arnie', and move off. Afterwards I ask the Corporal about the incident and he replies, 'they are all more or less new lads, two of them have only been with the Battalion about a week, so I'm just making sure we don't all end up in the shit'.

Instances where NCOs are 'dropped in the shit' constitute a breaching of the working relationship, and depending upon how serious they are and how much trouble the superior finds himself in, a tightening of disciplinary measures is likely to result.

Good Superiors

The working relationships established between privates and their superiors obviously vary in strength, the most worked out and consistent being those between privates and junior NCOs, for the reasons I have previously mentioned. Depending upon how deep and consistent such relationships are, privates classify their superiors, negatively and positively. This classification and the conceptions which go along with it, however, do not depend solely upon the superiors' inclination to interpret military law flexibly. Although this is the main criterion, there are others which are important. In contrast to the Depot, relationships between privates and their NCOs within the Battalion are built up over a much longer period of time involving much more mutually shared experience and a greater relaxation of formal roles. As a result, the criteria privates establish and use for evaluating superiors are themselves more complex.

On occasion when doing field research I came across privates using the term 'let-offs', and when asking its meaning, was told that having a working relationship with NCOs meant that on occasion you get 'let-off' activities that normally you would have to do. For instance, several privates, when on seven days 'Rickies' in Canada for being late on parade, were deprived of the opportunity to purchase presents to take home. Their SNCO, however, 'fixed it up' for them to have an afternoon off Restriction of Privileges, so that they could go shopping. Another example I observed involved a group of privates who, having performed inadequately on morning drill parade, had been ordered to attend an extra drill parade at dinner time. They returned to the barrack room almost immediately, announcing that the NCO who was to have taken them for extra drill, 'was a good bloke' as he had not given them drill but 'just fucked us off'. A further example is contained in the following statement by a private about an officer: 'Good bloke the Boss. In Ireland I was on orders for losing my ID Card (identity card), which is a straight hundred quid fine, and he cut it to fifty'.

As well as 'let-offs', there are 'get-offs' in which the superior takes some action to help the subordinate who is in trouble with other superiors. As a private explained: 'Say you get checked by the coppers [regimental policemen] and told to get a haircut, and report with it done, on staff-parade. You can go and see the SNCO and if he hasn't checked you for a haircut, he'll see what he can do'. Such actions are in effect a form of protection, provided within certain bounds, for misdemeanours by those superiors for those soldiers directly under their command. Obviously the more rank the superior holds the more protection he is able to give, and the more influence he wields when negotiating the issue with other superiors. The following comments by a private upon his former Company Commander indicate this: 'He's a good bloke, he'd look after us, stick up for us, whenever any other Company was getting on our backs for some reason. Say another CSM had gripped some of the lads. "Leave my boys alone", he'd say, "fuck off and leave my boys alone".' [16]

Another very positive trait which recommends privates to define superiors as good, is the behaviour embraced by their phrase 'not ballaching the lads'. 'Ballache' being the term generally used within the Battalion to describe unnecessary and onerous tasks. Privates being at the bottom of the Unit's hierarchy are more susceptible than any other group to have such tasks imposed upon them. There are innumerable occasions when superiors have the power to decide how privates' time is to be spent:

> Sitting on the edge of the 84 mm range (anti-tank weapon). Firing is a very slow business, as only two can fire the weapon at a time. The rest of the Company are stood or sat down doing nothing. A senior NCO arrives by Land Rover surveys the situation and promptly organises a game of rugby between platoons, using a steel helmet as a ball. The game is played with savage enthusiasm. Afterwards a number of privates proclaim the SNCO to be a good bloke, in one's terms 'a ballaching NCO would have had us picking up paper!'

'Doing things for the lads', is another reason privates cite for defining their superiors positively. 'Doing things' includes replacing lost equipment with their own spare equipment, such as ear-defenders and weapon magazines. Another example is the loaning of money to privates by senior NCOs and officers when the lads have run out of funds for beer, the amount to be paid back on payday. I also observed instances of superiors buying privates 'booze' when the latter had performed well in their military tasks over an extended period of time. Another seemingly mundane example, but charged with meaning for those concerned, was when certain NCOs made a practice of having a 'brew' ready for privates when they came off their 'stag' of sentry duty in the middle of the night while on field exercise.

A whole range of statements by privates indicated the importance they attached to informality in their relationship with superiors. 'Having crack with the lads' (informal talk) was cited repeatedly as a sign that an officer was a 'good bloke', rather than 'one of those posh fuckers', because 'he'll have a laugh with the boys'. Having 'crack' is especially valued for it allows one to 'have a laugh', which is the privates' term for the joking relationship I defined earlier: a relationship within which privates who are formally powerless can take some initiative, exercise some autonomy, and even score points off their superiors:

> CORPORAL(to his Section): O.K. Get fell in, in three ranks with your kit on.
> PRIVATE: Kit on?
> CORPORAL: Yes kit on?
> PRIVATE: For what good reason?
> CORPORAL: Cos I said so.
> PRIVATE: That's a good reason!
> (grinning)
> CORPORAL: Get in there you skeg! (spate of mock wrestling).

The form of this relationship allows the above kind of dialogue, and also allows superiors, as at the Depot, to administer cautions to their subordinates without resorting to any formal form of reprimand; what NCOs call 'friendly bollockings', which do not disrupt the overall tenor of their working relationships, and do not cause privates to change their assessment of superiors as being 'good blokes':

> Corporal speaking to a private who has failed to pack some personal equipment in his rucksack for a patrol. 'What are you going to do lad when some big bird wants it, and you haven't got any Durex, fucking useless you are!'
> Sergeant to a private who has his watch hanging on a pocket button of his camouflage smock. 'What are you doing looking like a fucking Christmas tree? Put it away or I'll stuff it up your arse! If you want to look like a nurse go draw a skirt!'

Bad Superiors—'Tick-Tocks'

There are other superiors who are defined by privates in negative terms. Although there is some form of working relationship with these superiors, the agreement—the bargain is always one which is much more problematic. Adequate performance is traded-off for a certain degree of flexible rule interpretation, but the levels neither of performance nor of flexibility are as deep or extensive as in the bargains arrived at with 'good superiors'.

Moreover, there is less evidence of the other subsidiary criteria which I have described in the previous pages. Such NCOs and officers are derisively labelled by privates as being 'Tick-Tock'. One thus hears expressions when privates are being harassed, 'ballached' in their terms, such as, 'he's swallowed an alarm clock this morning'. 'I bet he wanks by numbers', and 'his Misses starches his prick for him'.[17]

In their dealing with superiors, privates accept that those in command have their job to do. That is, they have to complete the tasks which are their responsibility, including if need be the enforcement of military discipline. Moreover, privates accept that if superiors do not do this they will themselves incur the displeasure of even higher authority. In one private's words:

> Sometimes they've got no choice than to charge you, if it's really serious, or if others know about it. I was down in town drinking and I had to be back on duty, but I said 'fuck it', and put a few down. Then I had a few more and rolled back to camp. He [his platoon sergeant] got no choice about it really, the CSM and the OC, they both knew I was late. Not just late put pissed, so if he didn't charge me, he'd be in the shit himself. Simple.[18]

The enforcement of discipline is perceived as part of the system of military law and discipline, under which they all exist, and viewed as inevitable, its dictates accepted somewhat fatalistically. Privates display resentment and anger rather at the imposition of unnecessary, pointless work, and the enforcement of what they view as unnecessarily rigorous discipline. What privates perceive to be unnecessary toil is not confined to activities like fatigues, but may also embrace various aspects of military skills. Here a private is criticising an officer after a simulated platoon attack for his lack of organizational ability and fieldcraft skill, deficiencies which had resulted in a general 'ballache':

> I can't understand it, it was a proper cock-up, a ballache. He couldn't have thought it out properly. We had all that ammo to carry and it nearly fucking killed me in this heat! Yet the attack phase lasted such a short time. My Gimpey (GPMG) barrel was pink when I finished. You're only supposed to fire a small amount before changing barrels, before they melt. I didn't fire half the ammo, and had to carry it all, stupid! Before, in the approach phase, he had us running with all that ammo in dead ground . . . That's ground where the enemy can't see you John. What a ballache. No need for any of it.

When such instances occur, privates often refer to their superiors' behaviour as 'tearing the arse out of it'. The following extract from my notes illustrates their dislike of superiors' behaviour when it breaches the bounds of what they see as reasonable:

> Sitting talking to 3 prisoners—all privates, in the dining room as they are having dinner. (The Regimental Police who are in charge of them are talking to the cooks). I asked what they thought of the police who were in charge of them, and received the retort: 'Well these are O.K. but some of them really tear the arse out of it . . . You know doubling us around the place. As soon

as we get out of sight, these stop doubling us, or slow the pace down. The
others who are on leave, are bastards though.' I then asked 'didn't you expect
them to give you a hard time?' And received the reply, "yeh, that's what
you're in nick for, to get punished, but some of them double you all the time,
never give you a rest, knacker you. They take it too far, power crazy set of
cunts."[19]

Bad superiors or 'Tick-Tocks' are perceived by privates to be in the
business of breaching the bounds of what is defined as reasonable
behaviour and tearing the arse out of it far too frequently. On such
occasions the additional moan of 'they're getting like that lot at the Depot'
is frequently heard, privates relating their present treatment to bad
memories of the more rigorous discipline of Basic Training.

Privates' Power and the NFI

Within the Battalion there was, then, an extended and deeper form of the
negotiated order encountered at the Depot. Although it is undoubtedly the
junior NCOs who have the most immediate and greatest need to arrive at a
satisfactory working relationship with their subordinates, higher ranked
individuals also need to accomplish this, if less immediately. That through
their capacity to be uncooperative, to perform poorly with a minimum of
efficiency, privates do have a form of power, was acknowledged by officers
of the Battalion, the group most removed from the day to day enforcement
of discipline. The following statements illustrate this awareness:

> MAJOR: You have to have a good working relationship with the soldiers.
> Otherwise if you don't, then you have a Company that has no flair. . . . Well
> the Company will function all right, but the men tend to switch-off. They
> have to perform their tasks anyway, it is how they perform them which
> makes all the difference. If you don't get on with them, they will not give you
> anything extra.

> LIEUTENANT: The difference between here and Sandhurst is that at Sandhurst
> you are told that soldiers will do exactly as they are told. You soon realise
> that it's not so, and that you have to watch them, otherwise they can make
> things difficult for you. It's not really power they have, its sort of non-
> cooperation. They can do things in a certain way, which can embarrass you
> in front of others.[20]

When the lads perceive themselves as being 'ballached' by a 'Tick-Tock',
they express this state of affairs with the phrases 'not impressed', or more
frequently 'NFI'—'not fucking interested'. Such performances are quickly
understood by superiors for they know intimately the capabilities of their
Platoon, Section, or Company. Inferior scores on the shooting range, a
slightly ragged response to commands on the drill square, slower times on
road runs or more individuals 'jacking their hands in' (dropping out) on
route marches. All these are swiftly discernable features, registering the
privates' collective state of NFI. A slower response to orders to form up for

parade, and a marked absence of informal 'crack' are other indicators of a state of discontent amongst privates, and a disruption of working relationships. This strategy of minimal cooperation, though rarely coordinated or planned in any fashion, is nevertheless consciously understood and implemented by privates, as one succinctly explained:

> Sometimes they fuck us around, if they're in a bad mood, somebody with more rank is fucking them about, well they take it out on us. They get it in the long run though, as we do as little as possible for them, and they drop bollocks from above.

IDENTITY AND 'REAL SOLDIERING'

I shall now change the focus of attention and examine the continuation of another social process which started at the Depot: the identification of privates with the soldierly role, and the internalisation of a self-image commensurate with this role. This identification is not purely an instrumental one. By that I mean that privates perform their roles efficiently not merely because they are aware that superiors will interpret military law flexibly, but also because they themselves are heavily involved with and committed to this role. It has a great deal of meaning for them and they display a craftsmanlike pride which is far from being purely instrumental.

This involvement is founded upon a self-image of soldierly proficiency. As their service with the Battalion develops, privates come to an acute understanding of what activities constitute their craft:

> It's weapons and tactics, that's what the job's all about. Fieldcraft, all that sort of stuff, like how to set up a trip-wire and how to get past one. That's what the jobs about, not polishing your boots, doing fatigues, or doing drill.

Proficiency in such core skills are important and meaningful to the private, and being able to perform well in these skills is seen as an indicator of adequacy, not just by superiors but also by peers. For instance, during weapon training classes or tests there was keen interest, with privates discussing esoteric technical points concerning the merits and demerits of weapons. There is a strong desire to do well in such tests, and when a bad performance occurs numerous excuses are offered, usually concerning the weapon's technical deficiencies, rather that the individual admitting to any ineptness. This type of bad performance elicits derogatory comments from peers, especially if the individual being tested displays anxiety—'stop flapping you cunt!' Those who are guilty of an inadequate display are swiftly told by others that such work is all that could be expected from a 'sprog'. And more veteran peers will grumble that they 'don't know what they're teaching them at the Depot these days'. A concern to do the job correctly is evident in the following extract from my field notes:

> Have just watched a simulated Company attack on a hill. 'The lads' are crashed out sweating profusely and drinking from water bottles. I am

catching a grumble from one private who moans, 'when we go to Ireland Billy is going to get us into some real trouble'. I ask why and he retorts, 'I've told him before about carrying the Gimpey, he carries it across his body, and it's dead easy to recognise that way. They're (the enemy) always trying to take the gunner out first. He should carry it like an SLR, they can't pin-point it so quickly then. If the gun [GPMG] gets taken out, that's seventy per cent of the fire power, and we're in real trouble, as they're not amateurs, they'll have a fucking M60 lined up on us. If he does it in Ireland I'm going to dig [hit] him'.

This concern with expertise extends to such subjects and activities, as map-reading, the use of radios, first-aid, all the core skills which are perceived as relevant to the role of infantryman.

Just as crucial to the self-image they hold is their capacity to endure discomfort. Peers who falter on a march, or drop out on a run, are encouraged or jeered at, depending upon whether others perceive them to be trying to give an adequate performance, or rather are 'jacking their hands in' (giving up without trying). In addition there is a continued concern with dress 'style', especially since within the relatively relaxed milieu of Battalion greater opportunities in this direction are possible. Uniforms become tailored to personal preference, berets become shaped even more idiosyncratically, and privates make an even greater distinction between style and 'bullshit' than they did at the Depot.[21] 'Bullshit', as it is demanded so rarely within the Battalion, creates an immediate and unwelcome contrast with normal standards of dress. 'Style' in contrast, is even more in the Battalion a part of the private's picture of his soldierly self. Through it he can signify his toughness and skill, and look sharp in a specific, if idiosyncratic fashion, which will be recognisable only to those who understand its nuances. The newcomer to the Battalion finds himself being told by longer serving peers that he looks like a 'sprog', his appearance clashing with their expectations of what a soldier's appearance should be. The following field-note extract illustrates this concern with style, and its connection with the soldierly identity:

Sitting on a bed in the barrack-room. Alan is just preparing to go and parade behind the Guard, as part of his 'Rickies'. He pulls on his camouflage smock, adjusting it carefully, does the same for his trousers, tucking, and folding their bottoms into his boot-tops, blousing them over with care, then stamping the ground hard, so they fall correctly into position. Finally, he adjusts his beret, patting, and pulling it into shape, before a mirror. This display brings forth a series of wolf-whistles, and comments such as 'got five minutes love?' He turns grinning to the Section, who are lounging on the surrounding bunks. And says 'load of Jack sprogs' [cocky novices]. More derision follows including the fact that he looks like a 'shithouse cleaner'. He smiles, looks at himself in the mirror, giving his beret a final adjustment, looks at his watch, and pronounces to the assembly, 'I'm sharper now than you lot are in your No. 2s' [best dress].[22]

This deep identification with the skills, qualities and appearance of the combat soldier, causes privates in the Rifle Companies to practise a humorous form of derision against their peers in the support and administrative echelons of the Battalion: individuals they see as not sharing all the hardships of the true infantryman's tasks and, moreover, not tough enough or skilled enough to do so.[23] Thus 'dipsticks', 'deadlegs' and 'FUBS' (fat useless bastards) are some of the terms used to describe storemen, medics, clerks, drivers and others. As one private put it when describing the performance of the Battalion's engineering craftsmen: 'They're all right when they're mending things, but when they've got to do sentry, or say an escort duty [on a vehicle] in Ireland, they moan like fuck, all they want to do is hand their tool-box in!'

The endurance of past hardships, particularly when on operational tours and field exercises, is a recurrent theme of privates' conversation. It acts both as a means of reinforcing the soldierly image they hold of themselves—of being action soldiers—and, by referring back to instances where conditions were worse, helps them to cope with what they are enduring at the time.

Insiders and Outsiders

This strong identification with the role of infantryman is fused with an identification with the Company, and its various subdivisions to which the private belongs. There was spontaneous cheering at winning competitions as mundane as an inter-company run at 6 a.m. In contrast grumbling and dissatisfaction occurred when privates saw peers in other companies 'getting away with things', that is, doing less work than them. When asking privates to comment on other companies, the answer was invariably 'a bunch of skegs' (no-goods). This identification and rivalry was explained to me by a private in the following manner: 'They're all horrible, all the other companies are horrible . . . Well they just are, they're not your Company, so they're bound to be horrible. Not serious like, I've got some good mates in them'. This identification extends to the Battalion as a whole, particularly so when its reputation and status is called into question. As I was informed: 'It's O.K. for anyone to slag down (make derogatory comments) the Battalion. It goes on all the time, when blokes get a bit pissed off about something. Yet anybody, like other squaddies, or civvies down the town, if they try it the lads will jump on them. They've got no right'. These forms of identification and the concern to perform their role effectively are seen together in the following comments by a private, about a field exercise:

> That exercise was fucking hard, the weather was awful. You sort of wanted to jack your hand in all the time. You couldn't though, you had to stay switched on, with the Paras as enemy. If they had managed to infiltrate our position, and gotten away with it! Well, we'd have never have lived it down from the other Companies, letting the Paras fuck-over the Battaion.

This strong identification is reinforced by the outgrouping of all other military units, derisory cliches and nicknames being used to facilitate this. Thus the Artillery are known as 'dropshorts', the Royal Green Jackets as 'falling-plates', and only two things fall out of the sky, namely 'Paras and birdshit'.[24] The strong identification with the skills and qualities of the infantryman and with their own Battalion, and the military comparisons they involve, are illustrated in the following fieldnote extract:

> Sitting together with two privates somewhere over Newfoundland, flying back to the UK after the termination of field exercise. They are recalling an exchange visit between themselves and members of the United States Army. Upon my question what were the Americans like, I received the following reply: 'They're a lot of wank really, nice blokes mind you, you couldn't ask for better, but not much good at their jobs . . . Well take map-reading, we took them out in the country and told them "OK your rations are in this grid square". All they had to do was to march to the square, look around and pick up the grub, which we put in an obvious place. They fucked it up, recruits could have done better. That's their Airborne, and if that the best they've got, then its not much of an Army, the Battalion could see them off without much trouble . . . We had a drinking contest with them, five of them and two of us. We hadn't even started and they were pissed, they're not like us, they're not real soldiers!'[25]

NOTES

1.   In Northern Ireland the Battalion's table of organisation changes somewhat. Given the nature of the conflict there, neither an anti-tank nor a mortar capability is required. Instead, another Platoon is established purely for the Northern Ireland operation, named 'Close Observation Platoon' (COP), whose duties are surveillance, intelligence gathering and ambush.

2.   In Northern Ireland preparation, such training is decentralised even further to the 'Brick' level, a patrol consisting of an NCO and 3 men.

3.   This lack of sleep was also a chronic problem for the reseacher. Attempting to be sociologically aware, and to write up field notes on a few hours sleep a night, creates observational researcher's neurosis!—the fear that I was 'missing things'.

4.   There appears to be a certain amount of evidence that very harsh measures have been or are being used by the British Army to cultivate 'toughness' amongst its troops (some would say brutalise). Several sources quote the exposure of troops to various forms of interrogation during field exercises. See Ackroyd (1977: 245), Fields (1973: 63) and a report in *Soldier Magazine* (1957: 16). I must stress that I myself never observed anything of this nature, during my periods of research with the Battalion or at the Depot.

5.   Only 13 per cent of privates Army-wide were married and therefore eligible to live out of barracks (figure supplied to the researcher by the Ministry of Defence in 1980).

6.   Roland (1955: 38) provides a very good picture of such positive changes, when moving from Basic Training to a Battalion during the interwar years.

7.   This decision to have a long weekend was made by the Battalion's Commanding Officer, on the grounds that for the first time in a number of years the Battalion was resident within its main recruiting area. It was thus comparatively easy for the single members of the Battalion to reach their homes on weekends. The C.O.'s decision was motivated by the fact that the Battalion had been away from England regularly on Northern Ireland duty and that it was

also shortly due to move to Berlin for three years. Normally work finishes for most Army units for the weekend at 1630 Friday, and commences at 0800 Monday.

8.   In relation to the need for the infantrymen to exhibit initiative and improvisation, see also the comments of Colonel Marshall (1978: 22), and those of Field Marshall Lord Wavell in an interview with *Soldier Magazine* (1945: 3). It is with the above objectives in mind that the Army has fostered a whole programme of adventurous training activities in recent years.

9.   See the following sources for instances of superiors turning a blind eye to the misdemeanours of their subordinates: Lloyd (1938: 91), Crutchlow (1937: 129), Hewetson (n. d: 67), Vivian (1930: 34), Bowlby (1969: 147) and Baxter (1959: 76).

10.   The formal role of the private within the Battalion was officially determined by the following sources of authority:

(*a*)   Rank.

(*b*)   Assignment, e.g. machine gunner, radio operator, rifleman etc.

(*c*)   Organisational subdivision—Section, Platoon, Company.

(*d*)   *The Manual of Military Law* and *The Queen's Regulations for the Army*. The legal codes and articles which cover conduct, discipline and punishment.

(*e*)   Battalion Orders, Company Orders, and Platoon Detail, which are published directives (sometimes daily).

(*f*)   The Commanding Officer's overall policy as implemented by the Battalion Adjutant.

11.   Goffman (1972a: 64) noted generally of 'the superordinate having the right to exercise certain familiarities which the subordinate is not allowed to reciprocate'. He also commented specifically on the military (1972b: 114) noting that 'an officer has the right to penetrate the life of a soldier serving under him, whereas the private does not have a similar right'.

12.   These tactical reasons in the first instance are primarily due to a fear of the enemy identifying and then liquidating superiors. Wingfield (1955: 56) cites an instance from his World War Two service, where the use of nicknames was substituted for the use of ranks, as enemy snipers understood the English for the latter.

13.   One of the first safety procedures soldiers are taught is that weapons are never pointed at anyone, other than targets on the range, or at the enemy.

14.   A brilliant fictional treatment of 'dropping someone in the shit', is contained in a fine play by John McGrath, *Events While Guarding the Bofors Gun*, (1974).

15.   Examples of exactly the same kind of breaching the bargain, through subordinates failing to maintain a formal 'front' with their immediate superiors, are to be found in the writings of both officers and soldiers. The examples I have come across are from the period of the first world war. See Graves (1967: 150) and Hiscock (1977: 132–3).

16.   Examples of superiors providing privates 'protection' are contained in the writings of Wingfield (1955: 124), Baxter (1959: 60) and Purdom (1930: 56).

17.   All these phrases are indicators of the rigidity and formality displayed by the superior. 'Tick-Tock' recalls the extremely formal behaviour demanded by participants on the Drill Square. All drill movements having to be completed in a regulation time, hence 'Tick-Tock'. Guard Duty consists of one of the few occasions in the Battalion's normal routine where there is a demand by superiors for 'bullshit', a process which involves privates using much starch on their uniforms. The word 'numbers' refers to the practice of breaking drill movements down in particular parts, and the chanting of particular numbers in regulation time as the movements are completed—a practice in force at the Depot, but not normally used within the Battalion.

18.   As Blau (1966: 77–8) has noted of supervisors in industry, they present as a justification for enforcing disliked practices, the rationale that they have no choice in the matter themselves, as commands are transmitted from higher up the organisational hierarchy.

19.   Privates determine whether a superior is 'tearing the arse out of it', by evaluating the action and its context against occurrences. Thus for instance, they hold little expectation of any informality being displayed by superiors when on a parade, or when those of higher rank

are likely to be in the vicinity. Privates have in effect a quite complex series of definitions of reasonable behaviour. Gluckman (1955: 128) has noted the operation of a similar code of reasonableness amongst the Barotse of Nothern Rhodesia. The norm of reasonableness, in some shape or form is widespread in human societies. 'Exchange theory', makes the norm of reciprocity central to human social life: See Blau (1964) and Gouldner (1960).

20.   For instances of privates embarrassing their superiors in front of even higher authority, see Ions (1972: 53) and Griffin (1937: 128).

21.   Obviously what I am talking about is a matter of degree. Privates cannot get away with diverging from the official dress norms to any great extent. 'Style' in fact consists of often minute changes to the formal forms of dress, and its nuances are often quite subtle. Hiscock (1977: 15) recalls a 1915 incident, when modification to his uniform in pursuit of style had gone too far for the liking of his Sergeant.

22.   Other examples of privates concerning themselves with styles are contained in Roland (1955: 37), Sims (1978: 21) and Baxter (1959: 84). Zurcher (1965: 399) has noted such unofficial style in the United States Navy. As Stone (1977: 101–2) has noted: 'In appearances, then, selves are established and mobilized. As the self is dressed, it is simultaneously addressed, for, whenever we clothe ourselves, we dress toward some audience whose validating responses are essential to the establishment of our self.' See also the comments of Clark et al. (1975: 56).

23.   Mack (1954) found a similar unofficial prestige system operating amongst United States Air Force Squadrons. Dunbar Moodie (1980: 562) has also noted such a system, grounded in concepts of masculinity, amongst South African gold miners.

24.   The nickname 'Dropshorts' is a straightforward questioning of the Artillery's competence. Dropping shells short of their designated target means one's own advancing infantry are in peril. See Wilson (1951: 224). 'Falling-Plates' are pieces of metal which are positioned on the rifle range, and are fired at during competitions designed to test speed and accuracy. The plates fall down when hit by rounds. In Northern Ireland the Royal Green Jackets have taken a large number of casualties, this factor together with their reputation for being 'flyboys' has caused this cynical nickname to arise.

25.   See Stouffer (1965: Vol II: 133) for a very similar (American) definition of 'real soldiers'. Also see Wilson (1951: 202).

Chapter Six

The Battalion:
'Us' and 'Them' Revisited

As I have shown in Chapter 5, there are various differences between the privates' new location and the Depot. Despite these changes the fundamental situation of the private does not alter. He remains at the bottom of the institutional hierarchy, possessing no official power, and still legally required to comply with all commands given to him by superiors. As a consequence, and no matter how informal and relaxed relationships are at times between superiors and themselves, privates still regard all those who hold rank as 'outsiders'. Even the most recently promoted Lance Corporal has the authority to give orders as well as the power to make life uncomfortable for his subordinates. The establishment of working relationships may often mediate and obscure to some extent this imbalance in power, but it becomes immediately and starkly evident once the negotiated order is suspended for whatever reason. When things go wrong, the 'us' and 'them' dichotomy swiftly comes into play so out-grouping all superiors. When the latter 'tear the arse out of it' or impose 'ballaches' the result is as described by one Captain:

> No matter how good the relationship is between you and them, once something goes wrong, they shut down completely. You might as well try to open them up with a chisel. They're like Fort Knox, you can get nothing out of them, for you're divided immediately. If you want to know something or a name, you have no chance. The Section Commanders are better at getting that sort of information, but even they get closed right off.

As he learnt at the Depot, the private finds that his ability to cope with Battalion life is enhanced through a process of active cooperation with his peers. Mutual aid remains of paramount importance helping all to deal not only with the constraints imposed by superiors, but also with work tasks and instances of personal need.[1] As one private remarked: 'You need a mate in the Army. Take something simple like camming up (camouflaging oneself). You can't see yourself so your mate helps you to do it.' Thus cold water shaves in the wilderness are avoided by passing around an electric shaver and, back in barracks when inspections are imminent, 'spare' equipment is lent out, so helping peers to avoid being deficient. Prior to pay day, with money in short supply, beer, soft drinks, and snacks in the

NAAFI are regularly shared between two or three individuals. Unfortunates who are rushing to prepare for their evening session of 'Rickies' are helped in the preparation of their uniforms. If there is a 'brew' going anywhere, anytime, everyone shares in it, automatically and without cause for comment. Privates thus hold strong expectations that those who have money, food and soft-drinks will share them with the less fortunate members of their Section (on occasion also extending to the Platoon level), a practice known as a 'crash'.[2] The following satirical comment by one individual whilst on field exercise illustrates the pervasiveness of the practice: 'I'll be glad when we get back to camp, so I can have a fag to myself. In fact I'm going to lock myself in the shit-house, and smoke a whole one all to myself! Know what I mean? [grinning to his Section]'

Old and New: Problems and Solutions

As a member of the Battalion the private finds he still confronts a number of the negative activities he encountered as a recruit, which he now terms 'ballaches'. Every five weeks his Company is officially designated 'Duty Company', and the Battalion's fatigues and Guard Duty are carried out by its members. Fatigues of a less structured nature periodically descend upon him and his peers, for his particular Company has its own administrative and domestic chores to perform. The same disagreeable tasks described at the recruit stage again provoke dislike and annoyance amongst privates. There are, however, a number of additional peculiarities of Battalion life which motivate privates to practise shortcuts, skiving and scrounging.

In contrast to recruit training, privates find themselves taking part in numerous extended field exercises: work which places great wear and tear on their clothing and equipment, and which also increases the possibility of them having it 'scrounged' from them, especially by members of other Army units. So there is additional incentive to acquire extra items and to forestall the Quartermaster's debits. Particular events will generate even further good reasons for such 'scrounging'. The following illustration was provided by a private during field exercise in a Canadian summer:

> It's always a good thing to have extra kit. Right now, we should have lightweight combat kit, but they haven't issued it to us. So if you've got spare sets of ordinary combats like this one, you just tear the lining out of it, and it's nice and cool. If you haven't got a spare one, you sweat your balls off. You can't do that if you haven't got a spare set, as you'll end up going diffy.[3]

The long periods of time spent on field exercises also provide incentive for a different form of scrounging, of the 'living off the land' variety. Prolonged periods of eating 'C' rations results in privates illegally seeking more attractive fare, namely the fresh produce and often stock of farms.[4] Field exercises also generate the motivation for privates to develop 'shortcuts' in attempts to make their work tasks easier. Rations usually consist of a pack containing 24 hours' supply and, apart from the much prized 'brew' kit, are consumed very quickly so as to lighten the load one has while marching.[5] The same reason motivates them to ditch as much blank ammunition as possible without being detected and, when returning from the field with weapons covered in filth and due for inspection, a quick shower eliminates hours of cleaning.[6]

Turning to the practice of 'skiving', the private encounters substantial new reasons for indulging in such behaviour. During the Basic Training stage, activities which recruits perceive to be central to their new-found infantryman's role—the core skills, such as tactics, weapon-handling, fieldcraft—are new and challenging. There is a degree of glamour and excitement in these activities, as seen in one recruit's comment on the firing range, 'you feel powerful, you can blow things to bits'. These activities after all constitute the action-packed life recruits have volunteered for, and have been promised by Army public relations. The novelty of such activities together with the desire to graduate from the Depot motivates recruits to display much enthusiasm and energy when completing them. Life at the Depot for recruits is a constant whirl of activity, a feature which official publicity material has claimed for Army life generally. For instance, a Royal Armoured Corps leaflet proclaims: 'There's no such thing as a typical day in a regiment'.[7] Life within the Battalion is, however, somewhat different in reality. As at the Depot, a training programme schedules major activities for the whole year. In between tours of Northern Ireland and the special counter-insurgency preparation they undergo for that theatre, the Battalion is involved in various field exercises designed to test its competence in other roles. These training periods, however, make up only a part of the soldier's year. Training areas have to be shared with other Army units. Furthermore, a not unimportant consideration is that field exercises are a very expensive business, and therefore not events which occur without careful budgetary calculation and planning.[8] So their number is limited, and the same financial constraints also apply to activities like adventure training of various sorts, such as canoeing, sky-diving, and sub-aqua diving. Opportunities of this sort are available to soldiers every year, but they are limited. As a consequence, the Battalion inevitably spends periods of time in barracks where smaller-scale training takes place.

The privates' time in barracks is largely occupied with activities such as physical conditioning through road marches, runs, assault courses, weapon training classes and occasionally lectures on subjects like first aid and the basic use of radio communication equipment. But there are limits to the variety which can be introduced to such training—limits depending not only on the ingenuity of those in command, but also on the availability of instructors, and other resources immediately available. For example, during my own research, the Battalion was located a considerable distance from the nearest suitable firing range, and this had to be shared with other Regular and Territorial Army units. So training activities within barracks are inevitably repetitive to some extent. There are also fallow periods of time in which activity for privates is reduced to a minimum. Those in command tend to fill in this fallow time by occupying privates with administrative and domestic chores. These chores are perceived by privates as 'ballaches', unnecessary, and understood for what they often are: an official means of passing the fallow time and maintaining a front of activity. Superiors are themselves well aware of the problems they confront in maintaining their subordinate's interest, during such periods. A Lieutenant recounts: 'They [his platoon] operate so much better when there is a definite aim. There is more spirit and the lads seem more together when we have got something to complete, particularly in the field. Here [in barracks] it's just a question of ticking the days off, and going through the daily routine. Weapon-training, runs, the usual thing.'[9] Frequent repetition of training activities spells boredom for the private, and periods of fallow time create the same state of affairs. Asked to describe life in barracks, one private clearly summed up the problem: 'Well a bit of firing on the range, clean your weapon, a run now and again. Then there's the odd jobs they find you. Mostly though it's trying to keep out of the way. The trouble is you get bored not doing much, and when you do it's the same stuff.' Unlike at the Depot, even the core skills that the private practises no longer have the same novelty and challenge. Once the newcomer to the Battalion has been instructed on the new weapons and tactics, they soon become common-place. As one private succinctly put it, 'they make you do something time after time to drill it into you, eventually you just get pissed off with it'.[10]

In a similar way, but to a lesser extent, the same problems of monotony and repetition confront the private on field exercises. Once he has completed half a dozen, the novelty and glamour wears off. Admittedly there are factors which mitigate these negative features, for instance, the greater degree of informality between all ranks in the field, and the variety of locations in which such exercises occur. However, excitement and glamour wear thin in the face of extremely hard physical work in uncomfortable conditions, often with a paucity of sleep. Another factor which motivates privates to view their involvement in field exercises with a less than unjaundiced eye is lack of realism. Field exercises are intended to simulate the conditions of war, and this is achieved by placing participants in situations of high physiological and, to a somewhat lesser extent, psychological stress. The one feature however which is generally absent from such exercises is the fear of an enemy and thus the fear of death or mutilation. These factors are important in motivating soldiers to remain alert, for upon such a state of affairs depends their survival when in actual combat.[11] This problem is partially solved by those in command by providing an 'enemy'. Troops from other Army units are the usual choice, although on occasion other NATO troops are used. Faced at least with an enemy of some sort privates respond more positively to field exercises. A threat from 'outsiders' reinforces their own identification with the Battalion, and creates a situation in which their self-image as competent infantrymen is tested.[12]

However, during field exercises 'enemies' are not always provided by 'outsiders', but by members of some other part of the Battalion. In such a situation there is not the same degree of threat, either physically or to one's individual or collective status within the Battalion. There is not the same motivation or incentive to stay alert and aware, to do one's job efficiently. In situations where the enemy invariably includes 'mates' who happen to be in other parts of the Battalion, privates tend not to take them seriously. After all, one is unlikely even to suffer a black-eye or a thick lip from a mate, let alone be killed or mutilated. Various instances from my field-notes illustrate this problem of alertness and realism and not taking the matter too seriously. During a simulated attack, the platoon I was with overran an enemy position. As it did so the hostiles stood up from their trenches, and gave the attackers 'V-signs', shouted 'bang-bang', and grinned broadly. A little later the platoon was ordered to regroup, and to go back and search the enemy dead for arms, ammunition and documents. When they did so, they found these 'casualties' had, in the words of one private, 'all fucked-off for a brew'. In a scenario where no enemy are provided, it obviously becomes even more difficult for privates to view the proceedings with much seriousness, or maintain a whole-hearted involvement in their roles.[13]

Doing the Job and Skiving?

In Chapter 5 I described how competence in what I have called the core activities of soldiering—in private's terms 'doing the job'—is an extremely pronounced element in the soldier's self-image. On the face of it at least, the practices which collectively constitute 'skiving' would seem to contradict the ethos of 'doing the job'. The contradiction is, however, more apparent than real: it arises from the difficulty, mentioned in Chapter 1, of 'telling it as it is'. It arises out of any attempt to describe the private's life in terms of beliefs, maxims, self-images and rules, guiding and shaping his conduct. That is because my descriptions of the privates' subculture inevitably have to be inferred, extracted and detached from the circumstances, the contexts, the exigencies, which give that subculture its life. But for the privates themselves, the self-images and modes of conduct are not seen as disembodied and formal rules detached from action and from the very circumstances which call them into play. The private soldier, like all social actors, is not a passive unreflecting puppet responding to the remote dictates of an external, 'objective', and reified culture. On the contrary, the cultural elements such as self-images, maxims, modes of conduct constitute a language used, in this case, by private soldiers to construct and account for their own social world. What this means in practice is that in order for the researcher to understand the meanings of all that is involved in 'doing the job' and 'skiving', he must be sensitive to the circumstances and the contexts in which the private uses these cultural elements to account for what is transpiring at a particular time. And what may seem a contradiction between two principles in the abstract may seem no contradiction at all in highly specific concrete situations.

Thus all the private soldiers I observed practised *both* 'doing the job' and 'skiving'. Both practices constitute part of the corpus of beliefs, conceptions, vocabulary, and so on that privates use to make their world accountable. But this corpus is in Zimmerman and Pollner's (1974: 94) terms an 'occasioned corpus' in which 'the features of the socially organized activities are particular, contingent accomplishments of the production and recognition work of parties to the activity'. In this respect then there is no intrinsic contradiction between 'doing the job', and 'skiving'. Rather, it is only by attention to the particularities of the occasion when such elements are used that one can understand how the private soldier puts together accounts of his conduct, the conduct of others, and circumstances he finds himself in. In using the expressions 'doing the job' and 'skiving' the private is not merely describing but, at the same time, judging and assessing. For example, it was clear to me that privates' performance and assessment of activities varied enormously. The assessment of weapons training by privates, to pick but one example, seemed to involve an amalgam of criteria such as: personal reputation amongst peers; whether the occasion was a formal test; the personality of the NCO in charge; collective advantage; the weather; the time of day, and so on. If they are firing a classification, the successful completion of which brings them infantry trade pay, then their shooting will almost certainly be up to par. At the other extreme routine practice firing in foul weather is likely to produce low scores and faster than normal firing. In this case personal and collective advantage would seem to reinforce each other in an effort to get off the range into somewhere dry and warm. Of all the elements I encountered on these occasions bad weather firings were regarded by all privates as a 'ballache', and almost invariably involves them in skiving by giving a sub-maximal performance. But there are many other occasions, especially when personal esteem is at stake, that no matter how bad the conditions or how desperate the private soldier is, 'skiving' is the last thing on his mind. On these occasions self-image and 'doing the job' are at stake. There were a number of instances I observed where very fatigued individuals refused to drop out of a line of march, or, as one respondent put it, he and his mates could never let 'the paras fuck over the Battalion'. On occasions like this there was no dozing off on sentry duty, or being less than fully alert when on patrol, or making unnecessary noise when in position for an ambush, or any of the other ways of skiving.

I hope this slight but important theoretical digression has made clearer the way in which the cultural elements I am discussing constitute the private's resources for socially constructing his social world; and that it has incidentally highlighted some of the difficulties I as a researcher experienced in trying to capture the essentially processual character of this world. The same considerations should be borne in mind now in turning to another element in the private's subculture, which I have called 'looking after number one'.

'Looking After Number One'

So far in my examination of Battalion life I have described how despite a change to a relatively more relaxed milieu, privates still indulge in practices which are, officially speaking, deviant. As his official career unfolds with his service with the Battalion, so his unofficial career also progresses. The unofficial learning process begun at the Depot continues within the Battalion. Previous knowledge, ploys, ruses and gambits, are built upon, elaborated, and added to. Gradually the private learns from his longer serving fellows and from his own experiences how to make his life more comfortable within the new environment. Therefore at this point let us look in depth at what the private terms 'looking after number one'. I do not intend to say much more about the practice of scrounging since I have already discussed the techniques involved and the reasons for it: equipment, clothing and rations, civilian farm produce or stock, whatever comes to hand, privates will attempt to scrounge it, acting either collectively or individually as the context demands.[14] Rather, I now wish to focus more closely upon the practice of 'skiving' which, within the Battalion, flourishes much more than at the Depot. As a result of less direct surveillance by superiors and a different perception of core activities, privates learn and use a much more varied set of techniques than they did when mere recruits.

The first technique concerns keeping out of sight, not being seen, not making oneself obvious to superiors. If one is too visible one is more liable to be nominated for all sorts of fatigues and administrative chores. The practice of anonymity has been familiar to the private since his recruit days, and within the Battalion it becomes almost an art form. The private takes care to avoid such locations as the Guardroom or the Battalion Headquarters where the individuals who are the very embodiment of disciplinary enforcement reside.[15] Elsewhere, if such troublesome individuals are seen approaching, privates smartly detour around buildings. Below is one private's description of the technique required for anonymity:

> You just sort of learn not to be there, if you think anyone is going to dish out jobs. It's sort of natural after a while, you know when to disappear. If you can't you just turn around and pretend not to notice him [a superior], pick something up, do something so you're busy, just for that moment when he's detailing blokes' jobs.[16]

I observed numerous variations of this technique, none a better illustration than the following example, recorded during a field exercise in Canada:

> The Company is preparing to get its evening meal. Just as the dixies [containers in which meals are kept hot] are being taken off the Land Rover, a Corporal says to a group of privates in his immediate vicinity, 'right you lot, let's have this ammo linked [joined in belts] before tea'. I am walking on the periphery of this group with a private, discussing football. Upon hearing the Corporal's command, he steps the other side of me, so I am between him and the Corporal. Still talking about Newcastle United, he guides me slowly

around a tent and a Land Rover, out of the view of the NCO. As we return to
the vicinity of the dixies, the Corporal has detailed some privates who are
duly setting about the task. My companion and I go and eat our tea. I ask
him about the incident and he replies, 'nobody wants to link ammo, it's a
ballache'.

Not being seen can be achieved by 'hiding out' in one's living quarters. The
accommodation includes some single rooms but in the main consists of
four-man rooms, and all the privates who occupy them possess their own
keys. Once privates have reached their room without detection, with the
door locked they can indulge in the favourite pastime of 'crashing the zzzz's'
[sleeping]. As there are only a limited number of master keys to the rooms,
privates are fairly confident of being secure from the attentions of their
superiors. Getting to the accommodation unseen, however, does present a
problem. One solution described to me by a private follows: 'We [3
privates] all got in the back of the Lanny (Land Rover), lying one on top of
the other. Joe drove us down to the lines [accommodation], and it looked as
if he had an empty wagon, as we were all below the level of the tailboard.
Smart, eh?'

Other techniques perfected by privates, and just as effective in
accomplishing a skive, can be summed up by the phrase 'saying and doing
nothing'. Sometimes situations arise when, due to an oversight by those in
command, privates are inadvertently left with no activity to complete and,
from their perspective, 'crashing the zzzz's' or sitting having a cigarette are
preferable to being given a task and under the control of a superior. One
Sergeant explained the tactic in the following manner:

> They [privates] can be very artful. For instance if you fail to detail one for a
> job in the morning, and remember shortly afterwards, pound to a penny he'll
> have disappeared. You'll eventually find him in the afternoon! You get given
> the old line 'nobody told me what to do Sarge', and then he'll tell you he was
> cleaning his kit, or some other excuse which will just about pass. They suffer
> the verbal abuse you heap on them, and get on and do about two hours work
> that day!

Other variations of 'saying and doing nothing' which I observed were
centred on occasions when activities finished early, and subsequently there
were no direct orders by superiors about what the privates were to do next.
The practice of 'hiding out' was then invariably put into operation. This
could involve moving location to a safer refuge such as the NAAFI, around
the back of various rarely used stores, or just staying in the same location.
Below a newcomer to the Battalion [a 'sprog'] learns at first hand the
importance of 'saying and doing nothing':

> Sitting in the dining hall with two privates who are on Rickies. They have
> just finished some fatigues and are having a brew. One who has been in the
> Battalion only a short while mentions that now they have finished the
> cookhouse task, hadn't they better report back to the Guard-room. An
> amazed look comes over the face of the other private, who then exclaims,

'you daft sprog! Isn't this cushy enough for you? Dipstick! D'you want to go back there and bump [polish] floors? Twat, Twat!' He leans across the table and whacks the other vigorously with his beret.

Another variation of this practice is concerned with making work look as though it takes longer to complete than it actually does.[17] This gambit is employed when privates realise that the next task may be more arduous, boring or uncomfortable.

A further means employed to 'look after number one' is the ruse of 'going sick', when privates want to evade activities they perceive as 'ballaches'. This involves reporting to the unit medical centre, with faked or self-induced illness, so as to be 'excused duties'. One is then legally allowed to miss whatever particular 'ballache' is imminent, be it a Company exercise or a weekend guard duty. Various methods and techniques for accomplishing such deception are common lore amongst privates. These range from continually wetting one's hand or ankle, and then tapping it gently with a spoon to induce a relatively painless swelling, to the simulation of chronic pains: techniques and ruses which appear to have been used by privates serving during other periods.[18] One conversation to which I was party involved a medic (medical orderly) giving another private copious advice on how to simulate the symptoms of stomach cramps.

'Having Mates Around'

As the private serves with the Battalion he gradually becomes aware of the advantages of having 'mates' in its various sub-sections. Those who serve in the rifle companies are for the most part without the unofficial resources to which their peers in other sub-sections have access. For instance, the Company Clerk can utilise official stationery for his personal use, and the Drivers in the M.T. (Motor Transport Section) are conveniently close to various oils and lubricants to ensure that their own vehicles are properly maintained. The private finds that 'having mates' in the various departments means it is on occasion possible to 'acquire' items or services, a practice which is officially deviant for both provider and receiver. In return, services as diverse as babysitting or extra pints of beer are provided. As Turner (1947: 346) has noted of the United States Navy, this exchange is essentially personal not impersonal—'the assumption is that the goods acquired are secondary to friendship'— and this is also true within the Battalion. Having a mate who is a medic opens up opportunities for acquiring everything from pharmaceutical supplies to the detailed symptomology of conditions required to be designated 'excused duties'. Friends in the M.T. and the Battalion's REME (Royal Electrical and Mechanical Engineers) contingent can be induced to provide advice and the loan of official tools if one's own transport is inoperative, while those who are cooks or orderlies in the dining hall and the Sergeants' or Officers' Mess obviously have access to sources of sustenance. Moreover, if the private is ordered to complete fatigues in such locations, knowing someone there increases the chances that the tasks he will be given will not be too arduous but rather 'cushy'. A mate in the Signals Platoon not only has the expertise to look at an ailing radio, but may also have some spare parts to remedy the affliction. And friends who are storemen are obviously a fine source for replenishing lost equipment, for which one would otherwise have to go 'diffy'. Similarly, if one is on good terms with the Clerk in the Company Office, the chances are that one can get one's leave applications processed quickly, as well as obtaining official stationery, and, just as important, from the same source one can receive advance information on forthcoming events, such as inspections and courses of instruction. The Company photographer is someone else with whom it is an advantage to be on good terms, for he can satisfy an appetite for glossy pin-ups, and 'warries' (photographs of oneself in full combat equipment, and in aggressive pose). 'Knowing' a Regimental Policeman is very important, for it not only prevents one being officially charged for having long hair or perhaps dirty boots but also ensures that if one is unfortunate enough to do a period of 'Rickies' or detention, one will be given a relatively easier time.[19]

Never Volunteer

In addition to the above unofficial and often deviant practices, privates also use ploys to 'look after number one' which do not transgress at least the letter of military law. Rather, they utilise these official practices to maximise personal advantage. One of the most pervasive clichés of military life is 'never volunteer for anything' which one hears from ex-servicemen when they are recollecting, and also from media depictions of the lot of the soldiery; the ITV series, *The Army Game*, with Alfie Bass and Bill Fraser, was a classic. Volunteering is the opposite of the practice of keeping out of sight—of being anonymous. Yet, in reality, the maxim by which privates actually operate is a slightly more extended one, namely, 'never volunteer unless you know exactly what you are volunteering for'. Privates will, and do, volunteer for activities they perceive to be personally advantageous, either in that they involve less work, easier work, money, opportunities to skive, to scrounge, or in that they impose fewer constraints upon them. The most obvious of these is volunteering for fatigues in the Quartermaster's Stores, during which opportunities to scrounge equipment are likely to occur. Whether or not the private volunteers depends upon his knowledge of the actual fatigue (for instance, it may be outside the stores, and thus yield no advantage), the Quartermaster, his staff and so on.

A more structured version of volunteering is when privates apply for courses of instruction well before they start, such courses being seen to hold a number of advantages. First, the activity may itself be intrinsically interesting, such as a Unit Photographers' Course. Secondly, it may, for its duration, remove various constraints: adventure training courses, for example, are usually completed in civilian clothes. Thirdly, attending the course is seen to be better than being with the Battalion, or with the Company and enduring its 'ballaches'.[20] Thus the more astute privates will, on occasion, volunteer for courses when the dates coincide with 'ballaching' events. The Battalion's ARU (Annual Readiness Unit) inspection, which entailed a temporary reimposition of a Depot type disciplinary regime and concern with 'bullshit', was the prime example of such an event. During my periods of observation, several privates managed to volunteer themselves onto a Joint Services Canoe course during this ARU period, a feat they gleefully proclaimed to their peers.

Awareness and Sensitivity

As privates serve within the Battalion and gradually learn to 'look after number one', they become acutely sensitive to all the possibilities for making out, for reducing discomfort, for making life easier. They learn that although fatigues are a ballache, some kinds are better than others. 'Salvage Detail', involving the collection and transport of rubbish, is usually over quickly, the general estimate being two and a half hours, allowing the participants ample opportunity to skive, since there was no officially designated time period for the duty. In contrast, fatigues in the cookhouse may well involve a seemingly endless amount of cleaning greasy pots and pans. One can of course be lucky and end up on fatigues in the Officers' or Sergeants' Mess, where superior fare may well be available. As one private announced on returning from a session of Rickies in the Sergeants' Mess, 'Boss [very good]! I had three steaks for my dinner, fucking boss!' As he acquires knowledge about the various compensations and pitfalls of different kinds of ballaches, he learns to take appropriate action, to make things easier when confronted with them or during them. Individuals differ considerably in how swift they are in initiating such strategies, some learn more quickly whilst others are slower and comprehend at more personal cost. The necessary technique of 'looking after number one' in such a context was explained to me by a private, in the following way:

> I'll give you an example from when you get detailed to go and do fatigues for the Colour [Colour Sergeant]. I went into his stores, and saw a big box of rubbish, so straight away I said, 'd'you want that emptying Colour?' He told me to take it down to the incinerator and burn it. That's at the bottom of the camp, what you'd call a long job. I knew as soon as I got detailed, that I'd end up bumping [polishing] the floor in his stores. That's usually a part of the fatigue, you know that before you do it. So you just keep your eyes open for something that'll get you out of bumping. By the time you get back, he's got someone else to do it.

Privates possess, then, a finely tuned awareness of the negative and positive possibilities inherent in the situations they are likely to encounter.

They indulge in a constant monitoring of these possibilities, ever ready to take whatever action is appropriate, to enable them to make life easier. For instance, there are occasions when to 'look after number one', is *not* to keep out of sight, *nor* to 'say and do nothing', but rather to gain advantage by making oneself visible to superiors. In the following extract from my field notes, three privates calculate such an advantage and decide positively to surrender themselves to their superiors:

> Three prisoners [privates] are in the dining hall on a fatigue detail. Since finishing it, they have been sitting down yarning and drinking tea, for a good hour. They decide to telephone the Guard Room, and announce they have finished their task. There is a consensus that it is 'cushy' sitting swigging tea, but there are other factors which mitigate against it continuing. The Battalion is about to leave Canada for the UK. The Quartermaster has a lot of work on, packing up stores and equipment. Moreover he is roaming the camp organizing this, and the cookhouse [dining hall] comes under his jurisdiction. The privates rationalise that if the QM spots them, he will detail them for some really dirty and arduous job. Therefore the best choice is to arrange it so they are quickly marched back to the Guardroom by a Regimental Policeman. This decision is enhanced by the fact that the two RPs on duty are 'cushy', the two who are known to be 'Tick Tock' being on leave. Therefore whatever work they do inside the Guardroom is likely to be easier than they will get if spotted by the QM.

It is this kind of acute awareness to events which motivates the more experienced privates, when they fire the 84 millimetre Anti-Tank weapon to perform well enough to qualify for their infantry trade pay, and to maintain credibility with their peers, yet not well enough to come top of those who are firing, thereby ensuring that they are not designated by superiors as the individual responsible for that weapon in their Platoon.[21] This particular strategy is motivated by the fact that the '84' is the heaviest and most awkward of the weapons used by the Rifle Companies. It is an awareness and sensitivity to events which enables privates to respond quickly to situations, with an action which is aimed to making the best of them, whether by volunteering for a 'cushy' fatigue or manufacturing an instant reply when being questioned by superiors.[22]

All the unofficial practices I have described are the means by which privates attempt to work out solutions to the problems they encounter whilst serving with the Battalion. These solutions broaden, build upon, and elaborate the strategies they developed while in the recruit stage. They are solutions which make the management of their daily lives easier, for as one private retorted tartly to my question about how he felt when doing things he was not supposed to, 'better than if I was doing the things I *am* supposed to'. Within these broad themes privates work out and employ countless variations, many of which are idiosyncratic to particular individuals, and learnt through being in particular contexts, at particular times, as the following extract recorded whilst on field exercise illustrates:

> The Platoon is practising anti-ambush drills from the back of a vehicle. This involves swiftly jumping off the tailboard, and as they do so one private falls

and injures his ankle. The radio operator is ordered to go back and escort the individual to the medical centre. Another private is immediately ordered by the Platoon Commander to carry the radio set, and the platoon continues practising drills for the next few miles, on foot. Afterwards in conversation with the 'new' radio operator, he volunteers that that's the last time he will get 'caught'. He informs me that in the future he will make a point of keeping well away from the radio operator, usual, temporary, or any operator for that matter! As he sees it such proximity has resulted in him having to carry a particularly heavy extra load.

Deviance, NCOs and Collusion

Where do superiors stand in relation to all these unofficial activities by which privates 'look after number one'? In particular, how do these activities fit into the bargain between privates and their immediate superiors, under which adequate military performance is traded off in return for a flexible interpretation of military law?

As remarked in an earlier chapter, this bargain necessarily involves superiors in breaches of at least the letter if not the spirit of military rules and regulations: the use of first names, 'let-offs', 'get-offs', the 'blind-eye', lending subordinates money, are all examples of this. In the Battalion, this involvement in rule-breaking entails an even more *active* collusion between privates and their superiors than was the case at the Depot. Baxter (1959: 60), writing of his National Service in the 1950s, recalls his Sergeant tendering him and fellow privates privileges and help when they were in trouble with other superiors ('get-offs'). In return the privates carried out certain domestic chores for the Sergeant and 'excused his frequent absences when anybody important enquired after him'. The same sort of collusion was evident within the Battalion I observed. All the evidence I encountered suggested that mutual involvement in deviance was primarily between junior NCOs and privates. Such collusion was motivated by a number of considerations, none more so than mutual advantage. Below, a private is describing such a relationship with a senior NCO (this happens less frequently and to a lesser degree):

> He's a good bloke, fair. You scratch his back and he'll scratch yours. . . . Well you're not supposed to use military vehicles for private purposes, and he'll ask you to pop down the town for birthday cards or something. Then when I need some time off one afternoon, there's no problem.

On occasion collusion is motivated by superiors perceiving that commands to which both they and their subordinates are subject are unreasonable for all. What follows is a Lance Corporal's explanation for him and his patrol skiving on a night map-reading exercise:

> We did a mass of night-navigation at Warcop, and out here we've had it three nights on the trot. It's just a way of keeping us working unnecessarily. So I

said fuck it, they're messing me around, and if that's the case they never get much out of me. So I took the lads up the track to the middle of the woods, and we set the brew-kit up for an hour, and then strolled back.[23]

Another example in the same vein concerned a live firing attack during the same field exercise. Because of shortage of manpower, the ammunition load carried by all concerned was excessive: live ammunition is *very* heavy. Orders from higher authority had stressed that the extra ammunition which could not be fitted into the custom-made pouches had to be carried inside the individual's combat-smock, something which is extremely uncomfortable. As a result, Section NCOs (Corporals and Lance Corporals) told the privates that if 'you put your ammo in your respirator container, we don't know about it, O.K.?' They themselves did exactly that, and the privates under their command followed suit, their actions directly contravening the order, which had also stated that respirator containers were not be used for holding ammunition, otherwise the respirators would not be released quickly enough should the need arise. On another occasion I observed a senior NCO and several privates who worked in his store rushing about in a atypical flourish of activity moving various bits of equipment rapidly about the store. On asking about the activity, I received the reply from the NCO (and broad grins from the privates) that 'we're just hiding all the buckshee [spare and thus illegal] kit, before the inspection tomorrow'.

On reflection it is not surprising the NCOs collude with their subordinates in what I have called acts of deviance, for certainly some of them, especially junior NCOs, still share certain of the problems which afflict privates, and they have, after all, been privates themselves. In this respect they possess both the knowledge and techniques needed to get around the letter of the military code successfully. Possessing 'scrounged' equipment and clothing has the same advantages for NCOs as it does for privates. And as I have mentioed, there are activities which all concerned view negatively, and which, if possible, NCOs will also attempt to avoid by skiving. Some of the constraints imposed upon the personal autonomy of privates also affect NCOs. A good example concerns single men who live in barracks, where they are not allowed to take women.[24] Nonetheless, females *were* smuggled into the barracks (usually in vehicles), by privates and junior NCOs.[25] Some degree of collusion between both privates and junior NCOs is inevitable in such an exercise, given the close proximity of their living spaces. The least it involves is a 'blind-eye' policy on both parts. The propensity of NCOs to indulge in deviant activity is, however, considerably less than that of privates, simply because the personal constraints and 'ballaches' they are subject to are less. For instance, while on Guard Duty, the private has to walk around the camp in all weathers, whilst the NCO mainly resides in the comparative luxury of the Guard Room. Obviously the higher the rank of the superior, the less he experiences such irritations—a state of affairs described by privates as

'R.H.I.P.—Rank Has Its Privileges'. In addition, if an NCO is caught in breach of regulations he has more to lose than the private; the cost is greater. An NCO is likely to be 'busted' (demoted) if found with a woman in his barrack-room, not only losing his rank, status and privileges and reverting to the bottom of the promotion list, but also the extra money that goes with rank. Be this as it may, the fact that NCOs do join privates in breaching military law, has consequences for both of them beyond the acts themselves. Such collusion deepens the working relationship established between them, by demanding a greater degree of trust on the part of all concerned.

NOTES

1. See the comments of Croft-Cooke (1971: 43) on the need for friendship in the ranks during the Second World War.

2. Instances of such mutual aid and sharing occur regularly in the memoirs of ex-soldiers; see Maitland (1951: 94), Griffin (1937: 28), Milligan (1976: 174), Lloyd (1938: 63), Ashton-Braithwaite (1969: 16), Roland (1955: 54–6), and Johnson (1973: 150).

3. The field exercise in Canada also provided the opportunity for privates to sell their spare (scrounged) equipment to their Canadian counterparts.

4. I actually saw no instances of this form of scrounging, the training area in Alberta being far removed from any farms. I base my judgement upon privates' comments concerning such practices while on exercise in Germany and the UK.

5. This practice is not encouraged by superiors, due to the fact that in actual combat the resupply of rations may be problematic.

6. The practice of giving a weapon a bath or shower is illegal as it encourages rust.

7. Recruiting pamphlet, 'Royal Armoured Corps . . .'

8. Large exercises are extremely costly. Radio and press reports put the cost of the major NATO field exercise in 1980 ('Crusader 80') at £8 million.

9. See the comments of Lieutenant Colonel Sharpe (1972: 42) on the problems of boredom in training.

10. This boredom would also appear to occur with combat veterans when they are out of the actual firing line, and are ordered still to practise core skills such as weapon training. See for instance Wingfield's (1955: 126) Second World War comments.

11. See Draper (1970: 44). See also the Second World War comments of Crimp (1971: 88).

12. There is a long history of fierce and often violent rivalry between different units of the British Army, a rivalry which promotes identification and solidarity with the private's unit. See Grant (nd: 82–3), and Morrison (n.d: 4).

13. The exception was the programme of Northern Ireland training which the Battalion underwent prior to an operational tour of that province. Privates' views of such training and their involvement in it were of a positive nature, as for them it represented the last chance to perfect their military skills and thus maximise their potential survival chances before entering a conflict situation. In their own terms Northern Ireland training represented the final opportunity to 'switch on' in comparison to 'switching off' or skiving.

14. Scrounging of the 'living off the land' variety takes on an added significance for the private during a major war, in which the provision of official rations may be problematic due to a lack of resources, enemy action etc. See for instance Smith (1922: 370), Wade (1959: 119),

Crimp (1971: 31), Haigh and Turner (1970: 95). Bagnall (1947: 92), Wilson (1951: 20), Bowlby (1969: 136) and Coppard (1969: 8). Recollections of National Service scrounging are contained in Johnston (1973: 96), whilst post-war (1945) examples are mentioned by Ions (1972: 225) and Ashton-Braithwaite (1969: 34), who were both regular soldiers.

15.   Baxter (1959: 74) recalls that Battalion Headquarters was a dangerous area, whilst Ions (1972: 24) describes the pitfalls of traversing the unit's main drill square, and becoming anonymous.

16.   Smith (1922: 378) provides a First World War example of this technique.

17.   For an example of making it appear that there is more work than there actually is, see the memoirs of Hartsilver (1960: 97).

18.   Wingfield (1955: 114–6) an infantryman in the Second World War, has recounted some ingenious techniques for accomplishing a medical skive, including the swallowing of cottonwool balls, so as to simulate stomach ulcers during X-ray inspections. See also Goffman (1976: 199–200) for his comments on the illegitimate use of medical services by asylum inmates, and Ellis (1980: 242–3).

19.   Zurcher (1965: 398–9) on similar networks of friends and the exchange of articles and services on board a ship of the United States Navy. See also Berlin (1961: 27).

20.   Crimp (1971: 83) recalls an incident where he volunteered for a signals course in order to avoid fatigue and drill parades, whilst Hiscock (1977: 138) admits to volunteering (to join the unit band) motivated by a desire to miss guard duty. See also Berlin (1961: 153).

21.   Crimp (1971: 14), recalling his Second World War service, stresses that his longer-serving peers had developed into an art form making things easier for themselves within the military environment.

22.   See a National Service example of a private manufacturing an instant 'cover' story in the face of a superior's questioning, in Chambers and Landreth (1955: 84).

23.   See the recollections of Frank Dunham, in Haigh and Turner (1970: 4), for an example of First World War privates and NCOs indulging in a spate of mutual skiving.

24.   The Commanding Officer of the Battalion had a firm policy on the matter of women being found in troops' accommodation, namely, 28 days' detention in the unit Guardroom. This was for privates; NCOs were liable to be demoted.

25.   See the inter-war recollections of Mays (1969: 102) on the subject of smuggling women into barracks.

Chapter Seven

The Operational Environment and Combat

The Battalion was deployed on a three and a half month tour of duty in Northern Ireland. Its operational area was South Armagh, and the particular Company I carried out participant observation with was based in Crossmaglen, hereafter known by its acronym as XMG. XMG, from the privates' viewpoint, was not a particularly salubrious venue, judging by the following graffiti scrawled on one of its toilets walls: 'If the world needed an enema, XMG would be the place they'd put the tube!' For members of the Company it consisted of a fortified base some three kilometres from the Eire border in the village of XMG. The base is about the size of a football pitch and is surrounded by machine gun posts, termed 'sangars', and anti-rocket mesh. The Company lived inside the main building which consisted of a heavily reinforced portion of an RUC station. Outside the living accommodation there was little else, for the remainder of the fortified area at the time of my research consisted of a building site as Army engineers toiled to improve the base's defensive capacity. Immediately adjacent to the base, but within a barbed wire perimeter, was a helicopter landing zone or, as Army argot has it, 'chopper pad'.

For privates, time spent in the base was very like living in a submarine: there were no windows, and all lighting, heating and ventilation was artificially produced. Privates lived twenty four to a room, in dim, narrow, cramped conditions, sleeping in three-tier bunks. NCOs and officers had their own accommodation within the complex. Senior NCOs and officers also ate separately from the remainder of the Company. Every inch of space was crammed with weapons, equipment and clothing. Members of each Platoon lived in each other's pockets rather as submarine crews are said to do. In an attempt to compensate for the deprivation troops suffered at XMG, a number of facilities were provided: colour television, daily papers, nightly film shows, a small multigym, small sauna, and a number of washing machines. There was also a small canteen where chocolate, coffee and the infamous two cans of beer per day per man could be purchased. The only time privates normally moved outside the base area was when they were actually on patrol. It was not surprising that all ranks referred to the area of South Armagh generally as 'Injun' or 'Bandit' country, for the similarity of their situation with the beleaguered inhabitants of a Wild West fort was striking. The Company lived very much within itself, an isolated, insular community, despite the provision of mail, telephones, and the mass media. It remained substantia'lly cut-off from the wider society surrounding it, a state of affairs brought about by the obvious and well publicised dangers prevalent in XMG.[1]

FEAR AND LOATHING AT XMG[2]

XMG is a most hazardous posting for members of the British Army. During the last ten years a large number of the Security Forces has been killed in its immediate area, many of them within the village itself. The local population is strongly Republican in sympathy and supports, either actively or passively, the PIRA. The elements of the PIRA who operate in South Armagh are highly skilled and well armed. To use one Warrant Officer's words, 'down here the opposition knows its business'. The chances of being maimed or killed by the PIRA through sniping, rocket, mortar attacks, or the use of radio-controlled explosive devices was thought by privates to be higher than anywhere else in Northern Ireland. Once patrols moved outside XMG base they were in hostile territory and consequently moved in a tactical formation. With the Eire border a mere two and a half minutes away by car, ambush and a successful escape by PIRA, members was always a high risk. I arrived at XMG after the Company had been resident for just over a month. During this period two privates were killed by PIRA action, and while I was there another casualty occurred, the individual suffering severe burning and having to be evacuated to England. The degree of threat can be judged by the fact that all movement in and out of XMG was either by helicopter or by foot patrol, movement by vehicles being judged normally too hazardous due to the expertise of the enemy in mining the roads. When a large amount of supplies had to be moved to XMG from Bessbrooke, other elements of the Battalion were deployed to secure the road, a tactic probably last used on the North West Frontier, and ringing with irony in this case. In XMG itself the Company's foot patrols usually had an armoured car in support during daylight hours.

The private's life at XMG consisted of a never ending cycle of four principal activities. That most liked was sleep and rest which occurred between work cycles, or the occasional time they were 'stood down' and given a rest period. Sleep was the dominant activity of any period when privates were not working, grabbed whenever possible, at every oppor-tunity, since the constant movement of patrols in and out of rooms at all hours ruled out uninterrupted slumber. The three other activities, each lasting for approximately three days, were static guard duty in sangars watching all the main approaches to the base, 'urban' patrol in XMG village and its environs, and finally 'rural' patrol in the surrounding countryside along the Eire border, which often involved sleeping out in the 'cuds' for two or three nights. The four-part cycle repeated itself endlessly for the Company's three and a half month tour, with only one scheduled interruption when individuals rotated on 4–5 days Rest and Recuperation leave (R & R) in England.

XMG, for members of the British Army at least, was and is a place of fear, danger and death, all courtesy of PIRA—a place of discomfort due to sleeping out in the 'cuds' or fields, from wearing heavy flack jackets when on the streets, and residing in what the Army officially calls 'sub-standard accommodation', and what privates termed 'a fucking hole'. Add to this scenario the restriction of two cans of beer per man, per day, no contact with the opposite sex, and we have good grounds for privates's dislike of their location.[3] Very evident amongst them were strong feelings of relative deprivation, reinforced by the knowledge that the other parts of the Battalion had easier, in the sense of less threatening or more comfortable, operational areas.[4] As one private informed me about the Battalion Headquarters at Bessbrooke, 'cushy up there, six man rooms, a table to do your ironing and the golly shops (canteen) twice as big as ours'. This then was the venue in which the most crucial state of the privates' career was enacted, and the dangers and discomforts of the situation were the factors to which they had to adjust.[5]

'Us' and the PIRA 'Them'

In a situation where they were surrounded by a generally hostile population, and under a constant threat, the social cohesion of the Company increased.[6] In XMG the internal division between 'us' and 'them', privates and their superiors, still operated but its import was considerably reduced in the face of a far more fearsome external 'them', the PIRA—a force which threatened not to 'ballache' privates or put them in detention, but to liquidate them. This threat together with their physical isolation from the civil population as well as the rest of the Battalion, evoked a high degree of identification with the Company.[7] The first two deaths the Company suffered at the hands of the PIRA reinforced mutual identification and solidarity amongst all members.[8] The privates themselves noticed this increase in cohesion, one for instance perceived the Company to be 'sort of together more now', attributing it to the fact that *all ranks* were 'always looking after each other out there (on patrol)'. Along with this increased cohesion, a grimmer attitude toward all who were not members of the Company or allies developed.[9] Animosity towards 'them' (PIRA), whether active supporters or merely sympathisers, was constantly generated by the fear of what 'they' could do to one when out on patrol. As one private recalled, 'it's hard to realise J's dead, you expect him to walk in any minute. I wish I could get the twat that did it, he'd wish he'd never been born'. The desire for retribution, to get back, was very strong, and in the following comment by a private is combined with frustration at the legal constraints to which the Security Forces were subject: 'We'd have had this mess cleared up now if it wasn't for that fucking yellow card (the written orders which every soldier receives, stating the conditions under which he can open fire). Instead of lift (arrest) on sight, it'd be shoot on sight. Get rid of some of these cunts, instead of like now, when we can't do anything.'[10]

The 'Brick'

Identification and solidarity were strongest at the level of the Brick, the four man patrol team normally used in XMG, principally because it was with this group that the individual private confronted the menace of the PIRA. Each brick was commanded by a junior NCO, and out there 'on the ground' the outgrouping of superiors by privates was largely suppressed— NCOs and on occasion even officers, being firmly regarded as part of 'us'. Solidarity was greatest at this level for, as one private commented, 'you just tend to work in little teams, always off doing things together, little worlds of your own': little teams which invariably regarded themselves as 'the best brick in the Company'; little teams which adopted strategies of making themselves more comfortable in the 'cuds', actions ranging from purchasing civilian Gaz burners to scrounging extra rations from the cookhouse.[11] There were groups, which on their one hour rest between urban patrols—themselves of one hour's duration—rotated in purchasing rounds of coffee and chocolate at the 'golly shop' (canteen).[12] There were teams, in which the more articulate members would write letters home for the less skilled, and in which individuals would rotate the task of doing each other's laundry. There were small groups which would share each other's parcels from home, in a display of mutual aid and teams in which an NCO would start a patrol with the announcement, 'I've come for my boys', and which had nicknames, based on their NCO's own name ('Kelly's Heroes', 'Charley's Angels'), their radio call signs ('One-Two-Fuck-Up'), and even on their appearance and demeanour ('The Rat Pack', so called because they were all crew-cut, and as their NCO explained, 'mean bastards we are!'). Self-contained groups that slept, ate, worked, and went on their R & R together.[13]

To recap, the most sociologically important feature of the operational environment, was the privates' change in attitude toward their superiors. A massive degree of external danger was the main problem which all ranks had to adjust and adapt to, and find a solution for. It was no longer the spectre of superior authority but the fear of being mined, sniped, rocketed, mortared and booby trapped that was the private's main concern. In the face of this threat, the Company and all who comprised it, *regardless of rank,* were resources which aided privates in *surviving.* Therefore on patrol, the internal dichotomy between those who held rank and privates was largely, put into abeyance.[14]

WORKING RELATIONSHIPS 'ON THE GROUND'

This change in how privates viewed their superiors acted positively to strengthen the working relationships between them, out there 'on the ground'. This relationship was further enhanced by superiors enforcing discipline at XMG in a particular fashion. As I have said, informality was largely the norm in peacetime barracks, particularly between junior NCOs and privates, and this was even more the case at XMG. Informality and tolerance of certain forms of rule-breaking were widespread, although the reverse was the case for other types of deviance. Any deviant act which was deemed to jeopardise the Company's operational functioning was heavily penalised. There were no Rickies at XMG, no parading behind the Guard, nor periods in detention, since such punishments would have removed privates from their operational role. Rather the main means of punishment were heavy fines, such as £200 for negligently discharging a weapon, £30 for smoking on 'sangar' guard, and £20 (a round) for losing ammunition. Furthermore there was a reduction in formal military display, no parades at all in the peacetime barrack sense, simply assemblies to mark the start and finish of the various work cycles. The use of first names and nicknames continued, and there was further reduction in how much superiors demanded that privates produce a smart appearance. Washing and shaving in the 'cuds' was unknown, boots were generally just blackened (as were faces!), and the length of privates' hair was noticeably longer than in peacetime barracks. Dress regulations were similarly relaxed and one noticed privates donning items of unauthorised apparel, ranging from American Army shirts, to civilian orienteering boots which were superb for keeping the feet dry in South Armagh, while flack-jackets sprouted biroed slogans idiosyncratic to the wearer.[15] This relaxation in appearance involved all ranks of the Company, even some NCOs and officers wearing items of unauthorised clothing. The slogans on individuals' flack-jackets were of the 'Newcastle for the cup' kind, rather than the overtly political, which were in evidence amongst troops of the American forces in Vietnam.

There was less emphasis on keeping the privates' accommodation sparkling clean; nothing apart from a periodic sweeping up was demanded. Fatigue details were kept to an absolute minimum, all attention being focused on the operational task at hand: combating the PIRA. There was little time or energy for superiors to indulge in military ceremony of any kind, other than the issuing of and complying with direct operational orders.[16] Moreover, XMG's isolation from the Battalion Headquarters provided fertile ground for the reduction of formal military behaviour. Privates, who had passed through the Battalion Headquarters at Bessbrooke on R & R, returned to XMG with woeful tales of encountering a sudden reintroduction of a relatively more formal discipline than they were used to.[17] As one explained: 'I'd rather be down here (XMG) but only for one reason. Back at Bessbrooke, there's nothing but ballaches. O.K. It's cushier but they ballache you up there'.

In the main, 'ballaching' the lads in XMG was a practice which the majority of superiors astutely realised had no place in an operational situation. Privates themselves quickly noticed such a change, particularly in relation to those superiors who in barracks were defined as 'Tick-Tock', as one explained:

> Here they're O.K. really, they've toned down a lot. Sergeant ————— was a regular gobshite always shouting at you in barracks. Not here though, it's all different, more like a real family, they don't shout at you, it's more, 'O.K. mate do that'. Much better.

The most negative consequence of ballaching was liable to occur out there 'on the ground'. One thing that superiors fully realised was that if the NFI (Not Fucking Interested) set in at XMG, disastrous results for *all* concerned were liable to occur. The almost total absence of NFI was very noticeable at XMG. In my time there I only heard the phrase used once, and then in relation to a direct 'ballache' by a superior. The occasion was when privates were criticising a tactical decision made by an officer. They maintained that if another option had been taken, there was a good chance the PIRA members would have been caught before they reached the border with Eire. The phrase was then used to sum up their frustration and their criticism of the decision. The absence of NFI I attribute to the lack of 'ballaches' and the fact that patrol activity was very meaningful to them, if for no other reason than doing it effectively kept them alive! It was this, in addition to a concern with their careers, which provided additional motivation for superiors to establish good working relationships with privates: something of which privates were fully cognizant, as the following statement indicates:

> They [superiors] don't really ballache you down here. You get pissed off and don't cover properly, and that's when they [PIRA] will hit you. They're always looking for the brick commander, the guy with the radio. If they get a chance they'll take him out first. I'm not saying blokes will not cover purposely, they'll just switch-off that's all, and the brick commander's the best target!

Performing well on patrol often required privates to act on their own accord—which the Army officially terms 'using initiative'. In such situations, a working relationship involves behaviour far removed from the conventional command and compliance. Below, a private describes how his Brick actually operates when on patrol:

> He's [Corporal] just like us really, O.K. so he's in charge when we get a contact (encounter with PIRA), but really out there he's sort of like a buckshee [private]. If we want a car stopped we say, 'Colin check it,' and he usually will. Or say if he tells Mike to go to a position and Mike finds he can't cover properly. Well Mike will just move until he can, that's the way we work out there.[18]

Not 'ballaching' the lads was, then, part of a familiar pattern of behaviour which superiors had manifested in the various other stages of the private's career, thereby providing further reasons for privates to regard many of them even more positively.[19] While in XMG there were few real 'let-offs' or 'get-offs' due to the reduced number of 'ballaches' generally, superiors still, 'looked after the lads'.[20] Instances of this ranged from a Corporal wangling an extra urn of tea from the Cook Sergeant (whilst his Brick was on standby duty and confined to the back of an armoured car, ready for immediate deployment), to creating an impromptu quiz game over the intercom system with members of his Brick who were all doing sentry duty in the various sangars ('to keep the lads happy', as the NCO responsible put it). Out on patrol 'looking after the lads', had added import. One Brick returned in a thoroughly disgruntled mood over a particular officer's behaviour, the NCO commanding it exclaiming:

> He's [the officer] a tuss [a pejorative]. In the square, all of a sudden it went deadly quiet, you know babies being whipped off the street. You know something's being set up. Some fucker opening up with an M60 and taking the whole Brick out. Anyway I said to him, something's up, let's fuck-off quickly? He wanted to stay and find out, in a set-up! I said to the blokes get in the can [armoured car], and they did, so he more or less had to come.

The above statement illustrates not only an NCO 'looking after the lads', but simultaneously displaying an expertise which constituted the extra dimension to the criteria by which privates judged superiors positively or negatively in XMG.[21] When on patrol this was the prime concern of privates, for in such a situation this expertise allowed the superior truly to 'look after the lads'. In contrast the behaviour by superiors which caused privates to view them negatively at XMG consisted of these superiors taking unnecessary risks and thereby not 'looking after the lads', but rather 'tearing the arse out of it': in the privates' view, jeopardising their existence unreasonably. The following are some examples of privates' negative feelings towards this type of behaviour:

> 'He's a stupid cunt, we were standing by the can and he said to me, this is boring I wish something would happen. Stupid, stupid cunt!'

> 'He's after his MM [Military medal], and he's going to get someone killed'.

> 'He kept us running about all the time on the street. You've got flack-jackets on and its very hot out there. He had us hard-targeting (moving very fast, and elusively) so much we were all knackered. If we had got a contact, we wouldn't have been able to do anything about it, the stupid git.'

> 'In on time and out on time [on patrol], an hour's what we're supposed to do on urban. He keeps us out twenty minutes longer than we're supposed to be. You don't need fucking 'O' levels to work out that's a third more risk.'

The last instance in particular was viewed extremely negatively by the privates concerned, and when such things happened at XMG, there was some evidence to suggest that they did use their power of non-cooperation in an overt fashion:

He [Platoon Commander] wanted to go down that street full of derelicts (houses), and you're not supposed to patrol down there, as its too easy for them [PIRA] to set up an RCD. Anyway it was a good shoot, long and straight, they could pick you off from up there on the hill. I thought this isn't on. Brian began to move toward the top of the street, so I signalled to him that I wasn't going down, as it was too dodgy. We both took up positions as Brian had sussed it as well. And then I told him [Platoon Commander] we weren't going down there as it was out of bounds. He couldn't do anything about it, not on his own, so we just got on with the patrol.[22]

In the main, however, and with far more immediate need on the part of both superiors and subordinates than in barracks, working relationships were maintained in XMG. The high degree of mutual interdependence required by all ranks to maximise their survival chances provided further reinforcement for the operation of *negotiated order*.[23] Some comments by a Lance Corporal exemplify this point: 'So I said to my blokes, you'll look after me and I'll look after you. I'll bring you all back home O.K. if I can, but a lot of it's up to you. We've got to get it right when we get out on the streets'. Getting it right means patrolling efficiently, being alert all the time, in the privates' terms being 'switched on'. It means that the three quarters of the Brick who are privates needed to use their own judgement, and often act on their own initiative. The Brick Commanders may, in the last instance, have made crucial decisions, but, nevertheless, their subordinates had considerable influence upon how things were managed when on patrol. The following extract from my field notes provides some indication of this:

Privates in Alan's Brick have negotiated with him, so that the GPMG is swapped around between them. The reasons for swapping are (1) the weight of the gun—it's heavier than the other weapons carried. (2) the gunner is always laying down on the ground, giving covering fire. This is particularly so at Vehicle Check Points. He therefore never (a) gets a chance to give the gobshits (PIRA supporters) a 'hard time', or (b) catches a 'Blimp' (a look at a good looking woman who is passing through the VCP in a car). Alan agrees on swapping the gun around, as long as all concerned know exactly how it's firing, high or low, left or right.

GOOD WORK AND 'BALLACHES': A NEW CRITERION

So far in this chapter I have examined the features of life at XMG which motivated privates and their superiors to establish even closer working relationships, behaviour which facilitated the achievement of official organisational goals. But what of the forms of behaviour which could be deemed to impede the attainment of such goals, and which I have shown to be in evidence at other stages of the private's career? To answer this question one needs to understand how privates viewed the various types of work they did at XMG. The deviant practices by privates at the Depot, and with the Battalion in its peacetime barracks, were provoked by strong dislike of certain kinds of activity. The means they found of diminishing or evading these disliked activities were, on many occasions, breaches of military law. As I have explained, boredom, repetition, and discomfort were some of the factors which created negative feelings about such activities as Guard Duty or fatigues.

At XMG much the same criteria were used, and a hierarchy of preference for particular activities was evident. For instance, doing cookhouse fatigues was seen as infinitely preferable to sangar guard. After all, doing the former one was warm, there was an endless supply of 'brew', music (on transistor radios), and talk with one's mates were all available, and there was no night duty. By comparison, being on sentry involved isolation, apart from an intercom, and a measure of physical discomfort. The sangars themselves were invariably cold and damp, and gazing out of an observation slit at the same featureless fields or nearly deserted streets for three and a half months constituted nothing but boredom.[24] Similarly, doing urban patrols meant that every other hour privates returned to the Security Forces Base to dry out, grab a quick 'brew' and relax for an hour. In contrast on rural patrol, two or three days were sometimes spent in the 'cuds', more often than not in soaking wet conditions in which one had to attempt to sleep, and eat 'C' rations rather than the hot cookhouse fare provided when on urban patrol. Yet, although such criteria (boredom, discomfort, isolation) operated at XMG, there was one factor which completely overrode them. The prime consideration behind whether privates viewed activities as good or bad, was the *degree of danger* they were subject to. Thus, on sangar duty the threat level was not high, the sentry being encased in a protective cocoon of steel and concrete with two GPMGs at his disposal. On rural patrol, however, the danger level increased dramaticaly, whilst 'being on the street' on urban patrol constituted the most perilous situation privates were to encounter. So much so that when finishing their cycle of urban patrols, one often overheard privates making remarks similar to the following: 'one more week of life [until the next urban cycle]', and 'I'd rather dig in than do urban'.[25] Therefore, regardless of the other factors, privates perceived all operational activities primarily in terms of how much they were likely to be physically threatened when doing them.[26]

This change in how activities were evaluated was part of an overall change in how privates saw their own position in relation to their work and their superiors. Both came to be seen as resources in the battle to stay alive. Given these changes, what were their effects upon privates indulging in unofficial activities at XMG?

Unofficial Behaviour at XMG

Just as in peacetime barracks, privates indulged in various forms of rule-breaking at XMG. For instance, there was so much scrounging of equipment between platoons that one Platoon Sergeant officially declared

his own Platoon's accommodation 'out of bounds' to all other privates who
were not members of it.[27] And sitting on my bunk in the base one afternoon
I was startled by muffled laughter, as two privates lugged into the room a
large container of ice-cream that had been scrounged from a resupply
helicopter they had just been unloading while on cookhouse fatigues. When
on sangar guard duty privates were habitually attempting to smuggle in
food, cigarettes, and the much prized 'wank mags' (pornographic
magazines), all of which were illegal since they could conceivably reduce a
sentry's alertness. These types of activity such as skiving and scrounging
were, however, in the main considerably reduced in comparison with the
peacetime barrack context, due to the overall reduction of 'ballaches'.

The Self-Image at XMG

As I have expained, at XMG privates assessed activities according to one
overriding criterion, the degree of danger to which they were subject. The
most dangerous, patrolling, constituted the core of their soldierly work and
was viewed, at best, with ambivalence. Throughout this account I have
stressed that when confronted with activities that they dislike, privates will
attempt to skive off in various ways: practices which they sum up in the
phrase 'looking after number one'. How then did this practice operate in
relation to patrol activity? In effect 'looking after number one' in this
context meant performing effectively—'doing the job'. For if one did not—
if one, in the private's terms, 'switched off'—disasterous consequences
could follow. To stay alive in South Armagh, and still more in XMG,
privates needed to maintain maximum alertness or, in their parlance, stay
'switched on'. Failure to move across a gap between two houses quickly,
failure to watch one's designated arc of fire, to hold one's weapon in the
'alert' position, all minimised survival chances. In the words of one private,
'doing your job saves your life out here'. On patrol in XMG the two
maxims—'doing the job' and 'looking after number one'— were combined,
and one could not be put into operation without the other. Skiving in such
a context would quite simply have constituted *not* 'looking after number
one'. Therefore in the most crucial of circumstances, out on patrol, any
contradiction between the two was minimised.
    To maximise their survival chances in XMG, privates needed to draw
upon all the core skills and experience they possessed. The self-image which
they held during peacetime service sharply confronted the stark reality of
life under a constant threat: a reality which was full of fear and loathing for
all concerned. There was then little time or energy for disillusionment over
the absence of glamour, the glitter being swiftly dispelled by the two
fatalities they had taken by the fifth week of operation. The demands of
their immediate situation required all their attention.[28] At the same time, it
was through participating in this harsh reality that the self-images they held
of being 'action soldiers', infantrymen, were reinforced and given some real

credibility. In XMG no war games or exercises were being played, for as one private grimly informed me, 'this is the fucking sharp-end'. The following statement by another illustrates how practice and self-image are mutually reinforcing and how they are enacted in the most perilous of situations:

> It'll have to be a clued-up twat if he's going to get us out there. We've got it worked out really good. Do it as it's supposed to be done, not like those other Bricks. Three go firm in hard cover, and the other moves fast. So he's got cover from three sides. Especially when there's a good shoot on, we cover it especially well.

Some indication of the meaning and strength of this combat soldier self-image can be gauged by the privates' desire for 'warries'. These are photographs of themselves armed and clad in full patrol equipment, including blackened faces. Taking them was a normal occurrence in a peacetime context, but it also happened in XMG. Thus I observed Bricks departing for patrol with members toting instamatic cameras. When questioned, replies were to the effect that such photographs were 'real warries', and thus highly prized. Such a practice was not considered to violate 'doing the job', for I was assured that it was only carried out when all patrol members were in 'hard cover' (secure, and in positions were they were adequately protected from enemy fire). At XMG, practice of the soldierly role and the self-image intertwined with each other in the daily battle for survival. Privates developed 'shortcuts' to facilitate their survival, which in themselves confirmed their expertise and their knowledge of the infantryman's trade. Thus, ploys such as taping open the cocking-handle of their SLRs so as to increase the speed with which the weapon could be fired in the event of a 'contact' were common practice. Or, in the same vein, purposely using the local civilians as cover when on patrol—even though this was officially disapproved—on the grounds that, 'PIRA are callous bastards, but they're not stupid enough to take out their own, just to get a few of us'. These 'shortcuts' constitute what privates termed 'knowing the score', being able to operate on patrol skilfully, minimising the threat at every opportunity: actions which daily substantiated the self-image they held of themselves, that of infantrymen serving in a highly dangerous location.

The location was made more dangerous from their standpoint by those in higher authority. Privates perceived the constraints of the 'yellow card', and the political veto on 'hot pursuit' of PIRA members over the Eire border, as evidence of the immorality of 'those FUBS in Whitehall and Westminster!' The yellow card guidelines forbade them to patrol with weapons cocked, meaning that in the event of a 'contact' precious time would be expended cocking their weapons and releasing the safety catches, before retaliatory fire was possible. Privates were well aware that a second was likely to be vital in such scenarios, and this official instruction was viewed with much cynicism, and perceived to be placing them in even greater jeopardy without good reason (see Chapter Nine for an elaboration on cynicism). As they saw it the tactical and political restrictions made their task in South Armagh more dangerous and difficult.[29]

'Not sticking your neck out'

First and foremost at XMG, privates wanted to survive, and this was the main factor motivating them towards a skilful military performance. However, this performance ('doing the job') did not entail what they termed 'sticking your neck out'. Taking unnecessary risks and chances on patrol, was perceived to be no part of 'looking after number one'.[30] Thus when, in the privates' view those of superior rank did so and endangered their team, they were categorised as 'bad' superiors by privates, for, after all, being a good superior involved 'looking after the lads'. A graphic instance of the latter type was when a Corporal announced to his Brick, when nearly at the end of an urban patrol cycle, that with just two one hour patrols to complete, none of the Brick were going to get out of the Saracen armoured car which accompanied them during daylight hours: a decision which evoked large smiles from the privates concerned.

While 'doing the job' in XMG involved exposing oneself to hazards, especially when on patrol, the other maxim influencing privates' conduct, and certainly a large number of junior NCOs, namely 'looking after number one', ensured that unnecessary risks were not part of the process.[31] The following comment from a private summarises this frame of mind:

> The [instructors] tell you that when a round is fired, cock weapon and go for cover. That's what they drill into you, before you come to Ireland. Out here though, its different, like when they (PIRA) got ———, it was go for cover and then cock your weapon. That's the way it is out here.

NOTES

1.   These factors of isolation and danger have been noted by Fitzpatrick (1980: 153) as the features which propagate a high degree of social cohesion amongst American coalminers.

2.   I am indebted to Hunter Thompson (1981) for the expression 'fear and loathing', which accurately sums up the ceaseless paranoia in XMG over one's safety—a justifiable concern in a location where everything from a matchbox to a milkchurn can result in one taking a trip to the morgue.

3.   When news reached the Company that members of the Battalion Headquarters echelon had played a game of football against the local RUC team, this heavily reinforced feelings of relative deprivation. The actual concept of relative deprivation was initially applied to the military, see Stouffer (1965: I, 122).

4.   The reasons privates gave for it being their Company designated to serve in XMG was that 'they' were the best, the most skilled soldiers in the Battalion.

5.   A description, in greater depth, of the day to day routines, constraints, and dangers, encountered by an Infantry Company on operational duty in Northern Ireland, is given by Bailey (1980: 20). Intensify all he describes and one has an approximation of life at XMG for the Company.

6.   Little (1964: 218), who did participant observation with the U.S. Army in the Korean War, has noted that the 'primary basis for solidarity in the platoon and company was the recognition of mutual risk'. On this point see also George (1971:294) and Stouffer (1965: Vol 2: 96). While both Turner (1967: 66) and Vaught and Smith (1980: 160) maintain that work groups subject to constant danger will exhibit a 'mechanical solidarity', as a matter of course. See also the comments of Salaman (1974: 120) on this topic.

7.   A high level of identification with their units, has been described by numerous privates when recalling their war service. See Crimp (1971: 117), Smith (1922: 309), Maitland (1951: 134), and Bowlby (1969: 113). Stouffer's (1965: Vol 2: 137) comments on the U.S. Army are also relevant.

8.   Privates were well aware of the civilian population's republican sympathies, and the fact that PIRA ambushes were set up in XMG with the aid of local people, who acted as 'spotters' (recording and examining patrol movements). When I arrived in XMG during the fifth week of the operational tour, there were various tales about the local population's hostility. The most often quoted concerned a local doctor who, it was said, refused to come to the aid of the Company's first casualty, as he expired in the street. The doctor was only eventually persuaded to come and render assistance by a cocked weapon levelled at his head. Privates saw this instance as a particularly bad example: that even a doctor would not come to their assistance hammered home to them that the Company was truly on its own.

9.   See the comments of Janis (1963) on group identification under conditions of external danger in the Army.

10.   The 'yellow card' is a guide to soldiers in Northern Ireland. If they follow its instructions and obey its guidelines—for instance when opening fire—then they will be deemed to have remained within the law.

11.   This narrowing of the active service soldier's world, has been described by those who saw service in the two World Wars: see Hamer (n.d: 13) and Coppard (1969: 20).

12.   Rivalry also existed at the Platoon level in XMG. Thus one often heard derogatory comments of the following ilk: 'Three Platoon's got all the fannies in the Company' and 'One Platoon can't handle the streets'. As in the peacetime milieu, such rivalry promoted identification and enhanced cohesion with the various levels of military organisation in which privates served. See Vaught and Smith (1980: 165) for a similar example amongst American coalminers.

13.   Little (1964: 217) has noted this embracing form of sharing amongst American troops in the Korean war. The 'Brick' in XMG closely resembled the classic military primary group, first defined in a combat context by Shils and Janowitz (1948). George (1971) has written a comprehensive review of the literature on the subject. The only work on the British military primary group I have come across is in Phillips (1965). The cohesion and efficiency of each Brick was a prime concern of the officers and senior NCOs of the Company. Privates were well aware of this concern prior to starting the Northern Ireland tour of duty. They themselves were concerned to soldier at XMG in a Brick commanded by a 'good' NCO. Conversations with them and their superiors, indicated that persistent complaints by privates about having to serve with a superior whom they did not get on with would sometimes result in the private being reallocated to another Brick. These moves were dependent upon the contingencies of manpower availability, and the desire to spread the experienced, those who had previously been on operational tours, through all the Bricks. The fact that such a reallocation did occur is another indicator of how privates were able to influence their superiors' decisions.

14.   Ashworth (1968: 420) in his analysis of 1914–18 trench warfare, maintains that a similar redefinition of group boundaries, the 'us' and 'them' dichotomy, happened. In this case all combat troops regardless of rank, 'constituted a quasi-group with a common purpose in resisting the demands of the military Staff'. He goes on to hypothesise that the horrors and carnage in which the participants were immersed eventually resulted in the incorporation of all fellow sufferers, including the enemy. As he puts it, 'the institutionally prescribed and dichotomous WE and THEY dissolved. The WE now included the enemy as the fellow sufferes. The THEY became the staff.' See also Stouffer (1965: II, 119) on this topic.

15. On the relaxation of formal discipline in combat see: Wilson (1951: 26), Robson (1960: 37), Bagnall (1947: 16–17), and Berlin (1961: 110). It is interesting to note that in time of a major conflict the Army's concern with ceremonial quickly diminished. Perusing Army Council Instructions published during the Second World War, one finds ACI's replacing brass buttons with plastic ones (ACI 1941, number 488), forbidding the polishing of the metal parts of personal equipment (ACI 1940, number 1423) and drastically decreasing the amount of drill troops were required to do (ACI 1942, number 597).

16. See similar comments by Stouffer (1965: I, 100).

17. Little (1964: 213–4) has noted the presence of a similar difference in discipline between parts of a US Army infantry unit, serving in Korea. This relaxation of formal ruling, and reduction of social distance between superiors and subordinates, also occurs amongst civilian workers in certain contexts. Graves (1958: 11) has noted that such changes occur amongst pipeline construction crews, as the difficulty and arduousness of their work increases.

18. Wingfield's (1955: 56) memoirs of infantry service in the Second World War provide a very similar account of how things were managed between superiors and subordinates when on patrol.

19. Little (1964: 211) cites a similar example of American privates evaluating their superiors. He uses the terms 'positive status legends' to describe the process.

20. It is interesting to note that the criteria which privates used to assess whether or not an NCO or officer was a 'good bloke' in XMG appears to be broadly similar to that used by American soldiers when making a similar evaluation. See Stouffer (1965: II, 407). See also Wilson (1951: 38).

21. This extra dimension to the criteria that privates used to evaluate superiors is, to a much lesser extent, evident in peacetime barracks. In such a context if an NCO or officer fails to map read properly, for instance, then not much more than sore feet is likely to happen to his subordinates. In contrast bad map reading in South Armagh, is likely to involve all concerned in trouble with PIRA. And if the Brick has strayed over the border into Eire, it means trouble with the security forces of that state. Numerous privates in the Company were well qualified to judge their superiors' military competence having completed operational tours of Northern Ireland before.

22. The features of this particular context are all particularly favourable to an explicit display of non-cooperation. The officer, if he had insisted on his initial course of action, would have himself been contravening standard patrol procedure laid down by higher authority.

23. See the comments of Stouffer (1965: II, 98) on the mutual dependence of American troops in combat.

24. Privates graded guard duty according to the sangar they were posted to. The criteria they used included warmth, the view, and the degree of access superiors had to the sangar. That is, how far each sangar was from the main command post, and also how easy it was for superiors to enter it. For instance, in certain sangars one just walked up steps to enter whilst in others one had to use a ladder and then open a trap door. In the latter sangars, the more noise and time involved opening them, provided privates with extra seconds to conceal cigarettes, 'wank mags', and chocolate. The view from the sangar was also considered important, primarily as some gave more access to 'Blimps' at night (women, dressing and undressing in their bedrooms), by means of infra-red image intensifying surveillance equipment. Such voyeurism has been noted amongst other male occupational groups; see the comments of Feigelman (1974) on construction workers.

25. 'Digging in'—digging trenches or shellscrapes whilst in the field, an activity which is the bane of all infantrymen. Casualties at XMG had invariably been inflicted by PIRA within the village itself, where there were greater opportunities for ambush, setting up ambushes (by local sympathisers), covering escapes to the Eire border, and utilising local civilians as decoys, sentries, and 'spotters' In contrast these advantages were not so great for PIRA in the countryside proper.

26.   A similar tendency to evaluate danger in terms of its specific manifestations and contexts has been noted amongst American miners by Fitzpatrick (1980: 138) and amongst high rise steel workers by Haas (1977: 164).

27.   The kinds of deprivation suffered by soldiers in Northern Ireland are not of the same order as those experienced by those who served in the two World Wars. The much greater physical deprivation experienced by the latter in terms of hunger and lack of shelter, occasioned a greater need to scrounge the basic needs of life, as their memoirs reveal. See for instance Hartsilver (1960: 86), Bowlby (1969: 136), Haigh and Turner (1970: 227), Wilson (1951: 21–22) and Bagnall (1947: 44–47)

28.   This absence of glamour, this disjuncture between reality and media depictions of combat, affected only those privates doing their first operational tour. Others who had served previously in Northern Ireland had no such illusions.

29.   One of the main concerns of government policy in Northern Ireland has been to win the support of the population in the campaign against PIRA. Yet as Moskos (1975: 28) has noted: for 'the soldier concerned with his own day-to-day survival, the decisions of state that brought him into combat become irrelevant. It is in this sense that the pros and cons of the basic issues of national policy are meaningless to the combat soldier'. The official policy of winning hearts and minds is meaningless to him. See also the findings of Stouffer (1965: Vol 2: 167).

30.   See Fitzpatrick (1980: 143) for similar findings amongst American miners. Yet the maxim of not taking unnecessary risks does not seem to hold for all dangerous occupations. Haas (1977: 157) has noted the opposite amongst high rise steel workers.

31.   This degree of caution and the taboo on taking unnecessary risks, in no way affected the private's conception of their masculinity. Rather they evolved a different conception of masculinity, appropriate to a situation where they were in constant danger. Little (1964: 205) noted something similar amongst American troops serving in Korea. See also Robson (1960: 114).

Chapter Eight

A Licentious Soldiery?—
Off-Duty Time

Privates are, among other things, part of an occupational community in that they have a common life together relatively isolated from the rest of society. Implicit in the term 'occupational community', is the idea that there is a special relationship between the domain of work and other spheres of a member's existence.[1] Non-work activities tend to occur in the company of fellow workers: and off-duty conversation, as Salaman (1974: 26) has noted, often centres around the subject of work. More specifically, Janowitz(1964: 177) has noted that 'the sharp segregation between work and private life has been minimized in the military occupaton'. This state of affairs applies particularly to privates, for the barracks constitutes the location where, for a considerable period of their service, they work, eat, sleep and socialise.[2] Whether in barracks or socialising 'down the town' the company and consequently the expectations of how one should act, tended to be similar.

As I noted in previous chapters, the self-image privates hold is a particularly masculine one, in the main arising out of their roles as combat soldiers. As a result I found that privates counterbalanced their hard, fatiguing and sometimes dangerous work by 'playing hard'. Their focal leisure activities centre on collective drinking and the eager pursuit of female company: a combination, on occasions, resulting in privates becoming involved in public fracas. Such activities, and the escapades which sometimes resulted from them, substantiated and mythologise the perception privates held of themselves, of being thoroughly masculine individuals. After all, this is what *real men* do; drink, pursue women, and if need be—fight. This self-image is not all that dissimilar from the traditional stereotype of a 'licentious soldiery', and there is no doubt that the social life of the privates concerned was rumbustious, although perhaps not as much as it used to be.[3] Whilst this reinforcement of their self-image by both work and leisure activities is important, there were also other significant features of their situation, which orientated them towards this type of off-duty behaviour.

Boredom and 'Blow-Outs'

Life in an Army barracks no matter how modern or well equipped places constraints upon the social life of privates. They are not allowed to bring women into their living accommodation, nor are they permitted to have alcohol there, the NAAFI being the only legal venue for drinking.[4] However, drinking in the NAAFI itself presented problems, for it was regularly patrolled by a Duty Corporal, known as the 'Canteen Cowboy', who was always alert for privates who were worse for wear. These constraints therefore, motivated privates, whenever they had adequate funds, to visit the nearest sources of civilian entertainment. In the case of the Battalion the amenities available to them in barracks were minimal, providing further incentive for them to conduct their social activity in either the nearby town or the more distant seaside resorts. In the words of one private, 'the NAAFI's boring, there's no cinema, it's miles from anywhere, and it's grotty. That's why the lads go into town and get pissed up'. 'Going down the town' had an added dimension for privates. There, military discipline did not directly apply. One could drink more or less with impunity, and one had access to women. This freedom from organisational control when in the civilian milieu was described to me by one private, as 'fucking Boss [excellent] times, doing exactly what we want, nobody telling us to do anything'. Although the constraints of a life in barracks made such leisure activity particularly welcome and significant, there were other factors which at least encouraged a rumbustious social life.

Military exercises are not picnics and privates suffer physical and social deprivation during them. In the operational context there is the additional element of danger. Moreover, at XMG, when off-duty—itself a rare event—there was nowhere to go and nothing to do but endure the boredom. As one private exclaimed, 'I write a letter, yeh. If I make a mistake I start again from the beginning, there's fuck all else to do.' During such periods of discomfort, deprivation and danger, a recurrent theme of privates' conversation was the 'good times' they were going to have when the period was over. These conversations were invariably accompanied by a 'days to do' syndrome, which entailed the individuals ritualistically telling each other how many days there were left to endure, before the 'good times' began; how many days were left before one got one's precious R & R in England, or how many days to do before the field exercise terminated. In addition to the practice of recalling their previous experiences of 'bad times' as a means of coping with present difficulties, privates also projected forward into the future and the 'good times' to come. 'Good times' were then particularly important not just for the enjoyment gained as they happened, but also because they were intensely looked forward to, thereby making it easier to cope with the 'bad times' of here and now.[5]

'Good times' represented the focal point of their social life and commonly involved going on a spree, a circumstance often made possible by the very deprivation and constraints they endured. After a period of field exercises or an operational tour, privates were likely to have a lot of accumulated back-pay. Partaking in a spree, in privates terms a 'blow-out', involved an excessive consumption of alcohol, and an equally excessive pursuit of women. One private described how he intended to celebrate the completion of the XMG tour of duty, in the following fashion: 'I don't care what she looks like, how old she is or anything. The first Dog [women] I see after this is finished is going to get some business from me.' Other 'amusements' which may evolve from these efforts, such as damage to persons and property, were perceived as part and parcel of having a good time. As I was pointedly told, 'you know yourself, after a good night out there's nothing like a friendly fight'. In Alberta, for example, the Company were pulled out of the field for two brief overnight respites during the field exercise. The first occasion resulted in numerous black eyes and the like, as the parade the next morning bore witness. On a subsequent visit to the local town a number of privates were incarcerated by the Canadian police on charges of drunkenness and stealing and smashing-up three civilian cars—an incident which caused the town to be put 'out of bounds' to the Company by the Battalion's Commanding Officer.[6] A 'blow-out', as defined by privates, involves such behaviour. It is excessive, hedonistic, uninhibited, and if possible extraordinary! In effect it is a celebration of their release, however temporary, from institutional constraints, discomfort, physical and social deprivation and perhaps danger. The fact that such behaviour may result in them falling into the unwholesome clutches of the civilian or military police is regarded fatalistically, and often rationalised with the phrase 'it was a good laugh'. And so there are good grounds for the whole cycle of bad times and good times to repeat itself once more. The following comment from a member of the car stealing group, made whilst still a prisoner and awaiting what turned out to be a heavy fine and a month's imprisonment sums up these sentiments: 'Wait until we get out of the nick, boy are we going to have some piss-up!' Such celebrations are truly hedonistic. For instance, during the Company's almost week-long Canadian R & R, the majority of the Company were back in Camp within three to four days. In that space of time, they had spent the major part of a month's pay, returning early because their pockets were empty.[7]

'Booze'

'Boozing', collectively and often to excess—'getting rotten' in privates' terms, is seen by them as an essential feature of their social life. It is viewed as something which *men* and, even more so, *soldiers* indulge in. Their perceptions of their own sexuality and their organisational role were intimately linked with alcohol.[8] In Canada during field exercise no beer was made available to the Company for over two weeks, which invoked much grumbling amongst the privates, particularly as the Officer-in-Charge had allegedly promised a supply of beer. This 'drought' was perceived as a violation of almost a *natural* right, as the following comment indicates: 'If you're going to give a bloke beer, you've got to give it to him. That's part of the squaddies life the ale, it's got to be.' Life in barracks for privates contained a fair amount of monotony and boredom, and consequently, as Bryant (1974b: 131) remarks about the American military, 'with nothing to do, nowhere to go, and often nobody (relatively speaking) with whom to do it with, drinking becomes an institutionalised way of spending one's free time'. Much social pressure was evident amongst privates for individuals to indulge in collective drinking, to be 'one of the boys', a feature which Gwinner (1976: 25) has linked with the relative absence of women from the military, and thus the removal of a significant control on heavy drinking.[9] Alcohol may also, of course, prepare soldiers for the ordeal of conflict and help them to deal with the traumatic memories which may arise in its aftermath. However, at XMG, with 'booze' rationed to two cans per day per man, there was no evidence of it serving privates in this fashion, although of course this function has been noted under conditions of general war.[10]

'Birds'

The fact that there was a relative absence of women in their lives made the pursuit of them even more significant for privates. So much so that barrack room conversaion was heavily monopolised by the topic of sexual activity. Masculinity being the nexus of both their sexual and occupational roles, privates perceived women in very much a traditional frame of reference. They categorised women into two distinct sorts, a military variation of the 'madonna and whore' syndrome, noted amongst young working-class males generally.[11] In short, privates made a distinction between females with whom they wished to have some kind of stable relationship and others with whom they demanded brief sexual encounters. This distinction was often expressed in the following fashion: 'Dogs are one night stands and women who hang around squaddies, not someone decent, who you go out with'.[12] This dichotomy between 'dogs' and 'decent' was maintained by an elaborate series of tales which circulated amongst privates, dwelling upon the attributes and lack of attributes of 'dogs'. Such attributes, no matter how expressed, were usually always portrayed in a negative fashion, focusing on a lack of physical attractiveness and also on certain kinds of behaviour considered to be non-feminine. This contrast between conduct considered to be womanly and its antithesis is implied in the following comment made by a private in a pub near the barracks. 'I saw one of them, show you what sort of dog she was, she came back from the bar with a pint!' In the main the only positive comments made by privates about such women concerned their granting more or less immediate sexual access, to whoever propositioned them. As one private observed:

> I go for the ugly ones, the real Dogs you know? If they're ugly you've got a
> pretty good chance they'll drop 'em, and you'll get your end away. The good

looking ones are liable to be a bit more fussy, a bit tight with it. They usually
fuck you off the first night.

These women were sexually objectified by privates in the grossest fashion.
By contrast those who were considered to be 'decent' were treated
somewhat differently.[13] They were still treated as sexual objects, but were
nevertheless attributed certain positive features, ranging from their physical
appearance, to their dress, and the degree of domesticity they displayed.

The role privates filled and the self-image that accompanied it placed a
great stress on virility, and in turn making explicit sexual overtures to
women. Certainly some members of the Company were more brazen than
others in this direction, yet all held to the same image, and conversations
were full of the ploys and techniques associated with such actions. This
practice of being sexually explicit was explained to me in the following
manner: 'I don't think we'd go down well with those university birds . . .
Well a squaddy's liable to say look do you fuck? Cos I'm not going to buy
you a drink otherwise.' A large problem for the privates in acting out the
virile demands made by their self-image was actually gaining access to
women. The Battalion, when in barracks, was located outside a small
town, thus creating a considerable demographic inbalance between the
ratio of young males to females in the area. Although the problem was
alleviated to some extent during the summer months by the not too distant
presence of seaside resorts, privates nevertheless faced much competition
from other members of the Battaion as well as the local male civilians when
seeking female company. The pursuit of female company in the immediate
area was largely confined for the privates to weekdays, since at weekends
there was a general exodus to their home towns. As the Battalion was at
that time located within its geographical recruiting area, large numbers of
privates made this exodus a regular practice. Visits to their home towns
were motivated in part by the knowledge that their chances of meeting
women were greater there than in the vicinity of their barracks. After all
they already possessed a social network which they could immediately plug
back into upon their return home. Their conversations also seemed to
indicate that the majority of stable relationships formed with women took
place in their home towns.

Faced with this problem of access—a real problem for many—collective
drinking tended to be the main pursuit in leisure time at least until the next
weekend or leave period. This pursuit also helped bolster the participants'
virile self-image (real men can hold their beer) while at the same time it
could be argued that it acted as a temporary substitute for sexual
encounters. As Bryant (1974b: 132) has noted about American troops,
'alcohol serves the function of relieving the tension of or blunting sexual
drives, acting as a kind of sexual anaesthetic, as it were'. Be this as it may,
despite the problems of obtaining access to women, particularly 'decent
birds', the pursuit of them continued, the difficulty, in effect, increasing the
challenge to the privates' masculinity.[14] In situations where the possibilities

of meeting either 'decent' or 'dogs' were both small, it was not unknown for privates to seek the services of prostitutes. During the field exercise in Canada, for instance, the small amount of off-duty time, coupled with a lack of knowledge about the morals of Canadian women, made involvement with prostitutes more likely than when the Battalion was in other locations.[15] (Complaints about the prices were how this information reached the researcher!) It was in conjunction with the combination of much alcohol and the ardent pursuit of women, that the third and less frequent feature of the privates' social life, was likely to occur, namely involvement in violence: in the privates' terms, giving or receiving a good 'wellying'.

Brawling

The private's existence was primarily a collective one. As I have noted, work and social life overlapped, and consequently when privates went out of barracks to socialise they did so in the company of other privates. Whether the occasion was a night out at the local pub, or a 'blow-out' to celebrate the end of a field exercise, as occurred in Alberta, it was unusual for privates to spend their leisure time on their own.[16] On the town with money in their pockets, groups of privates exuded a visible elan, a collective swagger.[17] The longer and more severe the deprivation they had suffered the more the swagger, and the greater the need to have a good time and the more money there was available to effect it. Thus, in Canada, on finishing the exercise in the 'badlands', there was a collective determination to celebrate not only the end of a period of hardship and their return to civilisation, but also the fact that they were tough enough to have endured the hardships. Putting it in the fashion privates themselves espoused, the collective goal of their R & R was to outdrink, out-fuck and if necessary out-fight all those with whom they came into contact. One therefore overheard numerous remarks prior to the R & R of the following kind: 'When we get to Edmonton, are those civvies going to be surprised!' Such a collective attitude and the élan that goes along with it, was nothing less than a direct challenge to the masculinity of other troops or civilians who happened to be in the vicinity.[18] A large amount of collective drinking, accompanied by the avid pursuit of that scarce resource, women, provided fertile grounds, when combined with everything else for brawling and public fracas.[19]

Particularly in a strange town or country where they are transients, privates were well aware that the consequences of brawling were likely to be limited to the short term. By that I mean that not having to live in the vicinity, they would be subject neither to social ostracisation through pubs or night clubs being placed out of bounds to them by the civilian owners or the military authorities, nor to long term retaliation by the males who resided in the area. Thus, after a visit to a distant resort, privates later remarked that they had been 'a bit rowdy in the discos'. Upon probing further I received the reply from one, 'well there was a punk-rocker bouncing up and down, who bumped into one of the lads, so we helped him bounce some more!' These types of confrontations, either with civilians or other troops, confirmed and reinforced the privates' self-image—that of rough, tough, infantrymen—as well as adding fuel to one of the popular images of privates, that of a licentious soldiery.[20]

As Blake (1970: 338) has noted, military socialisation and subsequent training is aimed at the production of efficient organisational killers. In preceding chapters I have elaborated upon the values and skills which such processes are designed to inculcate and foster. These features when present in the infantryman are likely to produce effective combat performance, a performance which by its very nature, as Bryant (1974a: 247) has pointed out, is concerned primarily with destruction. Given that the official organisational training procedures are orientated towards such an end, and that privates internalise a self-image which is largely sympathetic toward skilled military performance, it should not be too startling that on occasion they brawl in public. The application of violence to property and persons is, after all, the central feature of their occupation. What is perhaps more surprising is that such leisure-time behaviour is not more widespread.[21]

None of this is to say that privates did not go out for a quiet drink, or a film at the local cinema, or pursue more mundane and less dramatic hobbies. Rather what I am saying is that the trinity of booze, birds and brawling constitue the themes around which the myths of release from duty are played. These are very much intertwined with the masculine self-image that privates hold of themselves. The events described in terms of the themes quickly form a mythology of enjoyment and ways in which many of the privates I observed marked their time in the Army. In this way an unofficial career calendar is assembled and passed on from generation to generation.

OFFICIAL ATTITUDES

Official attitudes to privates' leisure activities are, to put it no stronger than this, ambivalent. While clearly deprecating the excesses that occasionally result from 'boozing' there are limits on how far those in authority can go in eradicating these excesses and turning privates into gentlemen.

The following is extracted from the initial address on discipline given to new recruits by an SNCO at the Depot.

> When you are allowed out and go down to town, keep out of trouble. By trouble I mean getting drunk and fighting with civilians. If you create a disturbance you'll get fined up to two weeks pay. That's military law, apart from what the civilian magistrate will do to you. Foul language in a public place, or urination, you'll have empty pockets for both offences. That piss will cost you roughly sixty quid. Keep out of trouble!

Yet despite the sanctions of heavy fines, swollen lips, and the possibility of venereal disease, privates still indulged in a rumbustious social life. The importance of such leisure should not be underestimated for, as I have indicated, it is directly linked to and feeds back upon the perceptions of the self that privates hold and which were themselves embedded in their military role.

The next question to be posed about this type of off-duty behaviour concerns its impact upon the military organisation. From one standpoint it can be seen as far from conducive to good military organisation. If, during a brawl, privates inflict damage to persons or property, this constitutes not only a contravention of civil but also of military law and hardly adds to the good image of the Army. Of more specific military concern, if after being on a drinking spree privates are manifestly incapable of performing their duty, this constitutes a breach of official rules and regulations. In fact, any form of conduct which is judged to bring the organisation into disrepute or to lower its efficiency is considered to be deviant. The Army, as a consequence, is concerned not only to maintain discipline amongst its members in their work environment, but also to maintain it as far as possible during leisure hours. This is particularly so in light of current Ministry of Defence publicity stressing that soldiers are 'professionals', and projecting a series of images which hinge on troops being skilled, self-disciplined, and technologically sophisticated. Drunkenness in public and the brawling that often goes with it smack of the traditional conceptions of a licentious soldiery, and mar officially projected images. Moreover, a rumbustious social life causes organisational problems of manpower deployment and increased administrative workload. Brawling may well result in troops being in hospital and therefore incapable of performing their roles. In addition, public rumbustiousness will inevitably involve Unit Commanding Officers with the police and civilian authorities, a dialogue involving its own administrative effort; and the problem may rapidly become a political one, if the location is overseas. Furthermore, attempts to control troops during their social activities, usually by the Royal Military Police, constitute another example of organisational resources being expended—resources which ideally should be directed toward propagating the organisation's main function of defeating the 'enemy'.

Yet this rumbustiousness, when examined from another angle, can be regarded as a positive force for the organisation as a whole. Brawling with civilians or other troops involves toughness, aggression, and the practice of violent skills. In addition, such occasions also demand solidarity in the face of opposition. Regardless of whether privates are fighting against another Army unit or the bouncers in a local disco, social cohesion tends to be generated during such occasions, loyalty is tested; in official organisational parlance, 'the team spirit is enhanced'. Just as in the case of facing PIRA (at XMG), external danger increases the solidarity of the group. Given that privates do become involved in fracas and brawls outside the combat situation, the cost to the organisation, in terms of administrative effort and manpower deployment, would seem to be a small price to pay for the reinforcement of core institutional values which are crucial to success in operational contexts. Examined from this standpoint, taking operational effectiveness as the first organisational priority, the rumbustiousness of off-duty privates must be seen to be a factor which is certainly not negative for the attainment of organisational goals. There is little doubt in my mind at any rate, whatever the ultimate truth of the matter, that the officers in authority appreciated the fact that the style of the privates' off-duty activities had these two sides to it. The result is that the officer is placed in an ambiguous situation. On the one hand he is explicitly charged with the duty of maintaining respect for the good name of the Army while, on the other hand ensuring that those under his command display all the valued qualities of loyalty, solidarity, aggression and so on. The result is that officers and men create, as I have noted before with respect to NCOs and men, a 'negotiated order'. In this case it is based less on stated trade-offs and more on mutual understandings about the limits that govern each party's response. In this sense it is an acknowledgement, largely implicit, of the unofficial roles each must needs play in order to maintain the official face. Privates know that officers have the duty of imposing such sanctions. As we shall see in Chapter 10 officers know and understand that privates, for all the reasons adduced earlier, will engage in off-duty behaviour which is likely to transgress the letter of military law. They also know that there are positive qualities involved in such off-duty behaviour. Accordingly there is a mutual awareness by officers and privates that while the 'game' has to run its course, if everyone plays their part the matter can be dealt with expeditiously and without the need for maximum penalties. If privates are caught publicly brawling (an offence for which they could potentially be dismissed from the service) and if they do not 'tear the arse out of it', in the sense that no-one is seriously injured, and there is no extreme damage to property, nor any involvement with civilian authorities, then the culprits will usually be treated leniently, within the framework of the 'game'. In other words the military authorities realise that privates will indulge in excesses, and on occasion subtly encourage them to do so. A parallel here might be with the paternal indulgence often accorded children; while authority and discipline must be maintained one should not, in doing so, crush the spirit.

NOTES

1.   Gerstl (1961: 38) perceives this relationship to be the most important characteristic of an occupational community.

2.   It is interesting to note that even married servicemen and their families (who do not live in barracks) are relatively cut off from the wider civilian society. Densham-Booth (1969) found that only 31 per cent of Army other-ranks' wives reported friendship in the civilian community, and 65 per cent had never attended civilian social functions.

3. Some indication of this decline, at least in drinking alcohol, can be gauged by *Soldier Magazine* (1961: 19) reporting in 1961, that the NAAFI sold nine glasses of milk, 50 cups of tea and ten cups of coffee, for every ten glasses of beer.

4. The official prohibition on drinking in barrack rooms has been in force, at least since the turn of the century. Thus both *King's Regulations 1902* (para 460) and *Queen's Regulations 1977* (para 5.084) contain the same restriction. In this respect the Army's legal code has not been liberalised with the passage of time.

5. Obviously privates also recalled previous 'good times', memories which served as part of the lore circulating in the Company, about its members capacity to have a good time in a thoroughly masculine fashion, as soldiers should do. There was as a result a 'when we were in . . .' syndrome in operation. See also Roucek (1935: 171) on this same topic for the American military, and a very similar rationale for 'good times' has been noted amongst Liverpool adolescents by Parker (1974: 156). Obviously the need for good times is heavily influenced by the contexts in which privates find themselves when things are bad. The Battalion's barracks for instance, were officially categorised as substandard by the Army. Obviously not all Army barracks suffer from such a lack of amenities, for many contain good modern accommodation, and facilities as diverse as swimming pools and ten-pin bowling alleys. However, the constraints imposed by military discipline are still evident within such superior locations.

6. During this same exercise the Canadian forces' bar in the camp where the Battalion was based was also put out of bounds as a result of fighting between members of the Battalion and resident Canadian troops.

7. Bryant (1974: 133) has termed such sprees amongst American troops, 'masculine rites of intensification'. Privates were able to indulge in such 'blow-outs' wholeheartedly, knowing that their food and accommodation would be provided by the organisation regardless of their personal poverty. Gwinner (1976: 25) has noted that the serviceman is protected from reaching rock-bottom by this element of organizational paternalism.

8. H. Elkin (1946: 410) has noted this connection between sexuality and alcohol amongst American troops, whilst Tunstall (1962: 136) has noted such a link amongst trawler fishermen. See also Mays (1969: 134) and Ashton-Braithwaite (1969: 16) for their recollections of drinking bouts.

9. Carney (1963: 169) has also noted this social pressure for troops to drink, amongst those serving in Cyprus. Ions (1972: 36) comments upon such social pressure, just prior to his Korean war service. Similar comments about American troops have been made by Long, Hewitt and Blane (1977: 116).

10. Mitchell (1969: 36), an infantry officer in the Second World War, recalls moving up to the front line prior to an attack with members of his platoon drunk. Alcohol may also serve an official ceremonial purpose, such as the American paratroopers' *rite de passage,* noted by Weiss (1967: 24).9, while at certain periods there appears to have been an official policy of issuing British troops rum to promote 'dutch courage'. Nasson (1980: 128) maintains such a policy was operating during the Boer war, while Brown (1978: 78) and Ellis (1980) cite it during the First and Second World Wars.

11. Various researchers have commented upon the 'maddona' and 'whore' syndrome evident amongst the male working class generally. See Robins and Cohen (1978: 58), Parker (1974: 135), R. Hoggart (1971: 100), Willis (1979: 44) and Wilmott (1966: 51).

12. It was interesting to note that upon meeting women whom privates classified as 'dogs', it became obvious that the women were conversant with certain aspects of the military milieu. For instance, they understood the argot used by privates.

13. See Guillaumin (1980) for an exposition of the sexual objectification of women.

14. The problem of meeting women is obviously greatly compounded when troops are stationed in large garrison towns, where the inbalance between male and females is even greater. On the Battalion's previous tour in Germany, the demographic problem was

compounded by linguistic and cultural difficulties, as one private explained to me: 'No way are you going to crack the women. In Minden there were five of our Battalions, and the German Army. The German civvies used to get pissed-off with their own squaddies, let alone our lads.' This situation in BAOR (British Army of the Rhine) seems to have changed little since the 1950s, judging by comments in Chambers and Landreth (1955: 112). Mays (1969: 168) provides a similar picture of garrison soldiering in inter war India.

15.   Prostitutes were then a third category of women and in terms of status, privates categorised them well beneath 'dogs'. In general, it would appear that troops' involvement with prostitutes is largely an overseas phenomenon, motivated primarily by the demographic, cultural and linguistic problems they encounter in meeting other kinds of women. Moreover the price of such services is more likely to be within the soldiers' budget in Third World countries, where the British Army has seen much service. Certainly my own recollection of serving in the 1960s are devoid of any memory of prostitution and troops in the UK, nor was it in evidence during field research. Involvement with prostitutes, or for that matter catching VD, elicits little stigma in the community of privates, above and beyond a humorous 'couldn't you get it for free'. Rather it is taken and treated as very much a normal occurrence. Mention of such an involvement can be found in the writings of Coppard (1969: 56), Crutchlow (1937: 57) and Crimp (1971: 31). Post-1945, a good source of information concerning soldierly involvement with vice, is the history of the Royal Military Police, by Lovell-Knight (1977). In it mention is made of such activity in locations as diverse as Japan (p. 215), Kenya (p. 161) and Sarawak (p. 174). See also Ellis (1980: 304–8).

16.   The exception of course was when privates formed stable relationships with women, for they then tended to spend less time socialising with their peers. This has been noted elsewhere: see Dennis, et al.(1974: 222).

17.   Hayner (1945: 219) has noted similar behaviour amongst the lumberjacks of North America, displays which often resulted in public brawling.

18.   The Battalion's location in the UK meant that there was no conflict between its members and other troops, during off-duty time, as it was the only Army unit in the area. In contrast, conversations with privates about their previous tour of duty at Minden in Germany invariably brought up the topic of brawling. The four other British units, a German Army unit, and local Italian immigrants, provided the opposition.

19.   I am not saying that every occasion privates went out of barracks involved them in brawling. Rather, it was apparent that such violence happened often enough for it to be regarded as a normal event. Individuals turning up on morning parade with swollen lips, closed eyes and the like, elicited from their peers, nothing more than a joke, and a cursory 'who done it?'.

20.   During participant observation at the Depot, I was asked by recruits who were still in their first month's training whether I was going to join them in celebrating, at the end of the month, their release from barracks. This invitation to a spree was tendered in the following manner, 'you'll have to come down to town with us John, squaddies on the piss! We'll have some good times pulling all the birds.' A few days later conversing with the same platoon of recruits, I mentioned that I had already visited the Battalion for a month. The recruits present who were destined to be posted to it were interested as to the nature of their future unit. The images they held of their future peers were all very much akin to the following response by one of them: 'I bet there's some hard lads there. Real piss-artists, give the civvies fuck all, eh John?' Given that these recruits had been serving for less than a month, and in fact had never been 'on the town' as soldiers, this would seem to point strongly towards the presence of a popular social image of a licentious soldiery.

21.   Short of extensively consulting official military records or newspaper archives, the degree of off-duty brawling by troops is difficult to gauge. Lovell-Knight (1977: 31) provides some evidence of it during the Second World War. The fact that it still goes on, and on some scale on occasion, can be discerned from the *Guardian* (1980: 4), which reported an extensive brawl in the garrison town of Tideworth: the result being 34 soldiers arrested, and eight police officers and one woman injured.

Chapter Nine

Occupational Values
and Beliefs

In this chapter I examine the values and beliefs which guided and regulated the patterns of private soldiers' behaviour I have described in preceding chapters. First, I will look at their value system, and the normative code through which it is enacted. In this account I will show the overriding principles of this code and, in addition, describe and illustrate how the code is implemented in practice. Essential elements of any normative code are the sanctions directed toward those who are deemed to have transgressed its precepts. Although there is evidence that NCOs, especially junior ones make use of it, the code primarily belongs to privates and, accordingly, it is the privates as a group who are responsible for judging transgressions by their fellows and administering any appropriate sanctions. In this respect it is an unofficial code. The next section is devoted to an examination of the private's view of the organisational processes which structure his existence. As I shall show, the private, on the whole, adopts a fatalistic, cynical and pessimistic view of the organisation: a view which is counterbalanced by a rich vein of humour. I stress how both the normative code and the attitudes and the beliefs comprising it, and the humour, all aid privates in adapting to and coping with the constraints, discomforts, and dangers they encountered during the stages of their Army career.

THE NORMATIVE CODE

The value system reflected in the privates' code was a product of a largely defensive orientation. As Becker (1973: 31) has noted:

> People shape values into specific rules in problematic situations. They perceive some area of their existence as troublesome or difficult requiring action. After considering the various values to which they subscribe, they select one or more of them as relevant to their difficulties and deduce from it a specific rule.

This normative code can be summarised by stating the one overriding concern, articulated by privates themselves, namely, 'look after your mates'. Privates are concerned to provide support in various fashions, to their peers in all possible situations, in the face of internal (all those who hold superior rank) and external (the 'enemy') opposition. The operation of this overriding norm of 'looking after your mates' serves to classify as deviant all behaviour, not conforming to its dictates. As a result, privates themselves placed limitations upon behaviour which, even though it may have made life more comfortable for an individual, was, nevertheless, likely to affect peers adversely.

The general norm translated itself into a number of specifics.[1] Privates expected each other 1. to reciprocate social obligations, 2. to do their share, 3. not get other peers into 'trouble', 4. not to 'tear the arse out of it', and 5. be loyal to peers.

Reciprocity involved privates in tendering all the forms of mutual aid I have previously described: mutual aid which helped all concerned to cope more easily with the constraints and dangers imposed by both the internal and external opposition. These ranged from supplying mates with a loan of money before pay day, to covering for them when their absence from duty was noticed by a superior—'he's just gone down the Q.M's stores Sarge'. The norm also demanded aid in dangerous situations whether at a dancehall brawl or during a 'contact' with PIRA at XMG.[2] Particularly in dangerous situations mutual aid is vital, and privates knew they were expected to conform in the expectation that similar support would be tendered to them.[3] Failure to adhere to the norm of reciprocal aid made the privates' existence more difficult to manage and certainly more uncomfortable. 'Ballaches' were more difficult to endure when imposed by the internal opposition and the threat from the external opposition was greater.

In the same fashion the norm of 'doing one's share' was intimately linked with all the contexts and activities in which privates found themselves. Much of infantry work is physically hard and gruelling, and therefore where there are facets of this work which impose an extra strain on particular individuals, this is shared by all immediate peers. On the march the heaviest loads such as the 'Gimpey' and the '84' are always rotated amongst the individuals present. Within barracks the numerous activities defined as 'ballaches' are similarly expected to be shared by all concerned. The norm stressed that all should cooperate and complete the distasteful tasks as soon as possible, each individual doing an equal share. In the combat context, doing one's share involved, in privates' terms, being 'switched on'. That is, being alert, accomplishing one's responsibilities, checking one's arc of fire, and covering others who form the patrol. Failure to do one's share, once again, results in a less bearable existence for all, in terms of either more work, boredom, discomfort, or danger.[4]

The third important norm which regulated privates' behaviour was one which stressed that members should 'never get peers into trouble'. Doing so in the argot of the privates, is 'dropping someone in the shit'. Any behaviour which resulted in this was strongly disapproved of. Individuals who caused others to get into trouble were invariably termed 'fuckups', and earned a reputation for causing individuals or the group to suffer either more work or the various sanctions imposed became of their inadequate performance.[5] On occasion 'fucking up' may be collective, as in the case I observed when a number of private soldiers who were new to the Battalion failed an equipment inspection during the unit's preparations for its ARU (Annual Readiness Unit) inspection. As a consequence, the whole Company had to stand another inspection the next day, an imposition which caused the Company's more experienced privates to display resentment towards the newcomers. Obviously, inadequate performance in the context of XMG constituted a particularly serious example of 'fucking up', in that the consequences were likely to be fatal rather than merely extra parades or inspections.

In contrast to the norm which demands an adequate performance so as not to get peers into trouble, the fourth norm called for moderation in all activities and conformity to a group standard. An excess of zeal by a peer was discouraged on the same grounds as those held by industrial workers, namely, that such behaviour might result in the group suffering undesired consequences. Just as in industry where the 'rate buster' (a worker on piece rates whose output is so high that it leads to the employer reducing the rate paid for each unit of output) is disliked by his or her peers, so privates also viewed such individuals with a jaundiced eye.[6] Within the infantryman's world there may be no such thing as piece-work or a production quota, but there are equivalents. Dress, for instance, and the degree of smartness associated with it, was a feature over which privates as a group attempted to maintain some control. At the Depot, recruits had no control over dress standards as the highest standards of smartness were demanded by the instructional staff. By contrast, within the more relaxed milieu of Battalion life this was not the case. As a consequence displays of ultra-smartness by privates were viewed with disapproval by their peers, primarily on the grounds that such a display reflected badly upon their own less smart appearance, and could possibly invoke an official demand by superiors for a higher general standard of smartness: a demand which would require more effort and time.[7] The same disapproval of an excess of zeal was evident in numerous activities ranging from the pace of a run to finishing an easy fatigue quickly (especially when more arduous or unknown work was likely to follow). This norm of moderation was also seen in the operational context of XMG. Privates expected their peers to do their job adequately when on patrol, so as to be able to render mutual aid and not drop anyone 'in the shit'. Yet there was also a strong taboo upon what they perceived as unnecessary heroics. The patrols were considered dangerous enough work without foolhardy action increasing the degree of peril—'sticking your neck out'. Individuals who took unnecessary risks were, by virtue of their actions, involving all of their patrol in extra danger, the consequences of which could always be fatal. This disapproval of heroics, when combined with the norm stressing an adequate performance, guided privates to a level of performance which constituted a middle way between 'hero' (or in barracks being defined as 'Tick-Tock') and 'fuckup'.[8]

The fifth norm guiding privates' behaviour was concerned with loyalty to one's peers. This form of conduct is of paramount importance to privates faced, as they were, for most of their service with constraints imposed upon them by the internal opposition, namely, their superiors.[9] Colonel Sprung (1960: 32) elaborates:

> Loyalty of one man to another even in the face of punishment is the backbone of the male society . . . A man's value is measured in terms of his strength and loyalty to his fellows . . . Soldiers in a platoon or company are 'all in the same boat' vis-à-vis their commander. The system forces them to feel this, even if it is not explicit. Anyone who 'breaks ranks' and destroys the strength of the common front is guilty of defection. If bad luck strikes and some punishment is due, a good team will suffer in common rather than permit one man to bear it all.

Yet it would be incorrect to presuppose that this loyalty is dispensed in a unregarding, unreflective, monolithic fashion. Rather, as in the case of the privates' definition of who deserved mutual aid (in barracks those who were peers, in XMG all members of the Company), more loyalty was given to some than to others. So some flexiblility could be observed in how closely privates conformed to the norm. An example of this concerned the practice of 'scrounging': when committed against peers this, one would have thought, was a clear instance of disloyalty, Yet, what I found was that the norm of loyalty in relation to scrounging extended only to a certain social distance from those who were initiating the scrounging. In the Battalion, for instance, privates repeatedly stressed that they would never scrounge from members of their own Company. As it was, events proved otherwise, with individuals frequently complaining that their equipment had 'walked'. And, at XMG, a particular platoon's accommodation was officially designated 'out of bounds' to all other privates who were not members of it, because of a proliferation of scrounging. Such factors all pointed to the platoon being the level at which peers' equipment and belongings were sacrosanct. This was also the case at the Depot. Privates, then, perceived scrounging to be a legitimate activity except within the confines of their own platoon. In contrast, when the norm of loyalty was applied in relation to those of higher rank, no such flexibility was displayed. Above all, for the privates there was no justification for what they termed 'bubbling'. 'Bubbling' constituted an individual providing any sort of information which resulted, or could result, in peers getting into trouble with superiors. 'Bubbling' was not acceptable on any grounds, even those instances where individuals had 'fucked up' and the group had to suffer sanctions for the former's misconduct.[10]

UNOFFICIAL SANCTIONS

This normative code then acted to regulate, justify and account for privates' behaviour, both in relation to peers and those of superior rank, and at XMG. All these norms were aimed at achieving and sustaining group solidarity in the face of the problems and dangers emanating from many sources. Violations of this normative code threatened group solidarity and, as such, solidarity was the source of what unofficial power privates possessed, all actions which breached it were regarded seriously and evoked sanctions, albeit unofficial ones. These sanctions increased in severity in relation to how seriously it was felt that the code had been violated. For instance, individuals who were classified as 'fuck ups' suffered a degree of social ostracism, a fate which largely precluded them from social activities and off-duty discussions characteristic of barrack-room life. Relative isolation and loneliness was the punishment meted out to these individuals, the power of such ostracisation stemming from the fact that for the majority of privates no other informal social group was available to satisfy their needs. 'Fuckups' were, then, presented with the alternatives of either enduring their isolation or, as the privates put it, 'switching on' and improving their performance so as not to endanger the group's interests further. There was, however, another option open to such individuals, namely, obtaining a transfer to another part of the Battalion.[11] Ostracisation did not merely inflict loneliness upon individuals, but it also involved the withdrawal of aid and, as I have indicated, privates, if they are to achieve a more comfortable existence, need such aid. The ostracised, therefore, found that life became much more difficult. The physical and emotional support they had previously enjoyed disappeared. For instance, if someone wanted to go to his home town for a weekend leave and found himself on guard duty instead, no-one would oblige and exchange duties with him.

In addition to the isolation and non-cooperation which ostracisation entailed, there were more aggressive forms of unofficial sanction. Name-calling and derision constituted the means by which the group made it known to particular individuals that they were approaching the limits of collective tolerance. In the following example a number of privates were discussing in his presence the 'bossy' behaviour of a fellow soldier. They attributed his conduct to his completion of a course of instruction designed for potential NCOs, and questioned his loyalty to the group:

> Jim announces loudly 'it's that NCO cadre that's gone to his head. Yeh, he'll be a right bastard when he gets a tape (gets promoted). Don't come and sit with the boys in the NAAFI, you can go and sit with the NCOs'. The alleged offender Alan, retorts sharply 'fuck off you silly cunt, did I ask for the course? No I got ordered to go on it, so shut it!' Loud assertions from the group follow, claiming that Alan is liable to go 'power crazy'.[12]

Once a peer had, in the privates' view behaved in a fashion which in any way indicated that his allegiance to them was questionable, a more specific form of verbal abuse occurred. The defendant would then be accused of 'brown-nosing', 'arse-licking', or 'sucking-up' to those of higher authority,[13] a state of affairs which privates saw as merely one step away from the offender indulging in 'bubbling'. Such conduct was stigmatised by the group on the grounds that the offender(s) was always willing to please those of higher rank. Always volunteering is another good example of this. A sustained critique of the individual's conduct was then liable to follow, termed 'a rifting'. In the following 'rifting', in this example for an entirely different offence against the code, a new member of a 'brick' is taken to task over his urban patrol performance at XMG:

> The lads have just come in off the street. They are rifting Big Jim [who has only been in the Company and XMG for three days] on account of his patrol performance. Dez is laying into him, 'you're always going for really good cover, OK fair enough, but half the time you're unsighted. You can't give cover to any of us, when we move. If you're going to go firm in good cover, you've got to make sure that it's good for us as well. Great if you're down behind a bloody great wall, and can't see us! You've got to get into a position where you can get a bit of both. It's not all yourself out there, we're covering you all the time'. Big Jim protests his innocence, and the two members of his Brick [joined by others in the room] retort bitterly 'you don't give a fuck about us'.

A third form of sanction for breaking the code, involved action by the group against offenders' property. As the transgression was breaching a code of conduct whose overall aim was to 'look after the lads', by definition the status of those who had broken the code was called into question. Mates, after all, do not get each other into trouble of any sort. Therefore, in such a case, the parts of the normative code which stressed trust, support, and loyalty, were held no longer to apply to the offenders, or were held in temporary abeyance until the 'fuckup switched on'. Those who constantly 'fucked up' on occasions found their equipment missing or perhaps broken. Alternatively sanctions would be applied not because the offender had given an inadequate performance resulting in harm to the group, but rather to check an excess of zeal which could have had the same consequence. Thus, a newcomer to the Company proceeded to 'bull' his working boots; a practice which violated the norm of moderation and could have caused supeiors to make comparisons to the detriment of other privates dressed less smartly. As a consequence, the said private found that someone had dropped his boots toecap down onto the floor, effectively destroying the 'bull' he had laboured to create: an action which constituted a salutory and effective warning.

The fourth and most extreme form of sanction which privates imposed against offenders was direct physical violence. This form of sanction occurred when there had been a serious transgression of the normative code, such as a clearly defined case of 'bubbling', or individuals who were caught *stealing* from within their own Platoon. Certainly in the operational context, violations of the code were usually met with direct violence, if not when actually when on patrol, then on return to the Security Force' Base. However, such sanctions were usually withheld if the offenders were, for instance, newcomers to the Company or an operational situation. Once this brief period of grace was over, further violations were usually met with violence: violence which ranged from a kick in the seat of the pants to being 'butt-stroked' (hit with a rifle butt). As one private explained:

> Yeh, say at a cross-roads if everyone is switched-on, you've got all round covering fire, for every bloke has a certain direction. A dozy bastard though, you've got them looking to see what the patrol commander's up to, instead of watching their arcs. And that's when ping! Someone gets it. With the dozy bastards you don't bother with the NCO, you just rift them once. If they keep switching-off you give them a good wellying!

Restrictions on Deviant Activity

As I have illustrated, the overriding concern of the private is to 'look after number one'. It is to this end that all the shortcuts, skiving and scrounging are orientated. However, the normative code which regulates privates' behaviour places certain constraints upon how number one is looked after. As a result, and in general terms, one never looks after oneself at the expense of one's mates. More specifically, the normative code places limits upon the various forms of deviance which contravene official regulations. Thus as far as skiving was concerned, I found that, from the private's standpoint, there was both good and bad skiving. It was considered all right if one skived, but never if it was at the direct expense of one's peers. If, by one's own guile, one managed to evade some 'ballache' before it started, then no norm was usually seen to have been broken. However, if a 'ballache' had begun and various privates had been ordered to complete the task, an individual skiving-off at this juncture was considered to be breaking the code.[14] No matter how artful the means by which the skive was accomplished, not doing one's share in such a context was seen as deplorable, since the rest of the group invariably suffered extra work—a clear case of the offender not looking after his mates. Moreover, whilst privates usually viewed a peer who had managed to accomplish an artful skive in positive terms, there were limits to their tolerance in this direction. An individual who habitually managed to avoid work, even when there was no *direct* repercussion upon his fellows, was viewed extremely negatively, as in the long term such a practice imposed more work on the group.[15]

Obviously skiving in an operational situation was likely to impose not so much extra work upon peers but, more important, extra danger. The following are the comments of one private upon doing skiving at XMG:

> I would never sleep in a sangar cos I'm always too scared of them [PIRA] trying an attack. It'd be on my conscience if they did get one of the boys when I was asleep. I'm really glad in a way that there's such a threat here. Like at Bessbrooke there's not much going on—it's quiet. On exercise you're always dozing off on stag, it's not real. Here in this arsehole of a place you've got to keep awake. Blokes do fall asleep in sangars but not on purpose, when it happens it because they're absolutely fucking knackered, you know yourself what it's like for getting any sleep around here.[16]

This is not to say that privates did not skive in XMG—they did. The practise of smuggling 'wank-mags' into sangars and perusing them as a means of alleviating the crushing boredom was common.[17] Yet, this action was not perceived by privates as breaking the normative code by causing their mates unnecessary danger. Rather, they made a distinction between reading pornography and sleeping in a sangar, a distinction based on their assessment of the degree of excess danger likely to result from these actions.[18] As they saw it, the odd glance at a 'wank mag' would not increase the danger level to any significant degree, the sangars and the Security Forces Base in general being fairly secure against any direct form of PIRA attack. The exceptions to this were attacks using rockets and mortars which would be launched from beyond the range of any sentry's vision, or the placing of vehicles containing explosive devices adjacent to the Base, a noisy and all too obvious ploy. Moreover, privates steadfastly maintained that the occasional glance at nude females helped prevent them falling asleep. In a case I have already cited, that of 'skiving' whilst on patrol, with members taking photographs of themselves ('warries'), the privates' rationale in this case was that such snapshots were only taken when all members of the patrol were in good cover or as safe as they could be, and consequently, there was no increase in the danger level.

Just as there was good and bad skiving, there was, for the privates, both good and bad scrounging. Legitimate scrounging occurred outside the private's platoon. Inside it, it was regarded with anathema and seen not as scrounging but as *stealing*. A further distinction related to the types of articles which were considered to be legitimate targets for scrounging. All military equipment, whether belonging to individuals or held in unit stores, was considered to come into this category. In contrast, it was regarded as bad scrounging and illegitimate to scrounge more personalised items such as a person's civilian clothing, and valuables.[19] This distinction was made regardless of the social distance between the victim and the scrounger, with the exception, of course, that individuals no longer considered to be mates were seen as legitimate targets.

These constraints which the normative code placed upon privates' 'looking after number one' served to prevent discord among peers who work, live, and socialise together: groups whose cohesion, particularly at the 'brick', section and platoon level, formed the bedrock of the privates' solidarity. Thus, privates conformed to this normative code not only through the fear of sanctions imposed by peers; as one private put it 'bubblers just couldn't survive', but, in addition, due to the realisation that looking after number one involved looking after one's mates also. To cope with the vagaries of an existence at the bottom of the organisational hierarchy privates needed such mutual support which, in its turn, bred solidarity. Moreover, faced with the most dangerous of situations, such as XMG, giving and receiving such mutual support was a paramount need: in this context, the desire to look after number one in any narrow individualistic sense being largely overridden. At no point was this more evident then in moments of crisis:

> XMG Security Forces Base. A 'contact' had just occurred with PIRA and I've just heard the explosion. The lads feverishly throw on equipment and weapons immediately, swearing and raging and wanting to get out on the ground, to help those who are involved in the contact. The lads pester the NCOs and receive a negative answer—support had already been deployed. They then cluster around the operations (telecommunications) room, anxiously waiting for news, names of any casualties etc. No orders were given for them to get their equipment on, they did so spontaneously, volunteering to go into a dangerous situation to provide support for the lads out on the ground. Talked to a Senior NCO who remarked that initially the Company had maintained a special QRF (Quick Reaction Force) at XMG to respond to contacts. In reality it was now maintained in name only, as it had been found that upon a contact, the lads were all eager to get on the street, without any orders being given.

'SQUADDIES' EYE VIEW OF THE ORGANISATION

As I have noted, the normative code was a product of a generally defensive orientation held by privates. The code itself was situated within a particular way of looking at and understanding Army life, also of a defensive nature. This way of seeing things was composed of a number of attitudes and beliefs that were fatalistic, cynical, and pessimistic.

Privates possessed no formal power to influence how their lives were ordered, and despite the presence of the negotiated order between them and their superiors, the main features of privates' existence remained largely outside their own control.[20] For instance, how a patrol was carried out may have been open to influence by privates, but they nevertheless had to take part in that patrol come what may. Therefore, while privates skived, scrounged and negotiated a more comfortable existence, they did so within definite parameters, and these were generally perceived to be unchangeable. Consequently their way of seeing things contained a strong element of fatalism. Hoggart (1971: 92) has summarised this way of looking at the world:

> When people feel they cannot do much about the main elements in their situation, feel it not necessarily with despair or disappointment or resentment but simply as a fact of life, they adopt attitudes towards that situation which allows them to have a liveable life under its shadow, a life without a constant and pressing sense of the larger situation. The attitudes remove the main elements in the situation to the realm of natural laws . . .

Military law, the massive inequality of power between superiors and privates, and the structure and programme of events which schedule their daily lives, were all taken for granted as routine features of life, and unchangeable. Privates were to a degree able to ease the constraints imposed by these factors, but their world was still largely controlled by 'them'. Fatalism is an attitude of mind which stresses coping, putting up with things, making the best of circumstances as they arise. Hoggart (1971: 92) also cites the various expressions common amongst the working class which summarise this coping perspective, such as 'soldier on' and 'it's no good moaning'. This kind of fatalistic rationale was generally used by privates, and it became particularly overt in circumstances they disliked. Thus, persistent grumbling at the course of events was strongly discouraged by the use of verbal rebukes. On field exercise, for instance— 'if there's one thing I hate on runs and marches, it's fucking moaners!' Putting up with things did not mean that privates were passive, the whole range of deviant ploys and skills pointed to the fact that they were not, for coping means making the best of the circumstances.[21] At XMG a certain brand of fatalism was in evidence. Faced with a highly dangerous situation, privates were forever uttering phrases such as 'if you're going to be a loaf of bread [dead], that's the way it'll be', and 'if your name's on the round [bullet] that's it'. This is not to say that they did not make the best of their circumstances. They did, by practising their patrol skills intensively and to the best of their ability. Pressing the point with them, one uncovered the element of chance, the belief that no matter how skilled they were in reducing the risks of death and injury, luck played a part in the course of events. Whether the action was an all day march in blistering heat, a drill parade, or a patrol along the Eire border, a fatalistic attitude was nearly always in evidence.

Closely interwoven with fatalism was the cynicism with which privates perceived the organisation they served: an organisation which, it must be said laid great stress on superiors looking after the welfare of their subordinates. These welfare responsibilities ranged from the provision of adequate sporting and recreational facilities to helping an individual private sort out his marital problems. There were also the informal, and thus unofficial, welfare practices instituted by immediate superiors which privates termed 'looking after the lads'. Despite these, privates, nonetheless, tended to view the organisation in cynical terms. This cynicism was grounded in the inequalities of power evident between privates and their superiors. Privates, in other words, were fully aware that the informal welfare practices were part of the superior's side of the bargain and the working relationship they offered was in return for an adequate military performance. Failure on their part, the privates knew, would result in such informal aid being immediately cut off. There was, then, some awareness that the basis of the working relationships with superiors was, at its core, an instrumental one, and any disruption of its functioning, would result in the inequalities of power becoming, once more, starkly revealed. It was this state of affairs which largely bred a cynical attitude amongst privates, summarised succinctly by one, who responded to my comment about superiors being indistinguishable from privates when all were wearing camouflage clothing with the retort, 'ah well, wait until they start shouting then you'll know soon enough!'

In relation to the officially instigated welfare practices there were other good grounds for the development of cynical attitudes. For, as privates well knew, all these welfare measures were aimed at maintaining a high degree of morale, so that privates would be as near to peak efficiency as possible in the event of them being called upon to go into combat.[22] Given that the organisational goal of the Battalion was that of closing with and liquidating the 'enemy', welfare practices functioned, in effect, to propel troops into perilous situations, and privates were well aware that their superiors were quite prepared to commit them to action. This is not to say that they thought that their superiors, especially those within the Battalion, would commit them rashly or unwisely, but rather that, after evaluating all possible contingencies, superiors would commit them with the full expectation that casualties would occur. They also recognised that their immediate superiors might also be in a position of not having any choice whether or not they were to be committed to action and that, for the organisation as a whole, they were expendable commodites when battlefield objectives had to be taken. This disjuncture between welfare and sacrifice motivated privates to view the former with a jaundiced eye.[23]

As a consequence all altruistic measures by those of higher rank were initially regarded by privates with a degree of cynical suspicion. Even the most mundane of altruistic actions evoked a particular brand of cynical humour. The following interchange was between a Corporal who had arranged a vehicle for his detachment to travel the mile and a half to the rifle range, and his subordinates. He announced 'OK lads on the Bedford and down to the firing point'. This was immediately met by the detachment gasping in mock astonishment, and the collective retort of 'Christ we're not actually getting a lift down there!'[24] At XMG there were additional grounds for privates to hold such cynical attitudes. In XMG they often referred to themselves as 'bullet-catchers' or as 'number elevens' (a man size target used for shooting at on the weapon ranges—it is the largest target and thus the easiest to hit). The political decisions which restricted hot pursuit of PIRA into Eire, and the constraints upon initiating action imposed by the Yellow Card, like not being allowed to have one's weapon cocked, fuelled their cynicism, a cynicism arising from the fact that they were in a very dangerous location, and were not being given (from their viewpoint) the licence to operate effectively. Cynicism was bred by the realisation that such measures reduced both survival chances and efficiency, in the very context where all efforts should have been orientated towards maximising these factors.[25] Cynicism was also provoked by the contrast between the official information they had been given concerning their role in XMG, and the actual reality they encountered. In the words of one private, 'the trouble is before we came here, we were told that we were coming to help the civvies. Well you can stuff them, they wouldn't piss on you if you were on fire! They're all for PIRA'.

The third feature of the private's view of the organisation I wish to examine concerns pessimism. As I have already stressed, privates do not routinely have enough power to change the structure of events which order their lives. Operating in tandem with this lack of control is a lack of information. Whilst the Army nowadays places much more emphasis on keeping ordinary soldiers informed of the events concerning them, there are, nevertheless, features of the military organisation which work against this policy, especially since rank and access to information are intimately related.[26] The higher the rank of the individual, the more comprehensive a grasp of the situation at hand he is likely to have. As Feld (1959: 19) has noted there are reasons why those lower down the chain of command should receive less information:

> The structuring of information is an integral part of military discipline. Security is not only a precautionary measure, it is also an instrument of authority. It apportions knowledge to rank and thus enables commanders to maintain control over subordinates at times when nothing else responds to their will. Confusion and uncertainty strengthen their hand. In the absence of any other tangible criteria rank decides. The assertion of superior knowledge and the assertion of authority are often one and the same act.[27]

Feld is correct in his contention that security and control are two of the prime reasons why access to information within the military is correlated with rank. However, there are other reasons why privates were often without specific information concerning their work tasks. In their own words they were 'mushroom soldiers', kept in the dark and fed on shit!' The Army is a large and complex organisation, and requires a mammoth amount of detailed planning and administration for it to operate at all. At the level of the Battalion the same needs, albeit less complex, were evident. Plans and programmes of events were drawn up, decisions made, orders given, and at the bottom of the chain of command the private was expected to respond obediently. Yet priorities changed, superior authority counter-manded orders, equipment and men were redeployed, all at short notice and the least notice being given to those of the lowest rank. There were periods when the private was kept waiting until the last moment before he actually knew what he was going to do, or knew what work tasks had been allocated him. Thus within barracks, the Company's training programme designated periods of activity for platoons to work on their own, usually entitled 'Platoon Commander's Discretion' and, as a result the exact content of such training periods was generally not known by privates until just before they began. In all these cases privates were the last to know their own fate, given the least notice, and expected to obey post haste. I frequently overheard the following sort of complaint: 'The trouble is you get fucked around a lot, go here, do that, too many chiefs. And by the time you get to the Indians the orders have changed twice, or you have got to do the initial command that was countermanded. It's then you get really pissed off.'

In situations where information was seen to be inadequate, privates perceived themselves to be 'ballached'. As one elucidated, 'it's really evil

when you don't know the crack [understand the situation]'. A lack of
information, or information that has been countermanded, produces not
only confusion but irritation. Equipment and weapons are pulled on for a
route march, and suddenly it's 'field administrative practice' instead and
nobody seems to know what that constitutes. During field exercises and
when at XMG, the fluidity and unpredictability of simulated or real combat
compounds the problem, and in such locations, cries of 'ballaches' and
'organised chaos' abounded. Privates, possessing no access to the general
picture of events, placed the blame squarely on the shoulders of their
superiors. As one put it to me, 'ballaches—that's something unnecessary.
Really it's to do with bad administration from up there, they're not
organised, and then it's passed down to the NCOs, and to us. So it ends up
with us, we get the greatest shit.'[28] As a result of this lack of information
and control over their lives, privates tended to adhere to a particular cynical
maxim that of 'believe fuck all until it happens'. Consequently they
adopted a cautious and essentially pessimistic attitude towards Army life.
Future work activities were viewed and thought about from the standpoint
of expecting the most undesirable outcome to happen. If more positive
events followed, well and to the good, but this did not deter privates from
once again expecting the worst eventuality.[29] Thus, I overheard some
privates digging a trench on field exercise, one saying to the other, 'you bet
we get this half-done, and we'll have to move to another location, and dig
another fucker!' Or, while in barracks, asking the time of an instructional
period, I received the reply: 'If this lot say we're going to finish at a
particular time, you can always add a few hours on.' And again,
commenting to a private that there did not seem to be any hills in Alberta, I
received the retort 'they'll find some'. Upon inquiring further as to the
private's meaning, the retort was 'they'll find some and make us run up
them'.

Privates draw upon their experience of the problems they encounter due
to a lack of information and control, to validate such a pessimistic stance.
After all when these problems occur, as one private described, 'we get the
greatest shit'. Such occasions as when orders go awry, are countermanded
and so on, provide a focal point for the privates' pessimism, and are termed
by them 'fuck-ups'. (There are situations which are designated in this
fashion, as well as individuals).[30] As with all large complex organisations,
the Army's administrative practices sometimes malfunction, and at the level
at which privates experience such events, the consequences spell boredom,
more work, and occasionally more danger. For instance, during the airlift
to Canada for the field exercise, departure times were delayed due to a
mechanical failure with the aircraft. a mishap which confirmed the privates'
gloomy assessment of future events. Even before the delay was announced,
my questions to them about flight details were met by the relevant
information and followed by a qualifier—'if there are no fuck-ups'. 'Fuck-
ups' were then seen to be inevitable, invariably resulting in 'ballaches' for
the lowest ranked. This is not to say that such administrative mishaps were

always happening within the Battalion, only that such occasions were frequent enough to provide further justification for privates to maintain a pessimistic attitude towards organisational processes.[31]

The attitudes and beliefs embraced by fatalism, pessimism, and cynicism formed an overall defensive orientation with which privates viewed Army life: a way of seeing things which was a direct product of a particular milieu. That milieu was one where there was always an inequality of power to the privates, disadvantage, often constraints and discomforts of various forms, and sometimes danger. It was a world view which stressed coping and making the best of circumstances, a view which was suspicious of official pronouncements, and one which initially stressed the possibility of a negative outcome when assessing future events. As such it was a world view aimed at 'looking after number one' in both physical and psychological terms: expecting the worst prepares one for it. When and if it occurs, it also minimises disappointment and shock.

Humour

The words fatalism, pessimism and cynicism conjure up images of a dour and gloom-filled existence. Yet the reality of the privates' world was far from that, permeated as it was by a rich vein of humour; humour which served a number of functions and enabled privates to manage the problems and constraints imposed by Army life more effectively. As I have indicated, the privates' fatalistic rationale involves making the best of adverse circumstances and coping with them. In such situations, the privates used humour to make light of their predicament. The adverse situations which the privates faced can be grouped into a number of categories, those emanating from 1. the climate 2. the enemy—the external opposition, and 3. from superiors—the internal opposition.

As infantrymen the privates were subject to the vagaries of both British and other climates. Hard physical work and long periods of waiting for events to happen, for instance on sentry duty or lying in an ambush awaiting for it to be sprung, all took place out of doors. Frozen in winter, roasted in summer, and often covered with nothing but a sleeping bag and a poncho, the privates soldiered on. Whilst in barracks, a drill parade, guard duty, or a trip around the assault course, found them having to endure similar albeit less severe discomforts. During such events, humour played an important part as a coping mechanism because it was used to make light of their predicament. During field exercises in Canada, torrential rain lasted for two days and nights, resulting in the Company having to endure soaking wet conditions, which coupled with a large temperature drop after sundown, made existence very uncomfortable. The response of privates to these conditions was a spate of humour focusing upon their plight. Quips about joining the Navy, becoming frogmen, the Quartermaster issuing flippers, and about going to the pay office to draw a 'wet allowance', were much in evidence.

The second use privates made of humour (and one which similarly made light of adverse circumstances) was concerned with the main problems they faced in the operational situation at XMG. Their fear of death and mutilation was a constant companion, one which they never got used to but whose effects they combatted with what Obrdlik (1942) had called 'gallows humour'.[32] Faced with a day to day existence full of precariousness and uncertainty, this form of humour acted as a compensatory device making the fear and tragedy of the moment seem only temporary. It was also a means of controlling group behaviour and sharing such burdens. Thus, at XMG privates would joke about appropriating each other's possessions in the event of any of them being killed by PIRA. Individuals cheerfully laid claim to boots, watches and even parcels from home! On occasion, some of this humour approached the grisly, yet simultaneously mocked the most horrendous features of the situation in which they found themselves. In the aftermath of the Company's second fatality, as the result of an RCD (in effect, an incendiary bomb), privates were ordered to wear their camouflage trousers whilst on urban patrol; instead of the olive drab variety they usually wore. The reason given to them was that the camouflage trousers comprised two layers of cloth, and that the last fatality had been found to have been less severely burned on the parts of his anatomy clad in camouflage. A silence followed this disclosure by a Corporal, and then one private announced, 'Fucking hell, fancy going to identify a pair of legs!' A response which produced much collective laughter.

As I have stressed, shortcuts, skiving and scrounging, were practices employed by privates to counter the institutional constraints imposed upon them by superiors. Therefore it was not surprising to find that humour was used in this fashion, particularly when privates perceived the superiors to be 'tearing the arse out of it'. When used in such a fashion humour was decidedly offensive, rather than being defensive or passive. Stephenson (1951: 569) has this to say on the subject: 'The conflict function of humour is expressed largely by means of irony, satire, sarcasm, caricature, parody, burlesque, and the like. The particular adaptability of humour as a conflict weapon lies in the fact that humour may conceal malice and allow expression of aggression without the consequences of their overt behaviour.' Privates realised all too well that other kinds of overt behaviour registering discontent ranging from verbal abuse of a direct sort to physical violence would quickly result in them being punished. Humour was, then, as Stephenson indicated, used as a means of 'getting back', of expressing dissatisfaction with events and superiors and it appears that privates have traditionally used it in such fashion.[33] The following example happened one morning in barracks, as a platoon was forming up for parade:

> The lads are taking longer than usual to form up into three ranks, and their Corporal becomes irate. 'Get fell in, I'll give you five seconds and then I'll start charging people!' Eventually with much grumbling the Platoon does so. The Corporal then angrily announces, 'you're like a lot of fucking women

this morning'. Quickly from the rear rank of the Platoon, a position obscured from the corporal's view comes an anonymous falsetto voice, 'I wish I was, I could make a few bob around here'. The Platoon dissolves into laughter, eventually silencing when the Corporal again threatens to charge them.

Various forms of humour were thus used by privates to help them cope with the problems they had to adjust to: problems imposed by the climate, superiours and the enemy. The use of such humour not only served to aid privates in such situations, but also functioned as Middleton and Moland (1959: 69) have noted, to create and reinforce a sense of solidarity amongst them. Both the normative code and the set of attitudes and beliefs towards organisational processes, together with the element of humour, were features which aided privates in their struggle to maintain a more comfortable existence. Combined together they helped him cope and manage with all the situations that occurred as his career progressed from raw recruit to XMG veteran.

NOTES

1. The problem with examining any normative code, and describing it in terms of mutually exclusive categories, is that in reiality such categories blur, overlap and fuse together. Sometimes they operate distinctly, while on other occasions they intermesh with other categories. The fact is of course that in reality (outside these pages) the code rarely, if ever, appears in such a formalised and discrete form. This should be kept in mind by the reader. See Weider (1975).

2. Military examples of the norm of reciprocal mutual aid, are to be found in Stouffer (1965: Vol 2: 143) and Little (1964: 201). For similar examples amongst occupational groups whose work involves danger, see Fitzpatrick (1980: 145) on coal miners, Faulkner (1974: 302) on professional ice-hockey players, and Cain (1973: 91) on policemen. See also Sykes (1958: 94) for a similar norm amongst prisoners.

3. As I have indicated the norm of mutual aid in dangerous situations, extended not only to the private's peers, but also (in XMG) to all other members of the Company, regardless of rank.

4. An American Army example of the 'do your share' norm is contained in Little (1964: 202). See also Fitzpatrick (1980: 144) for a similar norm amongst coalminers.

5. See Stouffer (1965: Vol 1:425) for an American Army example of 'fuckups'. Sykes (1958: 100) notes something similar amongst prisoners.

6. On rate-busting see the classic account of the 'Hawthorne Studies' in Roethlisberger and Dickson (1939) and the ethnography of Donald Roy (1952) as well as a more recent study by Herzog (1980: 116-126). Also Mars (1974: 225) cites an example of longshoremen placing informal limits on too much pilferage for fear of invoking official sanctions against their peers.

7. See the comments of Stouffer (1965: Vol I: 418) on American servicemen who were 'too G.I.'.

8. Little (1964: 203) found American infantrymen adopting a similar 'middle way' in Korea. See also Colonel Marshall's (1978: 149) substantiating comments about American troops in the Second World War. See also Fitzpatrick (1980: 145) and Faulkner (1974: 307) for examples of moderation in other high risk occupations.

9. Dennis (1974: 79) found this norm of loyalty to be the overriding concern of British coalminers.

10. Whilst the norm of never 'bubbling' anyone was strictly adhered to, in cases where the group suffers for one individual's misconduct, privates did nevertheless resort to their own form of sanction. I outline them later in the chapter. Thus on occasion various pressures would be brought to bear upon the offending individual(s). Privates termed this action 'bubbling' themselves'. The taboo against 'bubbling' is of course also found in industry, and prison. See Mars (1974: 223) and Sykes (1958: 87) respectively.

11. During my period of field research one individual did so, moving from the Company to the Unit Band at his own request. Little (1964: 203) cites a similar illustration of the socially ostracised obtaining intra-unit transfers. See Weinstein (1979: 94) for industrial examples.

12. Hodges (1974: 40) has recorded a very similar example amongst American troops.

13. A National Service example of harassing 'brown-nosers' is given in Baxter (1959: 65). Stouffer (1965: I, 264) and Anon. (1946: 369) noted it amongst American troops. Similar terms are used in industry to denote workers who are too friendly with foremen. See Miller (1969: 307).

14. At this point the act of skiving may mean the individual actually disappearing from the work location, or putting less effort into the work than his peers—in other words not doing his share.

15. Little (1964: 202) notes an American example of troops viewing individuals who made a practice of evading work at the expense of their comrades, in extremely negative terms.

16. See Barzilay and Murray (1972: 51) for an account by a Fusilier serving in Belfast, which mirrors the statement in the text.

17. See Milligan (1976: 90) for a good description of the crushing boredom experienced on active service sentry duty, in World War Two.

18. Fitzpatrick (1980: 149) mentions a similar practice of miners balancing danger against experience, skill, knowledge and their normative obligations. Haas (1977: 165) has also stressed that for high-steel workers, the problem of danger is a relative one, some sorts demanding much more caution than others.

19. A similar distinction has been noted amoungst stevedores by Mars (1974: 224)). The grounds for making such a distinction generally, have been examined in some depth by Henry (1978: 43-55).

20. Although acts of deviance could be seen as a form of resistance to higher authority, such acts were likely to reveal, in an extremely vivid and dramatic manner, the power of that authority to punish those who fail to obey it.

21. See the memoirs of Wingfield (1955: 57), Lloyd (1938: 199), and Gaze (n. d: 60) for insights into active service fatalism, also Baxter (1959: 17) for a National Service example. An American Army source is Stouffer (1965: II, 188), whilst Fitzpatrick (1980: 142), Hayner (1945: 224), Dunbar Moodie (1980: 562) and Tunstall (1962: 71) have noted its presence amongst civilian groups whose occupations are dangerous. The element of luck in combat, is mentioned by Graham (1919: 186), Haigh and Turner (1970: 71), Wingfield (1955: 122), Milligan (1976: 83) and Bagnall (1947: 210).

22. The development of the welfare function and its benefits for morale and the efficiency of troops, can be traced through examining the following sources: Wolseley (1918), 'Comrades in Arms' (1942), McMullen (1964) and McGhie (1973: 40). Soldier Magazine was featuring a supplement in 1979/80 in which there was a regular page entitled 'All in the Family', an indication of how extensive the institutionalization of Army welfare has become, extending not only to the soldier but also to his dependants.

23. See Goldner (1977) for an elaboration on the production of this type of cynical knowledge, in organisations where seemingly altruistic measures are seen by members not to be so.

24. See Wingfield (1955: 18), Bowlby (1969: 126) and Bagnall (1947: 113) for Second World War examples of privates' cynical attitudes towards organizational altruism. Stouffer (1965: I, 426) has noted it amongst American troops.

25. The fact that such cynicism over the constraints imposed upon them at XMG, did not result in privates losing faith in their leaders, I attribute to the fact that all ranks were subject to the same constraints, and that these were imposed upon the Battalion as a whole, by outsiders—official MOD policy. An example of an occupational group that manifests an even greater degree of cynicism and, as a consequence verges on the anomic, is that of the police (in America). See Niederhoffer (1967: 95–108).

26. An increased flow of information down to the private, relative to previous times, is due primarily to a need for a wider tactical dispersal of troops on the battlefield, and a consequent decentralisation of authority. This, of course, is the ideal. See for instance the stress laid by Brigadier Cooper (1973: 87–88) on keeping troops serving in Northern Ireland fully informed.

27. Marshall's (1978: 101) research on actual World War Two combat substantiates Feld's proposition, that the lower ranked are precluded from much tactical information.

28. See Stouffer (1965: I, 83), Feld (1959: 18), Marshall (1978: 90) and Ahrenfeldt (1958: 24). All stress disorder as being the overwhelming characteristic of battle. Complaints about a lack of information concerning the privates' immediate situation are contained in Hawke (1938: 97), Hartsilver (1960: 198), Moynihan (1974: 84) and Kelly (1954: 18–19). A peacetime example is to be found in Chambers and Landreth (1955: 198).

29. Stouffer (1965: II, 134) has noted a similar pessimism over future events, amongst American troops. See also the writings of Coppard (1969: 54), 'A Rifleman' (A. Smith) (1922: 286) and Bagnall (1947: 90, 98).

30. It is to prevent 'fuck-ups' that those of higher rank often order a degree of advanced readiness amongst privates, prior to activities commencing: a practice which can result in them suffering the 'ballache' of boredom, of fallow time. As one saw it, 'you're told to be here at so and so time by the Platoon Commander. So you're then told by the Sergeant five to, then five to five to by your Section Corporal, so you're hanging about. The extra time's to prevent fuck-ups, but they happen anyway, there's always fuck-ups.' A very similar comment by a Major General is to be found in Richardson (1978: 90). Mention of 'fuck-ups' can be found in the memoirs of Hamer (n. d: 21), Milligan (1973: 33) and Wingfield (1955: 138).

31. Eaton (1947: 90) has noted a similarly pessimistic view of organisational processes amongst American troops, and for the same reasons as in the text.

32. 'Gallows humour' has also been noted amongst American paratroopers by Weiss (1967: 26). An examination of the songs of the First World War soldiers, reveals its presence, none more so than in the classic 'Hush! Here comes a Whizz Bang!'. See Brophy and Partridge (1965: 54).

33. Examples of privates using humour offensively against superiors are to be found in the following sources: 'A Rifleman' (A. Smith) (1922: 8), Milligan (1976: 202), and Bowlby (1969: 56). If one examines the soldiers songs of both the two major world conflicts, much humorous derision of superiors is evident. See Page (1970) and Brophy and Partridge (1965).

Chapter Ten

Some Conclusions: Conflicts, Tensions and Paradoxes

In this final chapter I want to present some general conclusions arising from the material presented in the preceding chapters. In doing so I want to make some remarks on the relationship between the patterns of behaviour exhibited by privates and the official goals of the Army. Although my focus has been predominantly on what I would term the subculture of the private soldier, it would be foolish not to admit that this subculture and the patterns of behaviour it generates are situated in a wider context, namely, the Army itself. One of the main devices I have used in my account has been to show how the behaviour of privates departs from, is deviant to, can be contrasted with, the expectations and dictates embodied in the official manuals. This has enabled me to show how relationships between NCOs and men, officers and men, and men and men, are very much a negotiated order. An appropriate image here is that of a bargain in which the parties to the bargain, although in many respects unequal parties especially in terms of power and authority, must needs make concessions of various kinds in order to implement the very organisational goals they are required to meet. One could suggest, then, that the organisation itself needs to be looked at not as a failed idealisation of some plan but rather as a series of accommodations, negotiations, bargains. None the less the plan, embodied in this case in Queen's Regulations for the Army, is an ever present frame which members of the organisation use as a resource to manage their day-to-day conduct. One of the features of their day-to-day lives is the management of tensions between the subculturally induced inclinations of that often intractable material the private soldier, and the organisational goals. Questions about the integrative or disintegrative effects on the organisation of what I have summarily called the privates' subculture are relevant in this context, if difficult to answer in any unequivocal fashion. In what follows I shall try and throw some light on these issues by trying to evaluate the impact of the privates' behaviour upon organisational functioning.

Tensions

During my examination of the privates' career I identified what could be seen as a tension between certain elements within this subculture. On the one hand, by and large they perform their military duties effectively, motivated not purely by fear of coercive sanctions that may be imposed by superiors, but by a strong normative commitment to their role as infantrymen. Through initial organisational socialisation and life in a tightly knit occupational community, a particular self-image is internalised by privates. A craftsmanlike pride is evident, a concern to carry out efficiently all the *core* activities which they perceive to be central to their military role, in their terms 'real soldiering': forms of behaviour which were directly in line with official conceptions of soldierly conduct. Yet, as I have illustrated, the conduct of privates did deviate from at least the letter of military law in a fashion which was antithetical to officially prescribed conduct—deviance which was in a large part a response to and a remedy for the constraints and deprivations suffered as part of military service. As the private's career progressed this unofficial and deviant conduct was itself internalised as part of the self-image just as much as was officially approved behaviour. The self-image privates held was thus both a complex and composite one. There was a constant interplay, and often a resultant tension, between behaviour which was official and that which was unofficial in terms of organizational goals. Whether or not officially conforming behaviour is integrative in the sense of efficiently facilitating organisational goals and whether unofficial behaviour was disintegrative admits, at this stage, of no easy answer.

One of the general difficulties here has to do with the provision of criteria to evaluate efficient organisational functioning, criteria independent of whatever particular views or conceptions the inhabitants of the organisation may hold. This is a difficulty upon which much of structural functionalist thought in sociology has foundered.[1] Without going into details of this particular argument, from the perspective which informs this research, I take it first that some members of the Army, especially those in command, are concerned with the efficient functioning of the organisation as a task enjoined upon them as a condition of their role and, second, as far as the Army is concerned, the criteria of efficient functioning are to be found in *Queen's Regulations* and the *Manual of Military Law*. In other words, for those members of the organisation who have the responsibility for evaluating the performance of other members whom they command, the manuals of military conduct contain the ingredients out of which an evaluation may be made, and that it is their responsibility to show that this is done. What all these assertions imply, among other things, is that the judgement about whether or not behaviour does or does not serve official organisational goals is both a responsibility resting on some members' shoulders and fundamentally a matter of interpretation. By calling it a matter of interpretation I do not mean to imply that it is a whimsical affair, although on occasion is may well be, but that it is very much a process in and through which the reality of the organisation is created and sustained.[2] It does imply a process that is very much an 'occasioned' matter—that the interpretative process has to be applied to personnel and events which are often unique, circumstantial, often idiosyncratic, exceptional, time bound, and so on. Another way of putting it is to say the rules embodied in the manuals of military conduct do not apply themselves, but have to be used on particular occasions, particular times, with respect to particular individuals and particular events. This applies not only to those responsible for evaluating military performance and making decisions as to whether a particular pattern of conduct is or is not integrative for organisational goals, but also to those who are evaluated, in this case the private soldier. In other words, private soldiers are very much aware of the constraints surrounding those who have authority over them and, although they are not able always to choose the occasions and the terms in which their own conduct will be evaluated, they do, none the less, through the self-images they hold and the normative principles they adhere to, contribute their own interpretations and accommodations to the prescriptions which govern all members of the Army. I will now illustrate some of the forms that privates' interpretations and accommodations take.

As I have asserted privates' conduct is very much a matter of occasioned interpretation, in which self-images, activity and context all play a part. Which form of behaviour was justified, which was considered appropriate, was situationally determined by privates 'on the spot'. The activity, context, and the individuals involved, all were evaluated, and the choice and form of action determined as the following passage from my field notes illustrates. Two privates and I are conversing out in the Albertan 'badlands'. The interchange concerns whether or not one of the privates, a recent arrival to the Battalion from the Depot, is going to report sick and thus be sent back from the field to the Battalion's base. This interchange illustrates the kind of expectations privates held about following the rule or principle in 'looking after number one':

BRIAN: Your're not going in with it then?

JIM: I could do but I'm not going to bother.

BRIAN: You're fucking crazy man, does the Boss [Company commander] give you any more money for staying out here? No. Ah, you're no fucking squaddie!

RESEARCHER: What's up?

(Brian turns Jim face on to me, and I see that one side of his face is completely swollen up by mosquito bites, the one eye almost closed.)

The self-image which privates held was one which stressed coping adequately with all the vagaries of military existence, be this a twenty mile march, or an imminent fatigue detail. The above comment 'you're no fucking squaddie', indicated Brian's scorn at what he considered to be an incorrect choice of action by Jim. The Company, whilst out in the field at the time, was not engaged in any core activity but resting prior to a night navigation exercise: a situation which presented no direct challenge to Jim in terms either of him performing core activities adequately, or letting his peers down in any fashion. This context as well as the condition of his face

presented him with a direct opportunity to 'go sick' and exchange the
forthcoming rigours of a night field exercise for a comfortable bed and a
chance to drink a few beers at the base—in other words, 'look after number
one'. Brian's scorn was a direct result of his perception that Jim was failing
to conform to this precept—failing, moreover, due to his 'sprog' status and
his consequent lack of experience.

Another point illustrated by this example is that privates hold to a strong
normative commitment not only to *certain* organisationally approved
modes of behaviour, but also to the canons of 'looking after number one',
and one's mates. Expertly dismantling an SLR in total darkness, or stealing
ice-cream from the cookhouse, were both conduct considered to be
appropriate for 'squaddies', and the self-image privates held reflected such
a perception. The term 'soldier' was very rarely used by privates when they
described themselves. Much more often, they used the terms 'the lads' or
'squaddies', phrases which embraced both official and unofficial forms of
conduct, and contrasting with 'soldiers' which, for them had strong
connotations of officially approved behaviour only.[3] The private's self-
image was, then, one which encompassed proficiency in dealing both with
the external opposition—by being proficient in military skills—and the
internal opposition comprised of those of higher rank, largely by
developing an expertise in deviant practices of many kinds.

The upshot of this was that I was faced with a social process in which
correct and officially approved performance and deviance were interwoven
with an often puzzling complexity. I have already demonstrated the
presence of cynicism in the way privates viewed organisational programmes and events; and in attempting to understand fully the relationship
between adequate military performance and deviance further variations of
this cynical outlook needed to be penetrated. In some respects this cynicism
represented a smoke-screen which privates used to gloss a normative
commitment to the soldiely role. Any attempt to question privates directly,
especially in the company of others, on this topic invariably led to a cynical
response and refutation. The most common retort was 'NFI' which in fact
was delivered at every possible opportunity by privates, regardless of the
work involved or the context (whether they were being questioned by me or
not). Such a negative stance performed for privates a number of functions,
perhaps the main one being a defence of status within the group. For
instance, if one started on a long march in an optimistic, enthusiastic or
even confident mood, and then failed to complete, a status loss amongst
one's peers was liable to result. Not só if one started by proclaiming NFI,
for, after all, if one dropped out ('jacked your hand in'), one was not really
trying anyway. Moreover, purporting to be in a state of NFI about
activities in general was but another facet of the 'there are always fuck-ups'
syndrome, and part and parcel of the general defensive orientation adopted
by privates. If, for instance, the work activity had a negative outcome for
privates, then a 'we knew it all the time' syndrome appeared, providing the
grounds for a further state of collective NFI. In addition, actually

proclaiming oneself to be in a state of NFI meant that one openly registered one's opposition to official duty and, in doing so, individuals confirmed their allegiance to the unofficial normative code and to their peers. In contrast when certain privates responded enthusiastically about forthcoming duties they were invariably criticised and accused of being 'Tick-Tock', or worse, a potential 'Brown-Noser'.

The trouble one faced as a researcher was in accurately discriminating between genuine NFI, when privates perceived themselves to be 'ballached', and when they uttered such pronouncements as a matter of ritual. The following explanation was provided by one individual:

> Well you don't really mean it and then you do, you're sort of NFIing all the time. Sometimes you're really as sick as fuck about something, like the ARU. And others, well it's sort of difficult to explain it, your sort of always saying NFI, and sometimes you don't really mean it.

I found that once I was alone with a single private, they were readier to express attitudes openly which indicated a normative commitment to the soldierly role as they perceived it—attitudes which, as I have stressed, in the presence of their peers would elicit derogatory comments.[4] I also found that there were often direct contradictions between what individuals said and what they actually did. For example, before a 22 mile march in extremely hot conditions and carrying a considerable load of equipment, one private loudly proclaimed that he was in a state of NFI about the march. Yet, during the march the same individual refused to exchange his GPMG periodically for a lighter weapon with the other members of his section as was routine practice. Rather, he carried the weapon on his own for a full 17 miles before suffering an attack of severe cramp and collapsing. Another example of such a contradiction happened during the same field exercise, as a platoon camouflaged itself in a wood. My ears were being 'bent' by a private who espoused total NFI due to heat, fatigue, mosquitos, boredom, and no beer! He was simultaneously camouflaging his position, taking minute care about it, even to the extent of rubbing earth into the broken sections of branches he was using to prop up his poncho, to blacken the white sections of the branches which, although small, could be detected by an alert observer. A similar incident occurred during a night navigation exercise—a map-reading test which involved traversing rough, wooded, country in darkness, with rain falling steadily. One private of the patrol involved was constantly proclaiming a state of being NFI as mosquitos bit, ankles were turned and water crept down the participants' necks. Members of the patrol were taking in turn the task of heading towards the various check points. When it was this particular private's turn, the Corporal in charge suggested that another private should provide additional assistance. Immediately, this private who, minutes before, had been announcing that he was NFI, hotly denied the need for assistance, and proceeded to complete swiftly and efficiently the task at hand. Yet another example of this contradiction between what privates espoused and what they actually did, concerned marriage. Two privates in a particular platoon were constantly proclaiming themselves to be NFI about Army life, and looking forward to the termination of their service. Both stated, however, that they intended to get married in their best uniforms, and some months later produced photographs depicting the events!

This tension between official conduct conducive to organisational goals and other kinds of behaviour, together with the composite self-image which serves to validate them, is illustrated in the following passage, noted at XMG:

> A rural patrol comes into their room throwing rucksacks onto the floor, they are filthy and sweating profusely. Another section from the same platoon are sitting on their bunks, and proceed to deliver a lot of banter to the incoming group. They state gleefully that they have had a real 'cushy' time, nine hours lying in the sun, operating a cordon. Laughing at the incoming rural patrol, who have been marching more or less constantly for the same amount of time, across the countryside. They emphasise their cushy time. The incoming patrol returns the 'crack' stressing that they are the best section, and good soldiers, not 'fat jossers', who have to be put on an easy duty, because they couldn't cope with the more arduous tasks.[5]

Whilst the above example does not concern activity which is directly deviant, it does indicate the privates' concern to make life more comfortable, which on other occasions manifests itself in rule breaking. The other part of the contradiction, their concern to be 'real soldiers', and to be proficient in core skills, is explicit.

At this point I wish to examine a tension of a different kind. Looked at from one point of view, that is, the strictly legal standpoint, the deviant practices which evolve from privates' attempts to have a more comfortable existence are dysfunctional for organisational goals. They contravene the seminal rule of obedience to orders, misappropriate military equipment, necessitate the expenditure of resources in attempts to control them, attract bad publicity, and so on. However, if one stands back a little and takes a less rigid perspective and examines the *normal* routine range of deviance from another angle, then its consequences are not wholly dysfunctional. For instance, collective brawling in public calls for aggression and the use of violent skills, all of which tend to reinforce group solidarity. Therefore in this case, it is not implausible to argue the seminal official virtues, skills and values can be seen to be reinforced by such deviant practices, which, in turn, can perhaps be seen as unofficial training. Another illustration concerns the particular style of dress affected by privates. As I have explained such style is concerned not only with cleanliness or uniformity, the official dress norms, but with expressing autonomy, with being personally distinctive. As such this personalised style is liable to contravene both official dress regulations for the Army and the particular policy laid down by the privates' superiors. Yet this style is by no means antithetical to organisational values and goals. Rather, privates are celebrating a degree of individuation as *military men*, and not as civilians. For the manifestation of style expresses a belonging to the subculture. Tapered camouflage clothing and shrunken berets are both expressions of individuation and of *élan*, recognised by other soldiers and by ex-soldiers. The manifestation of such style indicates that the individuals concerned are neither recruits nor newly trained soldiers. To express such style, those concerned need both to understand its nuances and to be accomplished in the various techniques needed to achieve it.[6] Style then is a statement of individuation and commitment to the role not so much of 'soldier', the official version, but rather of being a 'squaddie'.

Turning once more to the deviant practices indulged in by privates when they 'look after number one', one can provide much the same conclusions. Skiving, scrounging, and the use of shortcuts are all ploys which demand the employment of initiative, guile, quick thinking, subterfuge, and the like—the very qualities which the organisation officially tries to foster amongst privates, particularly since modern war has become characterised by a high degree of fluidity, and the decentralisation of authority.[7] Certainly, there would seem to be an obvious case for the use of such qualities in an operational situation, qualities which are needed to survive the enemy's attention, and bear the general vagaries of conflict. For example, in a general war, within which some degree of organisational dislocation is inevitable, the guile used in barracks for scrounging various artifacts could be put to good use when foraging for rations. 'Living off the land' is, after all, a traditional coping device employed by soldiers, often born of harsh necessity. Therefore, when one examines these deviant practices more closely, one finds that when evaluated with the criteria of operational efficiency in mind rather than the purely peacetime canons of discipline, the disintegrative impact of their normal routine forms is perhaps outweighed by their potential utility.

Moreover, pursuing this train of thought further, one finds, that again there are certain similarities between official expectations of soldierly conduct and those demanded by the unofficial normative code operating; a congruence which could be integrative for officially defined goals. Initial socialisation at the Depot and subsequent training within the Battalion both stress loyalty, mutual aid, identification with the group, and so on; features upon which one finds a similar stress when examining more closely the private's general rubric of 'looking after your mates'. Good privates are loyal, offer large amounts of mutual aid, and certainly identify very strongly with their immediate work groups. Whilst such unofficial norms originate and are maintained in direct opposition to superior authority, the advent of an operational situation containing a potent threat to privates saw all their resources switched to combatting this more serious danger. In a context such as at XMG—out there 'on the ground'—there was a high degree of 'fit' between the official expectations of soldierly conduct and the unofficial equivalent regulated by the privates' normative code: a 'fit' which was hardly antithetical to organisational goals in that most crucial of contexts. Furthermore, when one examines the normative code in detail, one finds that the taboo against seeking personal advantage at the expense of one's peers places effective limits upon deviance, and possible disintegrative consequences, whether the context is operational or not.

The impact of the nomal routine acts of privates' deviance upon organisational functioning was then reduced by a number of mitigating factors. The forms such deviance took, whilst admittedly contravening military law, must nevertheless in an operational situation be viewed as having considerable utility for the organisation. The price the Army has to pay in less crucial non-operational situations for this benefit would seem, in comparison, quite modest. In a similar way, the values and beliefs which structure privates' deviance both limit it and, generally but especially in the operational context, act to reinforce and substantiate conduct which is aimed at fulfilling the organisational objectives.

DEFINITIONS OF GOOD SOLDIERS

During my periods of observation with the Battalion, I became aware of a certain distinction superiors made when assessing privates whom they commanded. This distinction focussed upon competence in core skills either in the field or on operations on the one hand, and conduct in peacetime barracks on the other. Frequently, superiors ranging from Lance Corporals to Majors would complain about the conduct of some private who was being punished for some transgression, and then qualify their remarks with a comment that so-and-so was still a 'good soldier'. This qualification was applied even to privates who had spent time in the Military Corrective Training Centre at Colchester, and held as long as the individual concerned displayed competence in core skills particularly in operational situations. Numerous privates had already done various trips to Northern Ireland before the South Armagh tour of duty.

Just as privates held to a self-image which viewed certain deviant practices as normative, so their superiors also perceived privates as *naturally* inclined to such behaviour. Certainly, all NCOs intimately understood the nature of the problems that privates encountered and the responses they made to them, having been in a similar predicament when privates themselves. Thus, both officers and NCOs expected privates to be involved in a certain degree of deviance, and only when such deviance violated their conception of soldierly competence would superiors label offenders as 'bad soldiers'. For example, a private who went AWOL (absent without leave), whether in barracks or at XMG, would adversely influence the operational efficiency of the unit, and superiors would classify him as a 'bad soldier'.[8] Yet such serious crimes as going AWOL or assaulting a superior were not the norm. They did not constitute the everyday routine acts of deviance in which privates were involved. Rather, the normal pattern of deviancy was one of a never-ending series of misdemeanours, which were regarded as normal and natural by superiors. Officially, and by that I refer to the position they must legally hold under military law, superiors were duty bound to impose sanctions upon transgressions. Yet, as I have shown, there was much opportunity for superiors to interpret law flexibly or even disregared it. How they interpreted law and imposed sanctions was influenced by the kinds of deviance brought to their attention and their understanding of the organisational consequences, not just by the legal canons before them. Superiors' interpretations of privates' unofficial conduct, their deviance, and the latter's impact upon organisational functioning, were not limited to deviant acts. Thus, when discussing the no 'bubbling' norm, they were well aware that despite the short term problems it posed for them, in the long term and in operational situations, adherence to the norm was likely to have positive effects upon the unit's social cohesion. In the words of a senior NCO: 'it means they've got loyalty to each other and that's a good thing, when they'll take punishment rather than tell on their mates. It means that when we go to Crossmaglen they'll trust each other on patrol.' Some other examples from my field notes serve to illustrate superiors' perceptions on the matter. The following statements are all by officers who, let us remind ourselves, constitute both judge and jury when official charges have been brought against offenders:

> A Captain commenting on public brawling: 'We're in the violence business after all, is it surprising that sort of thing is accepted? In a way it's good training, and everyone talks about it, especially if you manage to knock a few of them about. It's a good thing as long as you don't get caught'.

> And a Major on the same subject: 'Yet it's inevitable after a while, for you get to know them. They wouldn't be soldiers if they didn't behave like that. I don't think the Army has ever had saints as private soldiers . . . It depends upon what has happened, obviously if someone has been very badly injured then you have no choice but to treat it seriously. However in some ways you like to know your soldiers have got character, they need a bit of form to be good.'

> Similarly a Lieutenant explains: 'If it goes too far you have to treat it seriously . . . well if they really badly damage people or property, if they start using the bottle for instance. Otherwise it's treated in a fairly tolerant fashion. Of course there's always the problem of getting mixed up with civilians, police wise that is. Yet in a sense it's a good thing, as it keeps the spirit up, makes us more of a family'.

As Bryant (1974a: 251) has noted of American troops, 'initiative, resourcefulness, aggressiveness, and decisiveness—all characteristics developed by stealing equipment from other units—are also traits that contribute to tactical proficiency and thus the effective soldier', and the same applied to privates serving in the Battalion. The superiors I observed were well aware of the integrative potential of public brawling. Often between themselves they expressed approval, and occasionally outright admiration, of the escapades of their subordinates. These are views which, due to their rank, position and authority—here I am speaking of officers and senior NCOs—are never officially communicated to privates. Junior NCOs in contrast, although also never officially condoning such activity, did on occasion join in with their subordinates, a collusion motivated by their sharing some of the same problems experienced by privates. Yet, even in a situation such as at the Depot, where the position of junior NCOs in terms of their status and authority was much more removed from recruits, various forms of deviance were implicitly tolerated, if not encouraged.[9] The following interchange between a recruit, with less than a week's service, and a Corporal, provides an illustration. The subject being discussed is the shining ('bulling') of boots:

> CORPORAL: You'll need an extra spoon for boning down your boots.
> RECRUIT: Did you say steal one Corporal?
> CORPORAL: No I didn't say steal one, just acquire one that's all!

Moreover, on occasion, even officers of quite senior rank communicate their implicit toleration, if not encouragement of rule breaking, when they make remarks which bolster the very self-image privates hold of themselves—remarks which reveal the image officers themselves hold of privates and the kinds of conduct they expected from them. This conduct, although deviant, was still defined as being appropriate to the soldiery. The following observation I recorded during my time in barracks, and it illustrates on the one hand an official caution against deviance, and yet on the other an admiration for it:

> Lecture being given by a senior officer to the Battalion. Subject is the preparation for the forthcoming ARU. Officer stresses the need not to be caught out by the inspecting team, anyone who lets the Battalion down will find himself in trouble. No deviance will be tolerated. He remarks that any personal vehicles which are parked in camp must have an MOT certificate, otherwise they have to be parked outside. He goes on to say that a considerable number of privates now possess their own transport, concluding with 'it's great to see you lads on motor cycles [grins] preferably your own of course!' (much laughter follows).

Superiors' attitudes towards the forms of deviance which they cate-gorised as not serious or as normal, as the understandable 'high spirits' of 'good soldiers', were often communicated to me by them using the phrase 'its OK if they don't get caught'.[10] Thus, after a brawl in a bar in Canada, next morning, before parade, all ranks of the Company joked together about the incident. No-one had been apprehended, no judicial process civil or military had been initiated, and therefore everything was OK. Another example concerned smuggling women into barracks. During my periods of observation it became obvious that both senior NCOs and officers knew about this practice generally, as well as in more specific terms. I was party to a conversation between a Lieutenant and a group of privates, in which it became evident that the former was fully conversant with the Company's women-smuggling folklore. He told one well known story concerning a particular individual who was observed copulating in a shower with a young woman, clad in a steel helmet and boots, which caused the privates present to embellish the tale further, to everyone's amusement. The tenor of the conversations and incidents I have just described was jocular and unconcerned; it was all OK for no-one had been caught. If, however, offenders were caught and official charges pressed then, depending upon the offence, and regardless of whether it was detrimental or not to the Battalion's operational efficiency, the due process of law had to be enacted. Thus superiors held both official and unofficial definitions of serious crime. The unofficial generally resulted in tolerance and lenient treatment of offenders. In cases of brawling, for instance, as long as there were no really extensive damage to property or persons, privates would generally not receive any significant punishment, once their pay had been debited for the damage caused. If caught, privates accepted fatalistically that they would be punished for their crimes. Yet, at the same time, they evaluated the degree of sanction imposed against them against a standard whose basis was this lenient interpretation. Violation of this expectation, in privates' terms 'tearing the arse out of it', aroused anger and resentment. Privates themselves were well aware of what the Battalion's normal crime constituted, and on the rare occasions when individuals went AWOL or assaulted a superior, they viewed it as inevitable that heavy punishment would follow. The levels of punishment they normally expected then, were, based on past experiences of previous indulgent interpretations of military law, and superiors when sentencing individuals for a normal crime—one which they themselves regarded 'unofficially' as not serious—generally held to such a standard. Such a relatively flexible use of sanctions effectively lowered the level of resentment at being disciplined amongst privates. Thus, even when the official judicial process was initiated against offenders, the threshold of potential conflict between privates and their superiors was raised, so serving to diminish the resentment and bitterness which could rapidly erode the basis of established working relationships.

CONFLICT

As I have shown in preceding chapters, adequate military performance by privates was traded-off in return for a relaxed interpretation of military law by their superiors. In this context the concept of a 'negotiated order' advanced in the work of Strauss is a useful one. Strauss (1963: 148) points out that:

> . . . the shared agreements, the binding contracts—which constitute the grounds for an expectable, non surprising, taken-for-granted, even ruled orderliness—are not binding and shared for all time. . . . Review is called for, whether the outcome of review be rejection or revision, or what not. In short the bases of concerted action (social order) must be reconstituted continually or as remarked above worked out.

Negotiation and renegotiation were then ever present features of the relationship between the private and his superiors, in particular junior NCOs. The private's main concern was with which rules and commands were enforced, and which punishments were imposed upon offenders. In turn his superiors were primarily concerned with obtaining a suitable performance from their subordinates, in the interest of furthering their military careers and survival. But these working relationships were never static, nor were they the result of well established once-and-for-all bargains. Privates in seeking to make their lives more comfortable routinely engaged in transgressions of military law. Up to a certain point such deviance was regarded as normal by all concerned, and by that I mean that privates and their superiors expected such conduct to occur. What, however, was also expected by superiors was that subordinates would perform their work adequately without jeopardising the reputation of those superiors. Additionally, a certain proportion of the normal crime committed by privates was not liable to have direct repercussions upon their immediate superiors with whom working relationships were the most important. Examples of such crimes were: brawling in public, scrounging from the Quartermaster's stores, or skiving off an irksome cookhouse detail. During such activities the private's immediate superiors were often not directly responsible for their subordinate's conduct. If privates were caught performing such deviant actions there were not likely to be negative repercussions for their Section Corporal or Platoon Sergeant.

By contrast, if a group of privates failed to arrive on parade early enough, or failed to keep an appointment with their Company Commander, the competence of the NCO in charge would be questioned. It was around this type of deviant actions that conflict, punishment and subsequent renegotiation of working relationships were focused. The expectations of both sides were disrupted in instances of the kind I have just mentioned, but they were also disturbed when, for instance, an officer announced that some rule which was previously ignored was now going to be enforced. As a result, the working relationships between both sides needed to be renegotiated. In the case of privates being punished for transgressions, two factors which influenced their subsequent actions were the degree to which, first of all, they considered any kind of punishment to be appropriate, and secondly, the extent to which they judged the particular punishment to be fair. If deviance was known to have occurred, not just by the private's Section Corporal but also by his Platoon Commander, then an official charge was regarded with fatalism by privates. On other occasions when immediate superiors possessed total discretion over sanctions, privates expected the whole range of unofficial and unrecorded alternatives (verbal reprimands, fatigues, parading behind the guard.) to be employed, rather than an official charge being resorted to. When this did not occur, or when the punishment meted out was judged to be excessive or unnecessary, anger and resentment were felt and expressed by privates. What followed was a period of renegotiation, of redefining what was acceptable to both superior and subordinate(s). How long such renegotiation took depended upon the seriousness of the offence and the sanctions that had been imposed.

On occasion, an initial negotiation occurs between privates and a newly arrived superior. The parameters of the working relationship negotiated in this case depended upon the expectations both parties held of what was an acceptable state of affairs—expectations themselves based upon past experiences which may well be dissimilar, particularly in relation to understandings of how rules are to be enforced. This can obviously lead to conflict, and when a new superior is appointed, this often happens. During such periods privates test out their superiors' tolerance to rule-breaking. Whether or not a Corporal allows smoking during a lecture, and the kind of response evoked when one is late for parade, whether verbal reprimand, fatigue, official charge, are all incidents which provide privates with information to help them assemble a conception of their new superior—a conception which will either motivate them to perform with a high degree of proficiency for those defined in positive terms, or merely in an adequate and perhaps grudging fashion for those defined as 'Tick Tock'.

These disruptions of working relationships—these negotiations and renegotiations of bargains and agreements—generate anger, resentment and punishment. Such conflict marks the limit of the negotiated order, for what one must keep in mind is that such an order is maintained and operated within bounds defined by those who hold rank, and not by privates. Superiors possess the power and authority to both define the limits to such negotiations and punish those who overstep them. The fact that such punishment may be unofficial and lenient should not obscure the power to define and enforce a power which even the most inexperienced Lance Corporal possesses. A private's direct refusal to comply with a command is going to propel him in one direction only—into the clutches of the Regimental Police!

I now wish to examine more closely the implications of this kind of conflict for the organisation as a whole. It occurs when privates are confronted with onerous tasks, further restrictions on their autonomy, and so on. Their deviance is aimed at alleviating such factors, and at achieving a more comfortable existence. There is much that is relevant to the privates' condition (poverty apart, since soldiers are now reasonably well paid) in Taylor, Walton and Young's (1975: 182) comment on deviance amongst working class youth generally:

> We believe that it is true that delinquency is in part the result of an external situation of inequality, poverty, and powerlessness, and can be seen as an attempt to assert control and thereby to re-establish some sense of self.

The question which now needs to be answered is why—given that privates' deviance and the conflict that accompanies it are routine features of Army existence, constituting an attempt by them to assert some control over their lives—was the Battalion not a hotbed of insurrection? At this point the work of Coser, building directly on the writings of Simmel, is of some help. Discussing Simmel's understanding of the functions of social conflict, Coser (1956: 73) notes:

> It would appear that Simmel has failed to make a distinction between conflicts which concern the very basis of a relationship and those which concern less central issues. Conflicts arising from within the same consensual framework are likely to have a very different impact upon the relationship than those which put the basic consensus in question.

The issues which provoke normal conflict between privates and their superiors do not directly call into question the military system of power and hierarchy. The routine deviance of those who hold no rank does not directly threaten the unequal distribution of rank and privilege, nor the existence of the authority structure within which it resides. Thus the *legitimacy* of superiors to command, to demand obedience, and to punish deviance was not seriously questioned by privates. Rather, both the negotiation and renegotiation and the conflicts in which privates were habitually involved were all aimed at influencing how this command was exercised, at diminishing its negative consequences, and evading apprehension for deviance. Indeed, such deviance may well act to reinforce the legitimacy of that authority by calling it into play as a routine and inevitable feature of military life. The basis of consensus concerning the legitimacy of superiors' authority was not impaired by this process. For instance, privates within the Battalion never questioned the right of superiors to command. Where there was questioning it pertained to specific individuals who were perceived to be unfit to command on the grounds of military incompetence, rather than of illegitimacy.[11]

Conflict, then, occurred regularly as working relationships were disrupted and mutual antagonism flared up between privates and their superiors. Discontent was expressed wherever and whenever contentious issues happened. But this animosity was not left to feed upon subsequent conflict, grow, and become funnelled into a single major cleavage. Rather, frequent conflicts over secondary issues which did not question the hierarchy of authority and power prevented such a build-up of conflict, and the possible erosion of the basic consensus. As Coser (1956: 80) has remarked: 'Far from upsetting the basic relationship, the direct expression of feelings of enmity can be a source of integration if participation is segmental rather than total.' Privates committed the majority of their deviance on an individual basis and a minority of it in small groups. Therefore, when discovered, the subsequent sanctions, official or unofficial, were generally imposed upon individuals and small groups rather than the collectivity such as a Platoon or Section. Thus, the conflict of interests and any resentment or anger at any one time, was experienced by a small number of individuals. For privates not affected, their working relationships with superiors suffered no disruption. Moreover, given that those who punished a proportion of privates' deviance were not their immediate superiors but those who occupied positions as diverse as RSM, Orderly Sergeant of the Guard, Adjutant, Commanding Officer, then resentment was both sporadic and diffused. In addition, such anger could be focused away from immediate superiors since its source was the result of actions of those further up the chain of command. On occasion, Battalion Headquarters' directives inconvenienced and annoyed all ranks in the Company, and a mutual empathy was evident—Battalion HQ—the FUBs—were ballaching 'us' the Company—an empathy which was often communicated quite openly between ranks ranging from Sergeant to private. The same process was seen when the source of inconvenience and resentment was external to the Battalion. This was particularly evident during the ARU when a senior officer opened a lecture to an assembly of all ranks, by describing the forthcoming inspection as a 'ballache': a task imposed by District Headquarters, and one with which even those in command of the Battalion had no choice but to comply. The Battalion as a whole—'us' was suffering at the hands of District HQ—'them' and some of the anger and resentment at the imposition of a whole set of restrictions and inspections was deflected onto an external source. Another mechanism which acted to defuse anger and conflict was the peculiar kind of rule interpretation, and the dual definitions of crime held by superiors upon which I have already elaborated.[12] So there were a number of reasons why feelings of enmity toward superiors were normally segmented rather than total, and diffused rather than concentrated into one large primary cleavage. In a certain, if perhaps paradoxical, sense it is possible to view the routine conflicts I have described as integrative for organisational goals, rather than disintegrative.[13] To quote from Coser (1956: 85) once again:

> When close relations are characterized by frequent conflicts rather than by the accumulation of hostile and ambivalent feeling we may be justified, given that such conflicts are not likely to concern the basic consensus, in taking these frequent conflicts as an index of the stability of these relationships.

I suggest that such a process occurred within the Battalion and that, routinely, the basic consensus concerning the legitimacy of those who held rank to command obedience remained unshaken. The antagonism bred over conflicts of power and interest between privates and their superiors was diffused daily over a host of small incidents, which were dealt with as working relationships were negotiated and renegotiated. More specifically, as I have shown in preceding chapters, such routine conflict fosters a high degree of solidarity amongst privates in opposition to their superiors. And provided that, as was normally the case, such conflict was both segmental and diffuse, antagonism and hostility centres on and is expressed over incidents as they occur. Therefore, when faced with a larger and more serious threat, such as the question of life or death, posed by the PIRA, feelings of internal opposition to superiors were not strong enough to inhibit social cohesion amongst all ranks at XMG. In that location, internal conflict within the Company was subsumed in the face of conflict with

PIRA, and led to privates redefining group boundaries to encompass superiors as being part of 'us'. This state of affairs could not have happened within the Company if there had been any primary cleavage evident prior to or during its operational tour. Had there been conflict over the legitimacy of superiors to command obedience, it is highly unlikely that such an increase in social cohesion, and redefinition of the 'us' and 'them' dichotomy, would have occurred. Thus Coser (1956: 93) when commenting upon the possible integrative consequences of an external threat has noted:

> The relation between outer conflict and inner cohesion does not hold true where internal cohesion before the outbreak of the conflict is so low that the group members have ceased to regard preservation of the group as worthwhile, or actually see the outside threat to concern 'them' rather than 'us'. In such cases disintegration of the group rather than increase in cohesion, will be the result of outside conflict.

Therefore, at XMG, that most crucial of contexts for both individuals and the organisation, the solidarity generated in opposition to superiors during the routine peacetime conflicts of interest formed the bedrock of social cohesion upon which a wider solidarity was founded, encompassing both privates and their superiors.

I have confined myself to examining the routine conflicts of interest between privates and their superiors. The normal state of affairs is one in which what Coser would term 'primary cleavages' are absent. Certainly my observations within the Battalion, and the Depot, produced no evidence of such a serious dissensus. Rather, my fieldnotes show that the unit had high morale, much tenacity in the face of adversity, and solidarity accompanying it.[14] The *abnormal*, of course, is a state of affairs which is, or is close to, a state of *mutiny:* a conflict of a centralised and collective nature which would fit Coser's concept of a primary cleavage. Although such a topic is outside the bounds of this book, during my research I did come across a limited amount of documentary evidence concerning mutiny in the modern British Army from 1899.[15] A reading of these sources reveals that a number of common factors tend to be associated with the outbreak of mutiny. Some of these are: mismanagement by superiors resulting in intolerable living conditions, where there is no justification for them; harsh, often petty, discipline enforced by a rigorous application of military law; and, as a consequence, the violation of troops' expectations of how superiors should treat them. Such circumstances would seem either to preclude, or seriously to breach effective working relationships between superiors and their subordinates. I must stress that the evidence I have come across is scant, and it does not provide sufficient grounds for maintaining that within each unit, at the particular time of each mutiny, either working relationships were absent or were seriously breached. Yet, as I have indicated throughout this work, there are normally good reasons for superiors to allow such relationships to flourish—in effect, they need them. The main reason is that for troops to display a high level of performance, a normative commitment to their role is needed: a commitment which is unlikely to be fostered if superiors interpret rules rigidly for this is inevitably accompanied by a high degree of coercion and, in turn, an alienated condition amongst privates. Reliable generalisations are not possible at the present time, although the common factors which appear to be present when mutiny occurs, at least in the instances I have come across, all point to an absence of or a deterioration of the kind of relationships observed within the Battalion—relationships which kept conflict between privates and their superiors diffused and segmented. The basic consensus and thus the legitimacy of those who held rank to command remained undisturbed.

CONCLUSIONS

What general propositions can be put forward for explaining privates' behaviour? What conclusions can be drawn concerning them as a group? What is their impact upon organisational functioning? In attempting to answer these questions I wish to draw some links with the work of Frank Parkin (1975). Examining class stratification in western societies, he distinguishes three major value systems—the dominant, the subordinate and the radical. Of the working class he maintains that their value system is a *subordinate* one (1975: 81–93), that is, 'a moral framework which promotes accommodative responses to the facts of inequality and low status'. It 'emphasises various modes of adaptation rather than either full endorsement of, or opposition to, the status quo'. He goes on to state that this value system is a 'negotiated version' of the dominant one, the moral framework which actively promotes the endorsement of existing inequality. 'That is to say, dominant values are not so much rejected or opposed as modified by the subordinate class as a result of their social circumstances and restricted opportunities'. Drawing on the work of Rodman (1963: 209) he proposes 'that the subordinate class has two distinct levels of normative reference; the dominant value system and a "stretched" or "negotiated" version of it.' Following this he concludes that 'which of the two frames of reference is actually drawn upon will be situationally determined'.

There is much of relevance in Parkin's ideas to the position and behaviour of privates, and I will now attempt to show how far these ideas fit the case in hand, and how far they do not. As I have shown there are paradoxes in the behaviour of privates in that much of it could be said to serve organisational goals, while in contrast much could be said to be potentially subversive of them. Underlying these different categories of action are two normative frames of reference (in Parkin's terms). One can be equated with Parkin's 'dominant' value system, while the other bears *some* similarity to his 'stretched' version of it. As I have illustrated, privates possess a self-image which stresses a definition of themselves as infantrymen, tough and skilled in their lethal trade. It is the internalisation of the normative frame of reference which generates this self-image and which, to a large extent, motivates them to produce at least an adequate and at times high level of military work. This normative frame of reference consists of officially fostered values aimed at propagating efficient role performance from all members of the organisation.

In contrast, the other side of the privates' self-image consists of perceptions of themselves as individuals who practise various ways of 'looking after number one', conduct which is often antithetical to the official definitions of correct soldierly behaviour. These deviant practices are themselves ordered and legitimated by an unofficial set of norms and values. As Stone (1962: 93) has noted, the substantive dimension of self is *identity* and privates behaved in a fashion commensurate with the identity of 'squaddy', an identity which encompassed both the official and unofficial normative frames of reference. Which frame of reference ordered and accounted for privates' actions depended upon the *context* in which they found themselves at the time.[16]

Parkin's ideas thus seem relevant to the subjects of this work. Privates do hold two normative frames of reference whose relevances are situationally determined.[17] Their values, norms, and actions neither fully oppose nor endorse the military status quo. However, where Parkin's ideas do not seem to fit the position of privates is in regard to his concept of a 'stretched' or 'negotiated' value system, a value system which he sees as a modification of the dominant one. The value system which is generated by privates is *oppositional* to those in command. While one can agree with Parkin that the privates' behaviour does not normally challenge the values underlying the existing organisational structure, in my experience the deviant and unofficial patterns they manifest are certainly oppositional and do challenge authority over factors which are of *immediate* concern to them. It is, after all, at this level that they confront the discomforts and constraints imposed upon them by superiors. Parkin's concept of a 'stretched' version of the dominant value system does not seem applicable to the privates' case. Rather this alternative set of values justifies and propagates actions which constitute attempts by them to achieve some form of control over an existence marked by a lack of autonomy and constraint. The conflict that occurred between privates and their superiors arose out of face-to-face disputes over micro issues of social control. They were localised, centring on specific issues, and did not normally extend beyond the boundary of the Company or the Battalion.[18]

Evasion by skiving, making life more comfortable by scrounging and giving barely or less than adequate work performances to embarrass superiors, the use of ridicule, mimicry and even the application of official procedures to inconvenience those in command such as 'saluting traps', were all gambits in evidence.[19] So, although in Parkin's terms, privates are a subordinated group, they are far from passive agents in the military process. As a consequence the official requirements of the organisation are mediated by the presence of their unofficial solidarity and cohesion.

Superiors are well aware that good working relationships are mandatory for units to function well, be they Brick or Battalion. The result is the operation of a negotiated order in the way I have described, in which a relaxed interpretation of military law is traded-off for effective role performance.[20] Whilst the limits to this negotiation are still defined by those who hold rank, that it exists at all, in an organisation which officially demands instant and total obedience, is an indicator of the private's unofficial power. The fact that such unofficial values and behaviour were often complementary to the official forms and on occasion reinforced them, should not obscure the impact such power has upon organisational functioning.

As I observed it, privates' conduct was a combination of conflict and cooperation with their superiors.[21] The subculture acted to serve rather than subvert the organisational goals. As Shibutani (1978: 435) has stated, for the military unit, morale and thus effective performance,

> . . . is high to the extent that its avowed objects are supported by the definitions spontaneously formed in its component primary groups. The beliefs that emerge in local units and the commitments that rank and file members form towards those whom they are in direct contact with are of decisive importance.

NOTES

1. See Cancian (1960), and also Demerath and Peterson (1967).

2. What I am suggesting here is that the imagery of efficient system functioning contained in much of structural functionalist theorising is, at best, a stricter version of imagery and ideas prevalent within our culture and which the members today, of that culture, on occasion, use to create and account for the social realities in which they are involved. It goes without saying that this is only one among a number of available images. In this respect the so-called laws that structural functionalism sought to discover are better understood as rule-like conventions rather than as statements of causal mechanism. See on this issue of laws vs conventions, Winch (1963), Taylor (1978), Hart (1961), Hughes (1980).

3. Becker (1977: 178–9) has noted the importance of occupational titles for specifying areas of endeavour, 'belonging to those bearing the name and locate this area in relation to similar kinds of activity in a broader field. They also imply a great deal about the characteristics of their bearers, and their meanings are often systemized into elaborate ideologies which itemize the qualities and capabilities of those identified'. The term 'squaddies' when used by privates should be seen in the above light, encompassing the qualities and capabilities and skill at arms, as well as those required to outwit those of higher rank.

4. Becker (1977: 48–51) has noted a similar relationship between cynicism and idealism amongst medical students, and he has stressed the difficulty the researcher faces when attempting to discern how people really feel about particular issues. His descriptions of the students ritual cynicism are similar to the privates' constant utterance of NFI.

5. Stouffer (1965: II, 290–316) found a similar ambivalence between having an 'easy time' and 'real soldiering' amongst American infantrymen, serving during Word War Two. See also Wilson (1951: 96–7) and Berlin (1961: 71).

6. Not all the modifications which privates made to their uniforms and equipment were purely stylistic devices. Some also had functional uses, for instance, when privates cut their puttees in half and fastened them around the ankle with a piece of Velcro (self-fastening

material), instead of the original tape provided. Or when they cut-off the rear ends of a spare pair of Northern Ireland patrol gloves and sewed them onto the sleeves of their camouflage smocks as cuffs. In the case of puttees not only did they look more stylish when fastened this way, but the modification enabled the wearer to don them in half the normal time, a not insignificant factor if one was late for morning parade! The modifications to smock sleeves also not only gave the garment a more stylish appearance, but simultaneously increased its warmth by achieving a tighter fit around the wearer's wrists—another not insignificant benefit after lying motionless in a night ambush position for hours.

7. Field Marshall Wavell at the end of the Second World War was quoted in *Soldier Magazine* (1945: 3) as stressing the need for ordinary infantrymen to display a high degree of personal initiative. Since then the Army has developed a large programme of adventurous activities, designed to stimulate such initiative and resourcefulness. The extent to which such qualities are officially considered to be desirable, can be guaged by a report in a more recent *Soldier Magazine* (1978: News 4) which featured an Army expedition to North West Canada. The assistant leader of this expedition was a member of the WRAC (Women's Royal Army Corps), a part of the Army which has no combat function.

8. There was in addition a subsidiary criterion in operation, which also influenced superiors' definitions of offenders. This was very much based on moral prescriptions, as one senior officer informed me, 'I treat offences which offend moral decency very seriously—crimes like beating up another man's wife which happened recently.' In the main, however, the central criterion was that of operational efficiency.

9. White (1964: 429) has noted a similar encouragement of deviance by American basic training instructors, and another American example is cited by Morroe Berger (1946: 86). Bryant (1974a) has gone so far as to say that military training per se is a criminalisation process, whilst Einstadter (1969: 77) has commented that 'military experience of a certain variety, for example, lends itself readily to robbery'.

10. See Shibutani (1978: 209) for an American Army example of deviance being considered acceptable by superiors, as long as no-one was caught.

11. Both Moskos (1970: 147) and George (1971: 307) note that military morale (and efficient performance) depends upon the soldiers acceptance of the legitimacy of organisational demands. Obviously if privates did question the authority of those who held rank and power over them, then primary cleavages would be liable to occur. The point is that when recruits enter the Army they are presented with its system of power and privilege *in toto*. It appears as natural, a dominant and unalterable reality. A reality which they have been influenced by presocialisation to accept as the right and correct social arrangements. The recruits then perceive this state of affairs as legitimate, in the same way as they did when encountering the structures of school and industry. Both Marx (1974: I. 817) and Weber (1930: 54) noted that the unequal distribution of power and resources in the capitalist state is presented to the individual as a natural phenomenon. Marx using the phrase 'self evident laws of nature', and Weber 'an unalterable order of things'. Contemporary critics of the distribution of power and privilege in modern industry, such as Fox (1974: 328) and Willis (1979: 161) have made similar comments. Thus one observes recruits on the second day of their military service, already outwardly complaint to authority. Such is the degree of 'naturalness' with which inequalities of power and privilege were viewed, that privates neither granted nor denied their superiors legitimacy. Rather what actually occurred was very similar to what Nichols (1976: 58) has described as happening in a chemical factory. Writing about whether or not workers viewed managerial power as legitimate he concluded: 'To write of 'granting' or 'denying' is in fact to pose the issue in terms either too positive or too negative. Management like the job, like the shareholders, like capitalism, just is.' Therefore what questioning was evident amongst privates, was as I have noted in the text, concerned with the fitness of particular individuals to hold rank and not with the power and privilege associated with superiors' roles. Privates were all too aware of the coercive power which their superiors could command. This realisation constituting another reason for the structure within which they existed being regarded as inevitable, unchangeable.

12. Officers' and NCOs' views on the normal forms of deviance practised by privates comes close to what Becker (1977: 336) has defined as 'conventional criminality'. That is, deviance which 'is seen, even by those who neither engage in nor profit from it, as part of the social structure, no more likely to disappear than schools or subways'. See also the work of Sudnow (1965).

13. In addition to Coser's (1956) theoretical work on conflict having an integrative potential, there are also empirical studies which point towards such a conclusion: see Gluckman (1952), Turk (1963) and Black-Michaud (1975). Van den Berghe (1963) had also looked at this hypothesis theoretically.

14. Both Lasswell (1933: 640) and Blumer (1969b: 108) see tenacity in the face of adversity as the most unequivocal index of high morale. I base my judgement of the Company upon such tenacity, which I observed on field exercise and particularly in XMG.

15. Obviously research into mutiny will encounter major difficulties, not the least being that the authorities are not enthusiastic about publicising instances of major organisational cleavage. The following references provide useful evidence on which to ground further research. See: Gill and Dallas (1975), Ahrenfeldt (1958) particularly chapter eight, Rothstein (1980), Brown (1978: 29–31), Sims (1978: 19), Bowlby (1969: 47–8), Nasson (1980: 220), Winteringham (1936,) Sandell (1978: 21). Dallas and Gill (1985) and Morrison (n. d: 35–6). Lammers (1969), Cooper (1972), and Shibutani (1978) provide sociological insight.

16. Obviously there is also a reflexive relationship in operation. If norms and consequent behaviour are situationally determined, then the presence of them will also influence the ongoing situation. See Mehan and Wood (1975: 8–19), and Wilson (1974: 79).

17. There is, however, a difference between Parkin's formulation of the two normative frames of reference, and the way they applied to the private's existence. Parkin (1975: 93) maintains that amongst the working class the dominant value system will be used ' where purely abstract evaluations are called for', and 'in concrete social situations involving choice and action, the negotiated version—or subordinate value system—will provide the moral framework'. In the case of privates there is an absence of the need to make any purely abstract formulations. Their world is and was overwhelmingly concrete. The two normative frames of reference are applied in concrete situations. Nothing for instance would be more concrete, than being in XMG!

18. In this respect such behaviour although accompanied as it was by strong perceptions of group interests (the 'us' and 'them' dichotomy) did not constitute class consciousness. Rather this awareness of differing interests was a parochial one. As Westergaard (1966: 107–8) has pointed out, the solidarities of class and the solidarities of community are antithetical rather than complementary. Parkin (1975: 90) defines a class outlook as one being 'rooted in a perception of the social order that stretches far beyond the frontiers of community'. The solidarity—the 'us' feeling generated by privates, in conflict with those who held rank was not of this order. Rather this consciousness was one which was limited to immediate groups of peers, primarily within the private's Company.

19. During my time with the Company I observed several instances of privates seizing the opportunity, when officers were either heavily laden or preoccupied, to exercise a 'saluting trap'. They would pointedly call out 'sir', to attract the attention of the officer, and then salute him in an exemplary fashion. The officer would then struggle with his equipment, or halt what he was engaged in, to return the salute, as demanded by official regulations. Privates derived much glee from this practice, and it seems to have been utilised in previous times, judging by Milligan's (1973: 113) comments.

20. There are other examples of a negotiated order in operation, within institutions where officially superiors have considerable or total power over subordinates/inmates. See Sykes (1958: 40–62) and Scheff(1961).

21. Cooley (1918: 39) long ago noted that 'conflict and cooperation are not separate things, but phases of one process which always involves something of both'.

Glossary

The following list consists of official Army terms and abbreviations, together with examples of argot I observed in use, when doing participant observation. The list is obviously not exhaustive and contains only those examples used in the text of this book. Examples of argot are indicated with an asterisk.

Adjutant	An officer—usually a captain, who is responsible for the unit's administration and discipline.
Adventurous Training	Training which encompasses such activities as rock-climbing, sub-aqua and canoeing. Pursuits which promote initiative and resourcefulness.
Alert-Ready Position	The holding of a weapon in a position of maximum readiness, so that it may be aimed and fired in the shortest space of time.
Ammo*	Ammunition.
Approach phase	The initial phase of an operation or exercise, prior to the actual assault.
Arcs	Predesignated zones of responsibility which each member of a patrol watches constantly. These zones are then the individual's arc of fire.
Arse licking*	see 'Brown Nosing'.
ARU	Annual Readiness Unit. A yearly inspection by higher authority, of the unit's operational effectiveness.
Attack phase	The final phase of an offensive operation (or simulation) after the 'approach phase'.
Backsquadded	Term used at the Depot to refer to recruits who have failed adequately to complete their training, and have to repeat parts of it.
Badged	Upon entering the Depot recruits are designated as potential members of particular infantry regiments, and after a month normally wear their cap badges.
Ballache*	Term used in the Battalion to describe unnecessary, distasteful and often petty activities.

Basha*	A shelter used on field exercises and operations, constructed out of a waterproof poncho, and a sleeping bag.
Battle Camp	A period of training which recruits spend on northern moors living in the field and practising infantry skills and tactics.
Beasting*	Term used by recruits to describe occasions when their superiors are adhering to a rigorous and rigid enforcement of disciplinary measures.
Bedford	An Army vehicle.
Birds*	Women.
Blanket-Stacker*	Pejorative for soldiers who work in unit stores.
Blimp*	To look, glance or letch at women, particularly attractive ones.
Blow-out*	A hedonistic spree.
Bollocking*	A severe reprimand from those of higher rank. One can then be 'bollocked', and it is thus possible to 'drop a bollock'.
Boning*	To smooth down a pair of Army boots by rubbing them with a hot spoon and melted polish. Once smoothed down the boot is ready to be 'bulled' (shined).
Booze*	Alcohol. Sometimes known as 'loopy juice'.
Boss*	Excellent, very good. Also on occasion used to describe superiors.
Brew*	Tea or Coffee.
Brew-Kit*	Tea, coffee, milk (condensed) and sugar, together with a small hexamine-solid fuel stove. All of which are contained in ration packs used in the field.
Brick	Four man patrol used in Northern Ireland. The smallest organisational sub-division.
Brown-Nosing*	Pejorative for currying favour with superiors. See also 'arse licking' and 'sucking-up'.
Bubbling*	Pejorative for providing information to superiors, which results in peers getting into trouble.
Bubbling themselves*	Individuals owning up to offences and thereby ensuring that other privates do not suffer at the hands of superiors for their deviance.
Buckshee*	Spare (and thus illegally held) items of clothing and equipment. Also the term can be used to refer to a private soldier.

Bull*   Excessive cleaning and shining of clothing, equipment and accommodation. 'Bullshit' is also used in this fashion.

Bullet Catchers*   Cynical expression used in Crossmaglen to describe the operational handicaps which the Company functioned under.

Bump*   To polish floors.

Busted*   The demotion of an NCO or Officer.

Butt-stroked*   To be hit with the butt of a weapon.

Camming-up*   To camouflage oneself or equipment.

Can*   An armoured car.

Canteen Cowboy*   A duty corporal who nightly patrols the NAAFI.

Changing Parades*   Unofficial punishments imposed by NCOs at the Depot. Recruits have to change rapidly in and out of various types of uniforms and equipment.

Charge   To prosecute offenders officially against military law.

Chopper*   Helicopter.

Chopper pad*   Helicopter landing and take-off zone.

Call Sign   Patrol identification device used over a radio network.

Civvies*   Civilians.

Clued-up*   Understanding the situation, or possessing much expertise.

C.O.   Commanding Officer.

Cocking-handle   Device on a weapon, which when pulled arms it. That is it transfers a round (bullet) from the magazine to the breach, making the weapon ready for firing.

Colour*   **Colour-Sergeant. The NCO in each Company responsible for stores and equipment.**

Company   **Primary sub-division of a Battalion.**

Company Commander   Officer in charge of a Company, usually a Major.

Company Detail   Written orders published every day or every other day.

Combat Kit   Camouflage smock and trousers.

Contact   Engagement with the enemy (PIRA).

COP   Close Observation Platoon. A platoon used in Northern Ireland primarily for surveillance, intelligence gathering and ambush.

Coppers*	Regimental policemen.
Corporal	NCO in charge of a Section. Also known as a 'Full Screw'*.
Cow-kicking*	An incorrect drill movement, bringing the foot down at an angle, instead of vertically.
C Rations	Composite rations used by troops in the field, which usually come in packs lasting twenty four hours. Also known as 'compo'.*
Crack*	Banter, information, event—a generic term.
Crash*	To offer mutual aid, usually cigarettes or drinks.
Crashing the zzzz's*	Sleeping.
CSM	Warrant Officer and the Senior NCO in a company. He is thus the Company Sergeant Major.
Cuds*	The countryside.
Cushy*	Easy.
Dead Ground	Ground which the 'enemy' cannot see from their position, usually folds or dips in the terrain.
Deadlegs*	Pejorative for useless individuals.
Decent*	Women with whom relationships are to be formed.
Depot Dance*	The once a week mass parade which all recruits attend.
Diffy*	To go deficient of equipment and be debited for replacements.
Dig*	To hit or assault.
Dig In	To dig a shell scrape or trench.
Dipstick*	Pejorative for useless individuals, see 'dead-legs'.
Dixies*	Large metal containers used to hold hot food.
Dogs*	Women of easy virtue.
Doing the job*	Performing military skills adequately.
Doing things for the lads*	Informal welfare practices performed by NCOs and Officers for their subordinates. Also used in this context is 'looking after the lads'.
Dropped in the shit*	Actions which cause another individual to get into trouble with those of higher rank.
Double	To run.

Ear Defenders	Protective rubber plugs placed in the ears, when live ammunition is being fired.
Eighty Four	Eighty Four millimetre anti-tank projectile.
Excused Duties	Official medical status excusing the individual from all or certain duties.
Flack Jacket	A partially armoured jacket used by troops when on urban patrol in Northern Ireland.
Falling Plates*	A derisory nickname for the Royal Green Jackets. Also metal targets used on the rifle range, which fall down when hit by fire.
Fat Jossers*	Pejorative used to describe troops who work in stores, offices and the like. See also FUBS.*
Fatigues	Domestic duties carried out in barracks ('cookhouse fatigues' etc).
Field	Countryside.
Fieldcraft	Soldierly skills required to operate effectively in the field, including techniques of camouflage and the use of natural features to conceal movement.
FUBS*	Fat Useless Bastards—pejorative often used to describe those troops who work in stores and offices. See Fat Jossers.*
Fuck-up*	An individual who persistently turns in an inadequate performance, and as a consequence brings down extra work or the wrath of superiors upon his peers.
Fuck-ups*	Instances of organisational dislocation, bad organisation, or bad administration.
Genolite	Industrial cleaning fluid with an acid base. Illegally used to clean carbon deposits off weapons, after they have been heavily used.
Getting rotten*	The process of getting drunk.
Get-offs*	Term used by privates to describe superiors attempts to intercede with other superiors on the formers' behalf, when they have been caught being deviant.
Gimpey*	General Purpose Machine Gun. See (GPMG).
Gobshite*	Pejorative used to describe individuals who are considered to be loud-mouthed.
Go firm*	Term used to describe a patrol (or individual members of it) stopping and settling down in tactical positions. For instance when a brick moved in XMG, three members of it would 'go firm' whilst the other moved under the protection of their covering fire.

Golly*	Asian sutler providing canteen facilities for the troops.
Golly shop*	Canteen facilities provided by the above.
Good shoot*	A long and clear approach to a target. One with no bends or obstructions. Thus troops at XMG were particularly vigilant when moving in the location of 'good shoots', as the danger level increased.
Go sick	Official term used to describe an individual reporting to the Unit Medical Officer.
Green Baggy Skin*	Army uniform.
Hard cover*	A position which affords the maximum protection to the individual. Thus at XMG patrols were always looking to use hard cover when they stopped (went firm) momentarily.
Hard Targetting*	The movement of a patrol in a (tactical) fashion, which is both elusive, evasive, and very fast. Thus whenever a patrol member needed to move he would 'hard target'. Patrols would not hard target all the time, as it is very exhausting, but rather use it when locations were extremely dangerous—'good shoots' etc.
Hero*	Pejorative used at XMG to describe individuals (usually NCOs or officers) who exposed themselves to excess danger and in turn their subordinates.
IA's	Official term for Immediate Actions drills-specific movements needed to remedy malfunctioning weapons.
I.D. Card	Identity Card carried by all troops, embossed with the individual's name, rank, number and photograph.
Indian Country*	South Armagh. Also known as 'Bandit Country'.
Jack*	To be cheeky, or cocky.
Jacking your hand in*	Giving up.
Junior NCOs	NCOs below the rank of Sergeant, namely Corporals and Lance Corporals.
Junior Officers	Officers below the rank of Major, namely Captains, Lieutenants and Second Lieutenants.
Kit	Army equipment issued to an individual.

Knowing the score*	Knowledge and expertise needed to operate effectively in particular situations, for example in XMG being tactically proficient.
Lance Corporal	Lowest ranked NCO.
Lance Jack*	Argot for the above.
Lanny*	Landrover.
Let-offs*	Term used by privates to describe flexible and indulgent rule interpretation by their superiors.
Lift	Arrest.
Lights Out	The time at which recruits are supposed to go to sleep. Lights in their accommodation are turned off at this time.
Loaf of Bread*	Dead.
Locker Layout	The officially designated way in which equipment and clothing has to be positioned in the recruit's steel locker.
Locking Pin	The pin which locks the lever of a grenade into place, thereby making it safe to handle.
Looking after Number One*	Phrase used by privates to describe the process of making their lives more comfortable. A process which is often deviant.
Looking after the lads*	See 'doing things for the lads'.
Looking after your mates*	Phrase used by privates to describe their overall normative concern to provide aid to peers.
Mags*	Weapon magazines. Metal containers into which are loaded rounds (bullets).
MCTC	Military Corrective Training Centre. The major service detention establishment in the UK.
Mongs*	Mentally deficient individuals. Term used by recruits to describe others who have been 'backsquadded'.*
M.M.	Military Medal.
M.T.	Motor Transport Section.
M60	American light machine-gun used by PIRA.
M16	American automatic rifle used by PIRA.
NAAFI	Navy, Army and Air Force Institute. Official forces canteen and welfare services.
NBC	Nuclear, Biological and Chemical warfare.
NCOs	Non-commissioned officers.
NFI*	Not Fucking Interested.

Nick*	Gaol.
Northern Ireland Gloves	Leather gloves used by patrols in Northern Ireland. They are made of leather with reinforced knuckles.
Not Impressed*	Phrase used by privates when they are disenchanted with affairs.
Not sticking your neck out*	Taking no unnecessary risks. 'Not pushing your luck'* is also used in this fashion.
Number Elevens*	Man-sized targets used on the rifle range. They are the easiest targets to hit. Also a cynical expression used at XMG.
Numbers Game*	Phrase used by officers and NCOs at the Depot to describe the policy of passing-out recruits, who are not up to the standard of proficiency they would like.
Number Twos*	Number Two Dress. The privates' best dress, worn for parade.
O.C.	Officer Commanding a company, usually a Major.
OK if you don't get caught*	Phrase used by superiors to denote their attitudes towards certain types of deviance, which whilst officially they may be serious are not regarded so by them unofficially.
Operations	Active service, official term for combat.
On the ground*	Phrase used to describe patrol work generally in XMG.
On the street*	Phrase used to describe urban patrols in XMG.
Out of bounds	Official designation for locations which are placed off limits to troops.
Paras*	Members of the Parachute Regiment.
Passing off the square	Initial rite de passage for recruits at the end of their first months training.
Passing out parade	Final rite de passage for recruits after 18 weeks training.
PIRA	Provisional Irish Republican Army.
Platoon	Organisational subsection between a company and a Section.
Platoon Commander	Officer in charge of a Platoon, usually a Lieutenant or a Second Lieutenant.
Provo Sergeant	Provost Sergeant. The NCO in charge of the unit's Regimental Police.
Puttees	Pieces of cloth wound around the boot top, so as to provide additional support for the ankle.

Q.M	Quartermaster.
QRF	Quick Reaction Force. Body of troops kept in readiness for emergencies.
R & R	Rest and Recuperation leave from Northern Ireland.
RCD	Radio Controlled explosive Device used by the PIRA.
REME	Royal Electrical and Mechanical Engineers. The Corps responsible for the maintenance of vehicle transport, instruments and weapons.
Reveille	The time at which recruits have to rise in the morning.
Round	A bullet.
RPs	Regimental police. Also known as 'coppers'.*
RHIP*	Cynical expression used by privates to describe the benefits of their superiors—Rank Has Its Privileges.
Rickies*	Restriction of privileges, minor punishment dispensed for misdemeanours, involving being confined to barracks, and made to do extra work such as fatigues.
Rifting*	A strong verbal reprimand, see 'bollocking'.*
Ring	The ring on the end of a grenade locking pin, which one pulls to release the pin, and thus prepares the device for throwing.
Room-jobs	Daily cleaning task to be carried out each day in troop accommodation by privates.
RSM	Regimental Sergeant Major. Also known as the 'Razzman'.*
Rubber Dicked*	Expression used within the Battalion to describe a hoax, sham or pretence.
RUC	Royal Ulster Constabulary.
Rural	A patrol in the countryside around XMG and along the Eire border.
Salvage Detail	Fatigue duty involving collecting the unit's rubbish.
Sangar	Fortified machine-gun position.
Scrounge*	To acquire illegally equipment, food, clothing.
Section	Organisational sub-division between Platoon and Brick.
Senior NCO	NCOs of the rank of Sergeant and above.

Senior Officer	Officers of the rank of Major and above.
Sergeant	Highest ranked NCO in a Platoon.
Service Number	The individual number each soldier is given when he joins the Army.
Sharp End*	A dangerous location.
Shell-scrape	A small trench.
Silent Hours	The hours between 12 p.m. and 0600.
Skegs*	Pejorative for useless soldiers.
Skive*	To evade or perform incorrectly a duty.
Slag-down*	To berate or criticise.
SLR	Self-Loading Rifle.
Spotters*	PIRA supporters who monitor and record the movement of Army patrols.
Sprog*	A private who has little service with the Battalion.
Squaddies*	Privates.
Stag*	The individual's shift of Guard Duty.
Sucking Up*	See 'Brown Nosing' and 'Arse Licking'.
Switch off*	To perform inadequately.
Switch on*	To perform adequately.
Tail End Charley*	Last man in a patrol.
Take-out*	To kill or injure.
Tape*	A stripe worn on the arm denoting the individual's rank. Thus a Sergeant has three tapes and a Lance Corporal one.
Tearing the arse out of it*	Behaviour by superiors which breaches privates' definition of reasonable conduct.
The lads*	Privates.
The Lines	Troop accommodation.
Tick-Tock*	An unreasonable and thus bad NCO, a martinet from the privates' viewpoint.
Trained soldier	A private who has graduated through 18 weeks basic training at the Depot.
Training Team	An Officer and NCOs who are in charge of a platoon of recruits.
Trog*	A recruit with less than one month's service.
Tuss*	Pejorative for a useless individual.
Twatting*	To assault or hit.
Urban	Patrol within the environs of XMG.
VCP	Vehicle Check Point. Location where troops search vehicles.

Wank Mags*	Pornographic magazines.
Warrant Officer	Senior NCO above the rank of Staff Sergeant, thus both a CSM and an RSM are Warrant Officers.
Warries*	Photographs of troops in full combat equipment and in aggressive poses.
Wellying*	Assaulting or hitting. See 'twatting' or 'digging'.*
XMG	Official acronymn for Crossmaglen.
Yellow Card	Card issued to troops in Northern Ireland stating the conditions üder which they may open fire.

Bibliography

Abrams, Philip (1965) 'The late Profession of Arms: Ambiguous Goals and Deteriorating Means in Britain'. *European Journal of Sociology* 6: 238–61.

Ackroyd, C. *et al.* (1977) *The Technology of Political Control*, Harmondsworth: Penguin.

Adult Recruit Training Syllabus (1980) Basic Training Depot.

Ahrenfeldt, R. H. (1958) *Psychiatry in the British Army in the Second World War*, London: Routledge & Kegan Paul.

An Introduction for Recruits and Others (1980) Basic Training Depot.

Anon. (1946) 'Informal Social Organization in the Army'. *American Journal of Sociology* 51: 365–70.

'A Rifleman' (A. Smith) (1922) *Four Years on the Western Front*, London: Odhams Press.

Arkin, William and Dobrofsky, Lynn R. (1978) 'Military Socialization and Masculinity'. *Journal of Social Issues.* 34: 151–68.

Army Council Instruction (1941: 488) 'Plastic Buttons in Lieu of Brass Buttons'.

Army Council Instruction (1940: 1423) 'Equipment Brasses—Polishing of'.

Army Council Instruction (1942: 597) 'Simplification of Drill'.

Ashton Braithwaite, J. (1969) *A Black British Soldier*, Toronto: 21st Century Books.

Ashworth, A. E. (1968) 'The Sociology of Trench Warfare'. *British Journal of Sociology.* 19: 407–23.

Ashworth, A. E. (1980) *Trench Warfare*, London: Holmes & Meire.

Bagnall, Stephen (1947) *The Attack,* London: Hamish Hamilton.

Bailey, Anthony (1980) *Acts of Union Reports on Ireland, 1973–79,* New York: Random House.

Baxter, D. (1959) *Two Years To Do,* London: Elek Books.

Baron, Paul A. and Sweezy, Paul M. (1968) *Monopoly Capital,* Harmondsworth: Penguin.

Barzilay, David and Murray, David (1972) *Four Months in Winter,* Belfast: Royal Regiment of Fusiliers.

Becker, Howard S. (1973) *Outsiders—Studies in the Sociology of Deviance,* New York: The Free Press.

Becker, Howard S. (1977) *Sociological Work—Method and Substance,* New Brunswick, N.J.: Transaction Books.

Bell, Colin and Newby, Howard (eds) (1977) *Doing Sociological Research,* London: Allen & Unwin.

Bensman, Joseph and Gerver, Israel (1963) 'Crime and Punishment in the Factory: The Functions of Deviancy in Maintaining the Social System'. *American Sociological Review.* 28: 588–98.

Berger, Morroe (1946) 'Law and Custom in the Army'. *Social Forces.* 25: 82–7.

Berger, Peter L. and Luckman, Thomas (1976) *The Social Construction of Reality,* Harmondsworth: Penguin.

van den Berghe, Pierre L. (1963) 'Dialectic and Functionalism: Towards a Theoretical Synthesis'. *American Sociological Review,* 28, 695–705.

Berlin, Sven (1961) *I am Lazarus,* London: The Galley Press.

Bettelheim, Bruno (1960) *The Informed Heart,* New York: The Free Press.

Bittner, Egon (1975) 'The Concept of Organization'. pp. 69–81. In *Ethnomethodology.* Roy Turner (ed). Harmondsworth: Penguin.

Black-Michaud, Jacob (1975) *Cohesive Force. Feud in the Mediterranean and the Middle East,* Oxford: Basil Blackwell.

Blake, Joseph A. (1970) 'The Organization as Instrument of Violence: The Military Case'. *Sociological Quarterly.* 11: 331–50.

Blau, Peter M. (1964) *Exchange and Power in Social Life*, New York: Wiley.
Blau, Peter M. (1966) *Bureaucracy in Modern Society*, New York: Random House.
Blau, Peter M. and Scott, Richard W. (1970) *Formal Organizations. A Comparative Approach*, London: Routledge & Kegan Paul.
Blumer, H. (1969a) *Symbolic Interactionism*, Englewood Cliffs, N.J.: Prentice Hall.
Blumer, H. (1969b) 'Collective Behaviour'. pp. 65–121. In *Principles of Sociology*. A. M. Lee (ed). New York: Barnes & Noble.
Bourne, Peter G. (1967) 'Some Observations on Psychosocial Phenomena in Basic Training'. *Psychiatry* 30: 187–96.
Bowlby, Alex. (1969) *Recollections of Rifleman Bowlby*. London: Leo Cooper.
Bradney, P. (1957) 'The Joking Relationship in Industry'. *Human Relations*. 10: 179–89.
Brophy, John and Partridge, Eric (1965) *The Long Trail*, London: Andre Deutsch.
Brotz, H. and Wilson E. (1946) 'Characteristics of Military Society'. *American Journal of Sociology*. 51: 371–75.
Brown, Malcolm (1978) *Tommy Goes to War*, London: J. M. Dent.
Bruyn, Severyn (1963) 'The Methodology of Participant Observation'. *Human Organization*. 22: 224–35.
Bryant, Clifton D. (1974a) 'Socialization for Khaki-Collar Crime: Military Training as Socialization Process'. pp. 239–51. In *Deviant Behaviour—Occupational and Organizational Bases*. C. D. Bryant (ed). Chicago: Rand McNally.
Bryant, Clifton D. (1974b) *'Olive Drab Drunks and G.I. Junkies: Alcohol and Narcotic Addiction in the U.S. Military'. pp. 129–145. In Deviant Behaviour—Occupational and Organizational Bases.* C. D. Bryant (ed.) Chicago: Rand McNally.
Bugler, Jeremy (1966) 'The Army Trade'. *New Society*. 7: 5.
Burnham, David (1969) 'Paper on Cooping Gets a High Grade'. *The New York Times*. August 3: 68.
Byrom, J. (1957) *The Unfinished Man*, London: Chatto & Windus.
Caine, Maureen (1973) 'On the Beat: Interactions and Relations in Rural and Urban Police Forces'. pp. 62–97. In *Images of Deviance*. Stanley Cohen (ed.) Harmondsworth: Penguin.
Cancian, Francesca (1960) 'Functional Analysis and Change'. *American Sociological Review* 24: 818–827.
Caplow T. (1964) *Principles of Organization*, New York: Harcourt Brace & World.
Carney, M. P. W. (1963) 'Alcoholic Hallucinos Among Servicemen in Cyprus'. *Journal of the Royal Army Medical Corps*. 109: 164–70.
Chambers, Peter and Landreth, Amy, eds. (1955) *Called Up*, London:Allan Wingate.
Clarke, John *et al.* (1975) 'Subcultures, Cultures and Class: A Theoretical Overview'. pp. 9–74. In *Resistance through Rituals. Working Papers in Cultural Studies 7 and 8*. Birmingham: Centre for Contemporary Cultural Studies.
Clausewitz, Carl Von (1968) *On War*, Harmondsworth: Penguin.
Coates, Charles H. and Pellegrin, Roland T. (1965) *Military Sociology: A Study of American Military Institutions and Military Life*, University Park, Md: Social Science Press.
Cochrane, P. (1977) *Charlie Company*, London: Chatto & Windus.
Cogswell, Betty E. (1968) 'Some Structural Properties influencing Socialization'. *Administrative Science Quarterly*. 13: 417–40.
Cohen, Stanley (1973) 'Introduction'. pp. 9–24. In *Images of Deviance*. Stanley Cohen (ed.) Harmondsworth: Penguin.
Comrades in Arms—Three Talks to Junior Officers or Officer Cadets to Assist Them in The Handling of Their Men. (1942) London: HMSO.
Cook, Fred J. (1963) *The Welfare State*, London: Cape.
Cooley, C. H. (1918) *The Social Process*, New York: Scribner's.
Cooley, C. H. (1956) *Human Nature and the Social Order*, Glencoe, Ill.: The Free Press.
Cooper, G. L. C. Brigadier (1973) 'Some Aspects of Conflict in Ulster'. *Military Review* 53: 86–95.
Cooper, Mark N. (1972) 'The Occurrence of Mutiny in World War I: A Sociological View'. *International Behavioural Scientist*. 4: 1–10.
Coppard, George (1969) *With a Machine Gun to Cambrai*, London: HMSO.

Coser, Lewis A. (1956) *Functions of Social Conflict*, London: Routledge & Kegan Paul.
Crimp, R. L. (1971) *The Diary of a Desert Rat*. Alex Bowlby (ed.) London: Leo Cooper.
Croft-Cooke, Rupert (1971) *The Licentious Soldiery*. London: W. H. Allen.
Crutchlow. William (1937) *Tales of an Old Soldier*. London: Robert Hale.
Dallas, G. and Gill, D. (1985) *The Unknown Army: Mutinies in the British Army in World War I*, London: Verso.
Dalton, Melville (1959) *Men Who Manage*, New York: Wiley.
Datel, William E. and Lifrak, Stephen T. (1969) 'Expectations, Affect Change and Military Performance in the Army Recruit'. *Psychological Reports.* 24: 855–79.
Davis, Arthur R. (1952) 'Bureaucratic Patterns in The Navy Officer Corps'. pp. 380–95. In *Reader In Bureaucracy*. Robert K. Merton *et al.* (ed.) New York: Free Press.
Day, Robert and Day, Jo Anne. V. (1977) 'A Review of the Current State of Negotiated Order Theory: An Appreciation and a Critique'. *Sociological Quarterly.* 18: 126–42.
Demerath, N. J. and Peterson, A. eds. (1967) *System, Change, and Conflict. A Reader on Contemporary Sociological Theory and the Debate over Functionalism*, New York: The Free Press.
Dennis, Norman, Henriques, Fernando and Slaughter, Clifford (1974) *Coal is our Life*, London: Social Science Paperbacks.
Densham-Booth, Lieutenant Colonel (1969) 'Social Planning in the 1970s and 80s' cited in *The Military Family: A Study of Three Communities in the British Armed Services.* Cousins, C. R. MPhil thesis, London School of Economics (1975).
Dornbusch, Sanford M. (1955) 'The Military Academy as an Assimilating Institution'. *Social Forces.* 33: 316–21.
Draper, R. Second Lieutenant (1970) 'Jungle Challenge'. *Officer.* 27: 40–5.
Dunbar Moodie, T. (1980) 'The Formal and Informal Social Structure of a South African Gold Mine'. *Human Relations.* 33: 555–74.
Eaton, Walter H. (1947) 'The Military Environment'. *Social Forces.* 26: 88–94.
Education for Promotion: Students Handbook. Management. EPC (Adv) level (1974) DA Eds Inspectorate and Research Department.
Education for Promotion Certificate—Military Management Students Handbook (1978) DA Eds Inspectorate and Research Department.
Einstadter, Werner J. (1969) 'The Social Organization of Armed Robbery'. *Social Problems.* 17: 64–83.
Eisenhart, R. Wayne (1975) 'You Can't Hack it Little Girl: A Discussion of the Covert Psychological Agenda of Modern Combat Training'. *Journal of Social Issues.* 31: 13–23.
Elkin, F. (1946) 'The Soldier's Language'. *American Journal of Sociology.* 51: 414–22.
Elkin, Henry (1946) 'Aggressive and Erotic Tendencies in Army Life'. *American Journal of Sociology.* 51: 408–13.
Ellis, John (1980) *The Sharp End of War. The Fighting Man in World War Two*, London: Book Club Associates.
Etzioni, Amitai (1961) *A Comparative Analysis of Complex Organizations. On Power, Involvement and Their Correlates.* New York: Free Press.
Faraday, Annabel and Plummer, Kenneth (1979) 'Doing Life Histories'. *The Sociological Review.* 27: 773–98.
Faris, John H. (1976) 'The Impact of Basic Combat Training: The Role of the Drill Sergeant'. pp. 13–24. In *The Social Psychology of Military Service.* Nancy L. Goldman and David R. Segal (eds). London: Sage Publications.
Faulkner, R. R. (1974) 'Making Violence by Doing Work. Selves, Situations, and the World of Professional Hockey'. *Sociology of Work and Occupations.* 1: 288–312.
Feigelman, William (1974) 'Peeping: The Patterns of Voyeurism Among Construction Workers'. *Urban Life and Culture.* 3: 35–49.
Feld, M. D. (1959) 'Information and Authority: The Structure of Military Organization'. *American Sociological Review.* 24: 15–22.
Fields, Rona M. (1973) *A Society on the Run. A Psychology of Northern Ireland*, Harmondsworth: Penguin.
Filstead, William J. (1971) *Qualitative Methodology*, Chicago: Markham.

Finer, S. E. (1976) *The Man on Horseback. The Role of the Military in Politics*, Harmondsworth: Penguin.

Fitzpatrick, John H. (1980) 'Adapting to Danger: A participant observation study of an underground mine'. *Sociology of Work and Occupations*. 2: 131–58.

Fox, Alan (1975) 'The Social Organization of Indistrial Work'. pp. 321–30. In *People and Organizations*. G. Salaman and K. Thompson (eds). London: Longman/Open University.

Franklyn, Harold E. Sir. General (1953) 'Systems of Army Training'. pp. 250–66. In *Brassey's Annual. The Armed Forces Yearbook*. H. G. Thursfield (ed.) London: William Clowes.

Garfinkel, Harold (1967) *Studies in Ethnomethodology*, Englewood Cliffs, N.J.: Prentice Hall.

Garnier, Maurice A. (1972) 'Changing Recruitment Patterns and Organizational Ideology: The Case of a British Military Academy'. *Administrative Science Quarterly*. 17: 499–507.

Garnier, Maurice A. (1973) 'Power and Ideological Conformity: A Case Study'. *American Journal of Sociology*. 79: 343–63.

Garnier, Maurice A. (1975) 'Organizational Culture, and Recruitment in the British Military Academy'. *Journal of Political and Military Sociology*. 3: 141–51.

Gaze, W. B. A. Private (n.d.) *Dunkirk Driver*, Imperial War Museum unpublished typescript. 523 (41). London.

van Gennep, Arnold (1960) *The Rites of Passage*. Transl. by M. B. Visedom and G. L. Caffe. Chicago: University of Chicago Press.

George, Alexander L. (1971) 'Primary Groups, Organization and Military Performance'. pp. 293–318. In *Handbook of Military Institutions*. Roger W. Little (ed.) Beverly Hills: Sage Publications.

Gerstl, Joel E. (1961) 'Determinants of Occupational Community in High Status Occupations'. *Sociological Quarterly*. 2: 37–48.

Gibbs, D. N. (1957) 'The National Serviceman and Military Delinquency'. *Sociological Review*. 5: 255–63.

Gill, D. and Dallas, G. (1975) 'Mutiny at Etaples Base in 1917'. *Past and Present*. 69: 88–112.

Glaser, Barney G. and Strauss, Anselm L. (1979) *The Discovery of Grounded Theory. Strategies for Qualitative Research*, New York: Aldine.

Gluckman, Max (1952) *Rituals and Rebellion in South East Africa*, Manchester: Manchester University Press.

Gluckman, M. (1955) *The Judicial Process among the Barotse of Northern Rhodesia*, Manchester: Manchester University Press.

Goffman, Erving (1972a) *Interaction Ritual. Essays on Face-to-Face Behaviour*, Harmondsworth: Penguin.

Goffman, Erving (1972b) *Encounters. Two Studies in the Sociology of Interaction*, Harmondsworth: Penguin.

Goffman, Erving (1976) *Asylums*. Harmondsworth: Penguin.

Goldner, F. H. *et al.* (1977) 'The Production of Cynical Knowledge in Organizations'. *American Sociological Review*. 42: 539–51.

Goodrich, Carter I. (1975) *The Frontier of Control: A Study of British Workshop Politics*, London: Pluto Press.

Gouldner, Alvin W. (1960) 'The Norm of Reciprocity', *American Sociological Review*. 25: 161–78.

Gouldner, Alvin W. (1965) *Wildcat Strike. A Study in Worker–Management Relationships*, New York: Harper Torchbooks.

Graham, Stephen (1919) *A Private in the Guards*, London: Macmillan.

Grant, F. (n.d.) *First a Lancer, Then a Tanky*, Imperial War Museum unpublished typescript 781 8/1. London.

Graves, Bennie (1958) 'Breaking Out: An Apprenticeship System Among Pipeline Construction Workers'. *Human Organization*. 17: 9–13.

Graves, Robert (1967) *Goodbye To All That*, Harmondsworth: Penguin.

Griffin, Frank (1937) *I Joined the Army*, London: Secker & Warburg.

Guillaumin, Colette (1980) 'The Practice of Power and Belief in Nature: The Appropriation of Women'. L. Murgatroyd (transl.). *Feminist Issues*. 2/3: 3–28.

Gwinner, P. D. V. Major (1976) 'The Treatment of Alcoholics in a Military Context'. *Journal of Alcoholism*. 11: 24–31.

Haas, Jack (1977) 'Learning Real Feelings—A Study of High Steel Iron Workers Reactions to Fear and Danger'. *Sociology of Work and Occupations*. 4: 147–70.

Haigh, R. H. and Turner, P. W. (eds.) (1970) *The Long Carry—The Journal of Stretcher Bearer Frank Dunham 1916–1918*. Oxford: Pergamon Press.

Halfpenny, Peter (1979) 'The Analysis of Qualitative Data'. *The Sociological Review*. 27: 799–827.

Hall, O. (1948) 'The Stages of a Medical Career'. *American Journal of Sociology*. 53: 327–36.

Hamer, E. C. (n.d.) *A Private Soldier goes to Tunis 1943*. Imperial War Museum unpublished typescript 523 (41) 4814. London.

Hart, H. L. A. (1961) *The Concept of Law*, London: Oxford University Press.

Hartsilver, J. (1960) *Take that Man's Name*. Imperial War Museum unpublished typescript 323. 1/Acc 51634. London.

Hawke, J. (1938) *From Private to Major*, London: Hutchinson.

Hayner, Norman S. (1945) 'Taming the Lumberjack'. *American Sociological Review*. 10: 217–25.

Henry, Stuart (1978) *The Hidden Economy*, London: Martin Robertson.

Herzog, Marianne (1980) *From Hand to Mouth. Women and Piecework*, Harmondsworth: Penguin.

Hewetson, H. J. (n.d.) *No Passports for Passchendale—Memoirs of a Field Battery Signaller 1914–1918*, Imperial War Museum unpublished typescript. 323 (41) 59625. London.

Higham, Robin (1962) *Armed Forces in Peacetime*, London: G. T. Foulis.

Hilmar, Norman A. (1965) 'Transition from Civilian to Military Life'. pp. 287–310. In *Military Sociology: A Study of American Military Institutions and Military Life*. Coates, Charles H. and Pellegrin, Roland T. University Park, Md.: Social Science Press.

Hiscock, Eric (1977) *The Bells of Hell Go Ting-A-Ling-A-Ling*, London: Corgi.

H.M.S.O. (1941) *Physical and Recreational Training*, London.

Hodges, H. Eugene (1974) 'A Sociological Analysis of Dud Behaviour in the United States Army'. pp. 27–43. In *Deviant Behaviour Occupational and Organizational Bases*. Clifton D. Bryant (ed.) Chicago: Rand McNally.

Hoggart, Richard (1971) *The Uses of Literacy*, Harmondsworth: Penguin.

Holdaway, Simon (1983) *Inside the British Police*. Oxford: Basil Blackwell.

Hughes, Everett C. (1959) 'The Study of Occupations'. pp. 442–58. In *Sociology Today*. R. K. Merton, L. Broomand and L. Cotrell (eds). New York: Basic Books.

Hughes, Everett C. (1971) *The Sociological Eye. Selected Papers*. Chicago: Aldine. Atherton.

Hughes, John A. (1976) *Sociological Analysis: Methods of Discovery*, London: Nelson.

Hughes, John A. (1980) *The Philosophy of Social Research*, London: Longman.

Huntingdon, Samuel P. (1957) *The Soldier and the State: The Theory and Practice of Civil Military Relations*, New York: Vintage Books.

Ions, Edmund (1972) *A Call to Arms*, Newton Abbot: David & Charles.

Jackson, Brian (1972) *Working Class Community*, Harmondsworth: Penguin.

Jackson, Brian *et al.* (1972a) 'The 100 you paid to die'. *New Society*, 22: 639–40.

Janis, Irving L. (1945) 'Psychodynamic aspects of Adjustment to Army life'. *Psychiatry* 8: 159–76.

Janis, Irving L. (1963) 'Group Identification Under Conditions of Extreme Danger'. *British Journal of Medical Psychology* 36: 227–38.

Janowitz, Morris (1959) *Sociology and the Military Establishment*, New York: Russell Sage.

Janowitz, Morris (1960) *The Professional Soldier: A Social and Political Portrait*, Glencoe, Ill: Free Press.

Janowitz, Morris (ed.) (1964) *The New Military*, New York: Russel Sage.

Johnson, B. S. (ed.) (1973) *All Bull—The National Serviceman*, London: Alison & Busby.

Johnson, Doyle P. (1974) 'Social Organization of an Industrial Work Group: Emergence and Adaptation to Environmental Change'. *Sociological Quarterly*. 15: 109–26.

Jones, Frank E. (1968) 'The Socialization of the Infantry Recruit'. pp. 353–65. In *Canadian Society—Sociological Perspectives*. B. R. Blishen (ed.) Toronto: Macmillan of Canada.

Journal of the 3rd Battalion The Royal Green Jackets (Northern Ireland) September 1972, duplicated.

Kahn, E. J. Jr. Chief Warrant Officer. (1944) 'Soldier Humour'. *Infantry Journal* (Overseas Edition for U.S. Armed Forces). March: 40–2.

Kelly, Frank (1954) *Private Kelly*, London: Evans Brothers.

Kiev, Ari and Giffen, Martin B. (1965) 'Some Observations On Airman Who Break Down During Basic Training'. *American Journal of Psychiatry.* 122: 184–88.

King's Regulations for the Army. (1902) London: War Office.

Klockars, Carl B. (1975) *The Professional Fence*, London: Tavistock.

Kluckhohn, Florence (1940) 'The Participant Observer Technique in Small Communities'. *American Journal of Sociology* 46: 331–43.

Lammers, C. J. (1969) 'Strikes and Mutinies: A Comparative Study of Organizational Conflicts between Rulers and Ruled'. *Administrative Science Quarterly.* 14: 558–72.

Lasswell, Harold (1933) 'Morale'. pp. 640–2. In *Encyclopaedia of the Social Sciences.* 10. New York: Macmillan.

Liebow Elliot (1967) *Tally's Corner. A Study of Negro Streetcorner Men*, Boston: Little, Brown & Co.

Lifton, Robert J. (1962) *Thought Reform and the Psychology of Totalism*, London: Victor Gollancz.

Little, Roger W. (1964) 'Buddy Relations and Combat Performance'. pp. 195–223. In *The New Military*. Maurice Janowitz (ed.) New York: Russell Sage.

Lloyd, R. A. (1938) *A Trooper in the Tins*, London: Hurst & Blackett.

Loether, Herman (1960) 'Propinquity and Homogeneity as Factors in the Choice of Best Buddies in the Air Force'. *Pacific Sociological Review* 3: 18–22.

Long, J. R., Hewitt, L. E. and Blane H. T. (1977) 'Alcohol abuse in the Armed Services: A Review. II. Problem Areas and Recommendations'. *Military Medicine.* 142: 116–28.

Lovell-Knight, A. V. Major (1977) *The Story of the Royal Military Police*, London: Leo Cooper.

Lyndon, Neil (1978) 'Private Lyndon's Weekend War'. *Sunday Telegraph Magazine.* 26 March: 79.

McCann, Eamonn (1976) 'The British Press and Northern Ireland', pp. 242–61. In *The Manufacture of News.* S. Cohen and J. Young (eds). London: Constable.

McGhie, J. Major General (1973) 'The Psychology of the Soldier on the Battlefield'. *Royal United Services Institute Journal.* 118: 39–42.

McGrath, John (1974) *Events While Guarding the Bofors Gun*, London: Methuen.

McMullen, T. B. Captain (1964) 'Man Management'. *Royal Engineers' Journal.* 78: 310–15.

Mack, Raymond W. (1954) 'The Prestige System of an Air Force Base: Squadron Rankings and Morale'. *American Sociological Review.* 19: 281–7.

Maitland, F. H. (1951) *Hussar of the Line*, London: Hurst and Blackett.

van Maanen, John (1976) 'Breaking In: Socialisation to Work'. In *Handbook of Work, Organisation and Society*, Robert Dubin (ed.) Chicago: Rand McNally. pp. 67–130.

Manning, Peter K. (1974) 'Talking and Becoming: A View of Organizational Socialization'. pp. 239–56. In *Understanding Everyday Life.* J. D. Douglas (ed.) London: Routledge & Kegan Paul.

Manning, Peter K. (1977) 'Rules in Organizational Context: Narcotics Law Enforcement in Two Settings'. *Sociological Quarterly.* 18: 44–61.

Manual of Military Law (1972) London: HMSO.

Marlowe, David H. (1959) 'The Basic Training Process'. pp. 75–98. In *The Symptom as Communication in Schizophrenia.* Kenneth L. Artiss (ed.) New York: Grune & Stratton.

Mars, Gerald (1974) 'Dock Pilferage. A Case Study in Occupational Theft'. pp. 209–228. In *Deviance and Social Control.* P. Rock and M. McIntosh (eds). London: Tavistock.

Marshall, S. L. A. Colonel (1978) *Men Against Fire*, Glouster, Mass: Peter Smith.

Marx, Karl (1974) *Capital. Volume One*, transl. by E. and C. Paul. London: Dent.

Maskin, Meyer H. and Altman, Leon L. (1943) 'Military Psychodynamics'. *Psychiatry.* 6: 263–9.

Mays, Spike (1969) *Fall Out the Officers*, London: Eyre & Spottiswoode.

Mays, Spike (1975) *The Band Rats*, London: Peter Davis.

Mead, George H. (1972) *Mind, Self and Society*, Chicago: University of Chicago Press.

Mead, Margaret (1955) *Male and Female*, New York: New American Library.

Mechanic, David (1962) 'Sources of Power of Lower Participants in Complex Organizations'. *Administrative Science Quarterly*. 7: 362–3.

Mehan, Hugh and Wood, Houston (1975) *The Reality of Ethnomethodology*, New York: John Wiley.

Middleton, Russell J. and Moland, John (1959) 'Humour in Negro and White Subcultures: A Study of jokes among university students'. *American Sociological Review*. 24: 61–9.

Miller, Raymond C. (1969) 'The Dockworkers Subculture and some problems in Cross Cultural and Cross Time Generalizations'. *Comparative Studies in Society and History*. 11: 302–14.

Milligan, Spike (1973) *Adolf Hitler—My Part in His Downfall*, Harmondsworth: Penguin.

Milligan, Spike (1976) *'Rommel?' 'Gunner Who?'* Harmondsworth: Penguin.

Ministry of Defence (n.d.) *Basic Battle Skills*, London: HMSO.

Ministry of Defence (n.d.) *Royal Armoured Corps—We Deliver the Punch!* London: Central Office of Information.

Mitchell, Colin (1969) *Having Been A Soldier*, London: Hamish Hamilton.

Morrison, A. (n.d.) *On the Road to Anywhere*, Imperial War Museum unpublished typescript 75/75/1. London.

Moskos, Charles C. Jr. (1970) *The American Enlisted Man*, New York: Russell Sage.

Mouzelis, Nicos P. (1971) 'Critical Note on Total Institutions'. *Sociology*. 5: 113–20.

Moynihan, M. (ed.) (1974) *People at War*, London: David & Charles.

Nasson, William (1980) 'Tommy Atkins in South Africa'. pp. 123–38. In *The South African War. The Anglo-Boer War 1899–1902*. P. Warwick (ed.) Harlow: Longman.

Natanson, Maurice (1956) *The Social Dynamics of George Mead*, Washington D.C.: Public Affairs Press.

Nicholls, Theo (1976) 'Who Benefits?' pp. 52–9. In *Workers Divided. A Study in Shopfloor Politics*. T. Nichols and P. Armstrong. Glasgow: Fontana/Collins.

Niederhoffer, Arthur (1967) *Behind the Shield: The Police in Urban Society*. New York: Anchor Books.

Obrdlik, Antoin J. (1942) 'Gallows Humour—A Sociological Phenomenon'. *American Journal of Sociology*, 47: 709–16.

Otley, Christopher B. (1970) 'The Social Origins of British Army Officers'. *Sociological Review*, 18: 213–39.

Otley, Christopher B. (1973) 'The Educational Background of British Army Officers'. *Sociology*, 7: 191–209.

Otley, Christopher B. (1978) 'Militarism and Militarization in the Public Schools 1900–1972'. *British Journal of Sociology*, 29: 321–39.

Page, Charles H. (1946) 'Bureaucracy's Other Face'. *Social Forces*. 25: 88–94.

Page, Martin (ed.) (1970) *Kiss Me Goodnight Sergeant Major*, London: Hart-Davis, Macgibbon.

Palmer, Roy (ed.) (1977) *The Rambling Soldier*, Harmondsworth: Penguin.

Pannett, G. H. Colonel (1964) 'Man Management'. *Royal Engineer's Journal*. 78: 431–8.

Park, R. (1931) 'Human Nature, Attitudes and Mores' pp. 17–45. In *Social Attitudes*. (ed.) Kimball Young. New York: Holt.

Parker, Howard (1974) *View from the Boys*, London: David & Charles.

Parkin, Frank (1975) *Class Inequality and Political Order*, Frogmore, St Albans: Paladin.

Phillips, M. (1965) *Small Social Groups in England*, London: Methuen.

Pleck, J. H. (1976) 'The Male Sex Role: Definitions, problems and sources of change'. *Journal of Social Issues*. 32: 18–27.

Polsky, Ned. (1971) *Hustlers, Beats and Others*, Harmondsworth: Penguin.

Purdom, C. B. (ed.) (1930) *Everyman at War*, London: Dent.

Queens Regulations for the Army (1975) London: HMSO.

Radcliffe-Brown, A. R. (1940) 'On Joking Relationships'. *Africa*. 13: 195–210.

Richardson, Major General F. M. (1978) *Fighting Spirit. A Study of Psychological factors in War*, London: Leo Cooper.

Robins, David and Cohen, Philip (1978) *Knuckle Sandwich. Growing up in the Working Class City*, Harmondsworth: Penguin.

Robson, Walter (1960) *Letters from a Soldier*, London: Faber & Faber.

Rock, Paul (1979) *The Making of Symbolic Interactionism*, London: Macmillan.

Rodman, Hyman (1963) 'The Lower-Class Value Stretch'. *Social Forces*. 42: 205–15.

Roethlisberger, F. J. and Dickson, W. J. (1939) *Management and the Worker*, Cambridge, Mass: Harvard University Press.

Roland, A. (1955) *Guardsman*, London: Museum Press.

Rothstein, Andrew (1980) *The Soldiers Strikes of 1919*, London: Macmillan.

Roy, Donald (1952) 'Quota Restriction and Goldbricking in a Machine Shop'. *American Journal of Sociology*. 57: 427–42.

Roucek, Joseph S. (1935) 'Social attitudes of the Soldier in Wartime'. *Journal of Abnormal and Social Psychology*. 30: 164–74.

Salaman, Graeme (1974) *Community and Occupation*, London: Cambridge University Press.

Salaman, Graeme (1979) *Work Organizations*, London: Longman.

Salaman, Graeme and Thompson, Kenneth (1978) 'Class Culture and the persistence of an elite'. *Sociological Review*. 26: 283–304.

Sandell, Charles (1978) 'Secret of an Eight Day Mutiny in the Guards'. *News of the World*. 6 May: 21.

Scheff, Thomas J. (1961) 'Control Over Policy by Attendants in a Mental Hospital'. *Journal of Health and Human Behaviour*. 2: 93–105.

Schneider, David M. (1967) 'The Social Dynamics of Physical Disability in Army Basic Training'. pp. 386–97. In *Personality in Nature, Society and Culture*. C. Kluckhorn and H. A. Murray (eds). New York: Alfred A. Knopf.

Scott, Robert A. (1972) 'A proposed framework for analyzing deviance as a property of social order', pp. 9–35. In *Theoretical Perspectives on Deviance*. Robert A. Scott and Jack D. Douglas (eds). New York: Basic Books.

Sharpe, R. D. Lieutenant Colonel (1972) 'Discipline'. *British Army Review*. 42: 40–4.

Shibutani, Tamotsu (1978) *The Derelicts of Company K. A Sociological Study of Demoralization*, London: University of California Press.

Shils, Edward A. and Janowitz, Maurice (1948) 'Cohesion and disintegration in the Wermacht in World War II'. *Public Opinion Quarterly*. 12: 280–315.

Sims, James (1978) *Arnhem Spearhead*. London: Imperial War Museum.

Solomon, David W. (1954) 'Civilian to Soldier: Three Sociological Studies of Infantry Recruit Training'. *Canadian Journal of Psychology*. 8: 87–94.

Spencer, John C. (1954) *Crime and the Services*, London: Routledge & Kegan Paul.

Sperber, Irwin (1970) 'The Sociological Dimensions of Military Co-optation in the United States'. *Sociological Inquiry*. 40: 61–71.

Spindler, G. D. (1948) 'The Military a Systematic Analysis'. *Social Forces*. 27: 83–8.

Sprung, G. M. C. Colonel (1960) *The Soldier in Our Time*, Philadelphia: Dorrance.

Stephenson, R. M. (1951) 'Conflict and Control Functions of Humour'. *American Journal of Sociology* 56: 569–74.

Stone, Gregory P. (1962) 'Appearance and the Self'. pp. 86–118. In *Human Behaviour and Social Process. An Interactionist Approach*. Arnold M. Rose (ed.) Boston: Houghton-Mifflin.

Stone, Gregory P. (1977) 'Appearance and the Self'. pp. 86–118. In *Human Behaviour and Social Process. An Interactionist Approach*. Arnold M. Rose (ed.) London: Routledge & Kegan Paul.

Stouffer, Samuel A. (1949) 'An Analysis of Conflicting Social Norms'. *American Sociological Review*. 14: 707–17.

Stouffer, Samuel A. *et al.* (1965) *The American Soldier*, 4 vols. New York: Wiley.

Strauss, Anselm *et al.* (1963) 'The Hospital and its Negotiated Order'. pp. 147–69. In *The Hospital in Modern Society*. Eliot Friedson (ed.) New York: Free Press.

Strauss, Anselm *et al.* (1975) 'The Hospital and its Negotiated Order'. pp. 303–20. In *People and Organizations.* Graeme Salaman and Kenneth Thompson (eds). London: Longman/ Open University.

Sudnow, David (1965) 'Normal Crimes: Sociological Features of the Penal Code in a Public Defender's Office'. *Social Problems.* 12: 255–72.

Sullivan, Mortimer A. *et al.* (1971) 'Participant Observation as Employed in the Study of a Military Training Programme'. pp. 91–100. In *Qualitative Methodology. Firsthand Involvement In the Social World.* William J. Filstead (ed.) Chicago: Markham Pub. Co.

Sykes, Gresham S. (1958) *The Society of Captives,* Princeton: Princeton University Press.

Taylor, C. (1978) 'Interpretation and the Sciences of Man'. pp. 156–200. In *The Philosophy of Society.* R. Beehler and A. R. Drengson (eds). London: Methuen.

Taylor, Ian, Walton, Paul and Young, Jock (1975) *The New Criminology. For A Social Theory of Deviance.* London: Routledge & Kegan Paul.

Thompson, Hunter T. (1981) *Fear and Loathing in Las Vegas. A Savage Journey to the Heart of the American Dream.* London: Paladin.

Tugwell, M. Major (1969) 'Discipline as a Positive Force'. *British Army Review.* 31: 78–80.

Tunstall, Jeremy (1962) *The Fisherman,* London: MacGibbon and Kee.

Turk, Herman (1963) 'Social Cohesion through variant Values: Evidence from Medical Role Relations'. *American Sociological Review.* 28: 28–37.

Turner, Ralph (1947) 'The Navy Disbursing Officer as a Bureaucrat'. *American Sociological Review.* 12: 342–8.

Turner, Ralph (1967) 'The Types of Solidarity in the reconstituting of groups'. *Pacific Sociological Review.* 10: 60–8.

University-Services Study Group Edinburgh. (1968) Report and Papers of the Group, Lent term.

Vaught, Charles and Smith, David L. (1980) 'Incorporation and Mechanical Solidarity in an Underground Coal Mine'. *Sociology of Work and Occupations.* 7: 159–87.

Vidich, Arthur J. (1971) 'Participant Observation and the Collection and Interpretation of Data'. pp. 164–73. In *Qualitative Methodology. Firsthand Involvement with the Social World.* William J. Filstead (ed.) Chicago: Markham Pub. Co.

Vidich, Arthur J. and Stein, Maurice R. (1960) 'The Dissolved Identity in Military Life'. pp. 493–506. In *Identity and Anxiety—Survival of the Person in Mass Society.* A. J. Vidich, M. R. Stein, D. M. White (eds). New York: Free Press.

Viteles, Morris S. (1953) *Motivation and Morale in Industry,* New York: W. W. Norton.

Vivian, A. P. G. (1930) *The Phantom Brigade,* London: Ernest Benn.

Wade, Aubrey (1959) *Gunner on the Western Front,* London: B. T. Batsford.

Warren, Roland L. (1946) 'The Naval Reserve Officer: A Study in Assimilation'. *American Sociological Review* 11: 202–11.

Watkins, H. B. C. Major (1960) 'Discipline'. *Journal of the Royal United Services Institute.* 105: 391–400.

Weber, Max (1930) *The Protestant Ethic and the Spirit of Capitalism.* Transl. by Talcott Parsons. London: Allen & Unwin.

Weber, Max (1964) *The Theory of Social and Economic Organization,* Glencoe, Ill.: Free Press.

Weber, Max (1977) *From Max Weber: Essays in Sociology.* London: Routledge & Kegan Paul.

Weider, Lawrence D. (1975) 'Telling the Code'. pp. 144–172. In *Ethnomethodology.* Roy Turner (ed.) Harmondsworth: Penguin.

Weigert, Andrew J. (1981) *Sociology of Everyday Life.* New York: Longman.

Weinstein, Deena (1979) *Bureaucratic Opposition. Challenging Abuses at the Workplace,* New York: Pergamon Press.

Weiss, M. S. (1967) 'Rebirth in the Airborne', *Transaction.* 4: 23–6.

Westergaard, J. H. (1966) 'The Withering Away of Class: A Contemporary Myth'. pp. 77–113. In *Towards Socialism.* P. Anderson and R. Blackburn (eds). London: Collins.

White, Howard B. (1946) 'Military Morality'. *Social Research.* 13: 410–40.

Williams, Robin (1976) 'Symbolic Interactionism: The Fusion of Theory and Research'. pp. 115–38. In *New Directions in Sociology*. D. C. Thorns (ed.) Newton Abbot: David & Charles.

Wilmott, Peter (1966) *Adolescent Boys of East London*. London: Routledge & Kegan Paul.

Willis, Paul (1979) *Learning to Labour*, Westmead, Farnborough: Saxon House.

Wilson, Gutherie (1951) *Brave Company*, London: Robert Hall.

Winch, P. (1963) *The Idea of a Social Science*, London: Routledge & Kegan Paul.

Wingfield, R. M. (1955) *The Only Way Out*, London: Hutchinson.

Wintringham, H. T. (1936) *Mutiny*, London: Stanley Nott.

Wolfe, J. N. and Erickson, J. (n.d.) *The Armed Services and Society*, Edinburgh: Edinburgh University Press.

Wolseley, Field Marshall Viscount (1918) *The Maxims of Field Marshall Wolseley*, Aldershot: Gale and Polden.

Wrong, Dennis (1977) *Sceptical Sociology*, London: Heinemann.

Zimmerman, Don H. (1969) 'Record Keeping and the Intake Process in a Public Welfare Organization'. pp. 319–54. In *On Record: Files and Dossiers in American Life*. S. Wheeler (ed.) New York: Russell Sage.

Zimmerman, Don H. and Pollner, Melvin (1974) 'The Everyday World as a Phenomenon'. pp. 80–103. In *Understanding Everyday Life. Toward the reconstruction of Sociological Knowledge*. Jack D. Douglas (ed.) London: Routledge & Kegan Paul.

Znaniecki, F. (1967) *The Laws of Social Psychology*. New York: Russell & Russell.

Zurcher, Louis A. Jr. (1965) 'The Sailor Aboard Ship: A Study of Role Behaviour in a Total Institution'. *Social Forces*. 43: 389–400.

Zurcher, Louis A. Jr. (1967) 'The Naval Recruit Training Centre: A Study in Role Assimilation in a Total Institution'. *Sociological Inquiry*. 37: 85–98.

Index